SPATIAL PREPOSITIONS

SPATIAL
PREPOSITIONS

A Case Study from French

CLAUDE VANDELOISE

Translated by Anna R. K. Bosch

THE UNIVERSITY OF CHICAGO PRESS

Chicago and London

Claude Vandeloise is associate professor in the Department of French and Italian at Louisiana State University.

The University of Chicago Press, Chicago 60637
The University of Chicago Press, Ltd., London

© 1991 by The University of Chicago
All rights reserved. Published 1991
Printed in the United States of America
00 99 98 97 96 95 94 93 92 91   5 4 3 2 1

Originally published under the title *L'espace en français: Sémantique des prépositions spatiales,* © Editions du Seuil, 1986.

Illustrations are by the author and Monique Beckers.

Library of Congress Cataloging-in-Publication Data

Vandeloise, Claude.
    [Espace en français. English]
    Spatial prepositions : a case study from French / Claude Vandeloise.
        p.   cm.
    Translation of: L'espace en français.
    Includes bibliographical references and index.
    ISBN 0-226-84727-6 (cloth) —ISBN 0-226-84728-4 (pbk.)
    1. French language—Prepositions.   I. Title.
PC 2335.V3613   1991
445—dc20   91-7149
                                                              CIP

♾ The paper used in this publication meets the minimum requirements of the American National Standard for Information Sciences—Permanence of Paper for Printed Library Materials, ANSI Z39.48-1984.

This book owes much to conversations I have enjoyed with Melissa Bowerman, Benoît de Cornulier, Gilles Fauconnier, Annette Herskovits, Yuki Kuroda, Ron Langacker, and Nicolas Ruwet.

CONTENTS

PART ONE / GENERAL CONCEPTS

1

Beyond geometric and logical descriptions of space: A functional description

The purpose of this book is the study of expressions describing space in the French language. These include

> *au-dessus/en dessous* 'above/below', *devant/derrière* 'in front of/behind', *à gauche/à droite* 'on the left/on the right', *dans/hors de* 'in/out of', etc.

What system most accurately describes these spatial expressions? Geometry and logic are frequently suggested as possible approaches to this question: it is thought that the rigor of these disciplines makes them useful tools for an objective analysis of language. I will briefly present the solutions offered by these approaches, demonstrating their limitations. Then I will propose a system based on a knowledge of the world, which provides a more satisfactory explanation of spatial prepositions.

1.1 The geometric description of space

Here I do not intend to focus on a particular geometry, whether euclidean, analytic, projective, or other; rather, this section addresses any description of space employing the tools of spatial analyses: straight lines, angles, and measurements. A geometric description claims to be independent of context and speaker—independent, also, of the function of objects situated in space. Spherical coordinates, for example, locate point A with respect to the origin O by means of the straight line OA joining these points, and the angles a, b, and c formed by this line and three orthogonal axes. (See fig. 1.)

When a speaker locates an object in relation to himself, he is the origin of the system of reference, and three transverse axes are easy enough to locate. The vertical, frontal, and lateral directions usually fill these roles. The usefulness of these notions in the linguistic description of space is indisputable. However, while the prepositions *devant/derrière* and *à gauche/à droite* are commonly associated with the frontal and lateral directions, respectively, these geometric notions provide an incomplete description of the spatial expressions. The examples below illustrate my point.

This chapter is a revised version of an article published in *Linguisticae investigationes* (Amsterdam: John Benjamins, 1985).

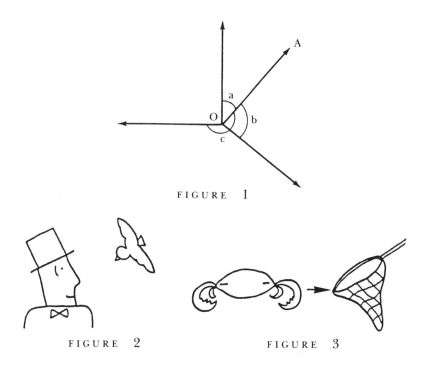

FIGURE 1

FIGURE 2   FIGURE 3

(1) *l'oiseau est devant le ministre*
the bird is in front of the minister

(2) *le filet est devant le crabe*
the net is in front of the crab

In the above scenes, the choice of the preposition *devant* is not explained by the frontal direction, but by the minister's line of sight and the direction of the crab's movement. These facts will lead us to develop a more complex concept than that of direction alone: the notion of orientation. General orientation, as we will see, is a *family resemblance concept* (Wittgenstein 1953), a concept that may be represented by various combinations of its traits. As a corollary, no single trait is a necessary and sufficient condition for the use of the word describing the family resemblance concept. For example, the concept of general orientation determines the use of the prepositions *devant/derrière*.

While the three dimensions of Cartesian space present a fairly accurate approximation of the way language describes space, no spatial preposition expresses absolute distance. For example, there is no pair of prepositions *blib/blub* meaning that the distance from object to subject is less than/greater than one meter. When I say that the grocery store is *near* the church, the distances expressed by the preposition differ depending on whether I intend to travel by foot or by car. In the same way, two galaxies separated by light-years can be considered close, while my fork might seem far away if it is out of reach.

In response to these problems, it is common to define *a est près/ loin de b* as a function of a distance that is less than/greater than a defined norm. When we consider the factors that determine such a norm, however (see chapter 5), we note that they follow from the physical accessibility of the subject/object of the expression to the object/subject. Isn't it more direct to define the prepositions *près/loin* according to accessibility/inaccessibility? Then distance itself would be only one of several possible factors influencing accessibility. Neither its geometric status nor its objectively measurable character justifies the privileged status usually accorded to distance in the description of the prepositions *près de/loin de*.

Other geometrical notions are often brought up in the study of spatial relations: the object of the spatial relation and the number of its dimensions, for example. H. H. Clark (1973) calls the English prepositions *at, on,* and *in* one-, two-, and three-dimensional, according to this criterion.

On what basis is such a generalization founded? Examples (3)–(5) present three uses of the preposition *à*, in which the objects have, respectively, one, two, and three dimensions.

(3) *le point est à l'intersection des deux lignes*
the point is at the intersection of two lines

(4) *le curé est à la plage*
the priest is at the beach

(5) *le ministre est à l'église*
the minister is at the church

How can the beach and the church be considered one-dimensional? It is generally agreed that the preposition *à* expresses coincidence of object and subject. Since the priest/the minister cannot exactly coincide with the beach/the church, the subject and object of the preposition must be understood as single points in space to satisfy this definition.

Two objections to this reasoning might be raised here. First, it is only a corollary of a specific definition of the preposition *à*. Suppose we substitute another definition, by which the preposition *à* expresses the coincidence of its subject with *a point of its object*. Unless there are imperative reasons to prefer the first definition to the second, we no longer need to reduce the beach and the church to unidimensional points. Nonetheless, we might indeed allow the cases of the beach and the church, since the idealization of the objects of a preposition is a fairly general phenomenon (see chapter 3). But why should these objects be reduced to precisely one point? We would like to discover how the unidimensionality of the object felicitously represents the speaker's idealization of it. This particular reduction, it seems to me, is only one of several possible interpretations, although it is particularly called to mind by the attraction of geometry and its three dimensions. I doubt that either the child or the naive speaker using sentences (4) and (5) has succumbed to the appeal of geometric principles. Instead, the child or the naive speaker might idealize the beach or the church as an indeterminate mass, where dimensionality plays no role. That is, rather than being represented as an object with a single dimension, the beach or the church might be represented as adimensional, having no dimension at all. An alternative definition of the preposition *à* by means of a functional concept, *localization,* will be proposed in chapter 11.

Similar criticisms can be voiced regarding the tridimensionality of the object of the preposition *dans.* The sentences below illustrate that the object of this preposition can be three-, two-, or one-dimensional.

(6) *les bijoux sont dans la boîte*
the jewels are in the box

(7) *la vache est dans la prairie*
the cow is in the field

(8) *le curé est dans la file*
the priest is in line

Hawkins (1983), forced to admit that the English preposition *in* is indifferent to the dimensionality of its object, invokes the concept of *natural categories.* Here the uses of a single word are classed along a scale of how well each use represents the category. Hawkins thus corroborates Clark's description, considering the three-dimensional objects of the preposition *in* more natural than the two- or one-dimensional objects. While this approach may be justified, I maintain that the role of dimensionality is indirect and secondary. It is in fact only one consequence of the meaning of the preposition *dans,* whose subject is contained by its object. This containment imposes one obvious condition on the object: it must be a potential container. Furthermore, three-dimensional objects satisfy this condition more often than one- or two-dimensional objects do. From the start, then, they are the ideal objects of the preposition *dans*. Note that, while a stone does have three dimensions, the sentence below sounds vaguely surreal.

(9) *le pain est dans la pierre*
the bread is in the stone

It is indeed difficult to imagine a stone containing a loaf of bread. On the other hand, as long as a one- or two-dimensional object could possibly contain the subject, we find perfectly acceptable sentences. For example, the corner of the page might illustrate this characteristic, while the whole page may not: consequently, example (10) is acceptable in contrast to (11), in which the entire page is the object.

(10) *la ligne est dans le coin de la page*
the line is in the corner of the page

(11) **la ligne est dans la page*
the line is in the page

Nevertheless, the above objects have the same number of dimensions in space. The difference in acceptability between the two sentences is explained by the object's ability or inability to be a potential container.

In summary, in a world where entities may be conceived of according to one, two, or three dimensions, it should not be surprising if the objects of spatial prepositions also illustrate this range of possibilities. However, the dimensionality of the object is often only a superficial consequence of the preposition itself, and not an essential characteristic of the use of the preposition. Seductive geometric generalizations, often based on simplified analyses, hide the true nature of the prepositions they attempt to explain.

This review of the geometrical qualities attributed to spatial words concludes with a return to the now classic article of Bierwisch[1] (1967)—a description of adjectives of dimension in German. Here dimensions are defined by the following features: primary (− 2d) for length or secondary (+ 2d) for width; principal (+ main) for length and width and nonprincipal (− main) for thickness.[2] It is my belief that Bierwisch has arbitrarily constructed a general rule out of a frequent—but not necessary—consequence of the use of terms of dimension, in rigidly defining the importance of these dimensions in the speaker's mind. I maintain instead that the speaker is free to consider one single object from an infinite number of perspectives, each of which may alter the importance accorded to any dimension. If we ignore this creativity, giving precedence instead to a "normal" conception of the world, we neglect one of the fundamental characteristics of language.

The example of *thickness* will illustrate my point. Bierwisch characterizes this dimension by the feature (− main). Does it necessarily follow that the thickness of an object only comes to the speaker's mind after the characteristics of length and width? It's true that the thickness of a wall or a table often characterizes the smallest dimension, but the size of the dimension should not be mistaken for its salience. The absurdity of this equation should be immediately apparent if we take the example of a bank teller, protected from a robber's bullet by a bullet-proof window. Although the thickness of the window is its smallest dimension, this dimension is vitally important to the life and safety of the teller. Locating thickness in a hierarchy of dimensions is not an entirely satisfactory way to describe it. Once again we must turn to a functional concept to understand the use of this word. In section 1.2 I will show that the notion of thickness depends less on the object's volume than on its strength. Only indirectly does a notion of thickness apply to the dimensions of an object.

One argument associating thickness and resistance, or strength, is indicated by the polysemy of the word itself. The thickness of an object may refer to its density (the thickness of the soup) or its smallest dimension (the thickness of the plank of wood). However, an object's strength is proportional to its density, as well as to its dimensions. Strength ties together the two possible uses of thickness. A second argument follows from the figures below.

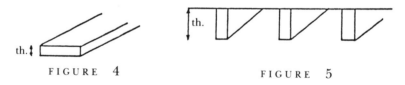

FIGURE 4   FIGURE 5

In figure 4, the thickness of the board is indeed its smallest dimension. This is not the case, however, when we look at the beam supporting the ceiling in figure 5. So the thickness of an object may be vitally important; furthermore, it may not invariably coincide with the smallest dimension of an object (as in figure 5). A geometrical analysis can only point out this exception without explaining it. This variation, we will see, follows naturally from a functional analysis described in terms of an object's resistance. In figure 4, where no outside force is indicated, the speaker judges the strength of the beam pessimistically: it is evaluated according to its greatest chances of breaking, that is, its smallest dimension. In figure 5, on the other hand, the ceiling bears down on the beams, and the architectural structure determines their chances of breaking. In this case the thickness of each beam is not measured by the smallest dimension, but by the force that is placed in opposition to the weight of the roof. Figures 4 and 5, and the bisemy of *thickness,* are naturally explained if this dimension is described in terms of a functional concept. Because it only draws on appearances without exploring their cause, a geometrical analysis ranking the various dimensions in terms of a hierarchy will associate thickness only with the usual factors related to resistance. Geometry neglects factors that less regularly affect the solidity of an object, or is satisfied with listing these factors as arbitrary.

I have focused on Clark's proposals concerning the dimensionality of prepositional objects and on Bierwisch's presentation of the hierarchy of dimensions because both approaches illustrate geometry's seductive appeal to linguistics. The basic goal of these works, however, is identical to the goal of this text: to establish a correspondence between the linguistic description of space and the extralinguistic knowledge of space that speakers share.[3] I have attempted to show that certain geometrical concepts have not advanced this goal significantly. Before introducing the concepts I believe necessary to the description of spatial words, I will examine the value of logic in this domain.

1.2 The logical description of spatial prepositions

The first studies of spatial prepositions formulated in terms of logic are found in the British literature and include Cooper (1968), Leech (1969), and Bennett (1968). Miller and Johnson-Laird (1976) devote an entire section of their book to this problem.

All the above works propose definitions of spatial prepositions that may be translated into first-order logic. Such an exercise is surely destined to fail if the distributions of prepositions are seen as classical categories governed by necessary and sufficient conditions of inclusion. No spatial word lends itself easily to such a strict definition, and counterexamples may be found for every proposed definition. I leave to the reader the exercise of convincing himself of this fact, given these four definitions of the English preposition *in.*

Cooper: x in y: x is located internal to y with the constraint that x is smaller than y.

Leech: x in y: x is enclosed or contained either in a two-dimensional or in a three-dimensional place y.

Bennett: In y: locative (interior y).

> Miller and Johnson-Laird: In (x, y): referent x is in a relatum y
> if: part (x, z) & Incl (z, y).

The inadequacies of these definitions will be apparent when we turn to a detailed analysis of the prepositions *dans/hors de*, in chapter 13.

If, however, we admit that language is organized into *natural*, rather than *classical*, categories (Lakoff 1982, 1987), then we allow certain usages of a word to be more representative than others, and a few counterexamples will not definitively condemn an analysis. Obviously the above formulas do not represent all (and only) the uses appropriate to the preposition *in*, but they could describe the most representative uses. Even though these definitions were not developed within this theoretical framework, this simple revision would allow us to believe (at least a little longer) in the validity of their description. By means of this model we can set out four essential features distinguishing logic and language.

1.2.1 The idealization of relational terms

Because the language of logic does not allow ambiguity, a word that is n times polysemic must be represented by n different symbols. If we look closely at the terms of a spatial relation, however, we notice that even this multiplication of symbols does not resolve the issue. Different symbols will be necessary, not only for the different uses of a word but also for the different perspectives according to which the designated object is examined. An example of this is illustrated by sentences (12) and (13), describing the figure below.

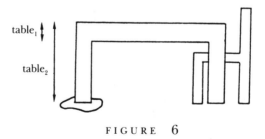

FIGURE 6

(12) *la chaise est en dessous de la* table$_1$
   the chair is under the table$_1$

(13) *le papier est en dessous de la table*$_2$
   the paper is under the table$_2$

According to the definition of the expression *en dessous* presented in chapter 6, example (12) is true if its object refers to the upper part of the table but false if, as in sentence (13), it refers to the entire piece of furniture. Logic must then designate one single table by several different symbols if its purpose is to represent the truth value of sentences (12) and (13) exactly. The multiplicity of symbols attached to one word evidently poses no problem to a logical analysis. Nevertheless this example illustrates how logical descriptions of space underestimate the complexity of spatial relations and of our perception of objects. I will return to this problem in chapter 3.

1.2.2 Asymmetry of the subject/object relation

The pairs of prepositions *au-dessus*/*en dessous, avant*/*après*, . . . are said to be converse since they illustrate the following equivalent relations:

$$a \text{ est au-dessus de } b = b \text{ est en dessous de } a^4$$
$$a \text{ is above } b = b \text{ is below } a$$
$$a \text{ est avant } b = b \text{ est après } a$$
$$a \text{ is before } b = b \text{ is after } a$$

Not all spatial prepositions respect these equations, however, as the sentences below illustrate.

(14) *la pierre est devant la maison*
the stone is in front of the house

(15) **la maison est derrière la pierre*[5]
the house is behind the stone

The asymmetry of the examples above is due to the function of these prepositions (see chapter 2), locating a small, moveable object of unknown position (the target) with respect to a larger, more stable object of known position (the landmark). The target is always the subject of the spatial relation, and the landmark, its object. Sentence (15) seems bizarre because it violates this constraint. When *a* and *b* can play the roles of both target and landmark, the prepositions *devant*/*derrière* are indeed converse, as sentences (16) and (17) illustrate.

(16) *le chêne est devant le peuplier*
the oak is in front of the poplar

(17) *le peuplier est derrière le chêne*
the poplar is behind the oak

The descriptions provided by predicate logic generally ignore constraints on target and landmark.

1.2.3 Additional constraints

Although logic is by its nature compositional (the meaning of two terms may be calculated from the meaning of each alone), this is not always the case with language. Herskovits (1986) cites the sentences below as an example.

> (18) *Annette est à son bureau*
> Annette is at her desk

This sentence expresses more than the proximity of Annette to her desk: she must be sitting, facing the desk, trying to work. The meaning of the expression *à son bureau* has become richer than we would suppose from the meaning of the preposition *à* and its object. Logic cannot express this additional meaning without sacrificing its own demands of compositionality.

1.2.4 Selection restrictions

Logical definitions of spatial prepositions are often too extensive and must be accompanied by selection restrictions. One example may be drawn from the target/landmark and subject/object relations of the prepositions *devant/derrière*. In his definition of the English preposition *in*, Cooper introduces another restriction, $a < b$, a restriction that is manifestly false when we consider the phrase *a tree in a planter*. Even in the ideal case, logic will correctly express these restrictions but fail to motivate them. Such artificial constraints seem to confirm the arbitrary character of language. I will attempt to show that, in fact, such constraints point up the inadequacies of the descriptive system that demands them.

Logic, in neglecting the functional character of language, reduces the study of spatial prepositions to a description of their formal usage, abstracting out of context. Other usages are not coincidental, and often the true function of a preposition is revealed by a detour demanded by a single unexplained occurrence. One of the major defects of a logical description is its need for unmotivated selection restrictions, which must be applied in order to restrict an overextensive definition. My intention here is not to deny the role of the arbitrary in language; however, the extent of this role is exaggerated by inappropriate descriptive systems. Because they ignore—and often contradict—the essential characteristics of language, geometric and logical descriptions emphasize the complexity of the distribution of spatial propositions, rather than explaining this distribution. These exact sciences claim to provide exhaustive and autonomous information to a speaker who is ignorant of the context of speech, but language maximally exploits the knowledge shared by the participants of the discourse situation. Both logic and geometry refuse the aid of this shared knowledge, although language itself is built on the foundation of the discourse context. The role of the arbitrary is restricted by this shared knowledge. Once the divergences between natural languages and formal languages are recognized, it should not be surprising that the latter only imperfectly describe the former.

1.3 A functional description of spatial prepositions

Rather than depending on a logical or geometrical system of description, I will offer a description of spatial words based on functional concepts[6] that are tied to the extralinguistic knowledge of space shared by the speakers of one language. Extralinguistic knowledge need not be considered a maze of information striking fear into the heart of a reasonable man; in fact, we do not have to advance far into the center of this maze to find concepts that enlighten our use of language. By means of a basic concepts I will develop a description of spatial expressions. The primitives I will discuss may differ from one another in nature, and only certain of these may be termed "functional," such as the relations *porteur/porté* 'bearer/burden' and *contenant/contenu* 'container/contained'. Other primitives discussed here relate to an anthropomorphic interpretation of the world and are tied to the form of the human body, or to its perceptual system. Several of these concepts, such as the concepts of frontal and lateral directions, have already been used in descriptions by Clark, Fillmore (1971), etc. Their use is necessary and inevitable. In this introduction I will particularly focus on the following key concepts: spatial location; concepts such as the container/contained relation, which are tied to a notion of naive physics; access to perception; potential contact; and general and lateral orientation. These concepts will point up connections among different uses of a single word, especially in cases where geometry and logic must appeal to chance or arbitrariness. The functional relationships discussed in this work will establish direct connections between these cognitive concepts and language.

1.3.1 Localization

One essential function of spatial relations is to situate objects that the discourse participants hope to find or contact in some fashion. The role of the preposition *à* facilitates this search by associating the target and the landmark, whether the target is static (chapter 11) or mobile (Vandeloise 1987). This preposition, essentially localizing in nature, can be distinguished from *sur* and *dans:* these latter prepositions basically describe situations reflecting the bearer/burden or container/contained relations. The preposition *à* seems to prefer situations in which knowledge of the landmark is shared by both participants in the discourse—thus, the preferred landmark will situate a target that may often be smaller, mobile, and far from the physical place of utterance or outside the visual field of the speakers.

1.3.2 Naive physics[7]

I do not know whether or not a naive conception of the world is universal, or if it varies with cultures of different linguistic communities. At any rate, certain world beliefs are most definitely shared by all speakers of a single language, for example:

1. A man stands up, a tree grows, a stone falls along one single axis, which we call the vertical direction. This direction will be used in the description of the expressions *au-dessus/en dessous* (see chapter 6).

2. If an object carries or supports another object, it is generally larger, closer to the ground, partially hidden by the supported object, etc. The nature of the bearer/burden relation plays an important role in the descriptions of the prepositions *sur/sous* (see chapter 12).

3. If an object contains another object, it often hides the contained object and has some influence on the shape and position of this object; the contained object generally moves to the container rather than the inverse; etc. The container/contained relation arises even in the logical definition of the English preposition *in,* proposed by Leech. I will show (chapter 13) that this functional relation describes the prepositions *dans/hors de* better than the topological relation inclusion/exclusion does.

Note that naive physics differs from scientific physics as radically as natural languages differ from formal ones. Even though the earth is round, no one takes into account the curve of the earth's surface in a linguistic description of space.

1.3.3 Accessibility to perception

Since all people share the same faculties of perception, we all perceive space in the same manner. In particular, the direction of our gaze is better represented by a straight line than by the corkscrew curl of a pig's tail; for the young as for the old, for the good as for the wicked, an object located behind one's back, behind an opaque object, or within an opaque object is invisible without mirror, periscope, or sorcery. Of these three causes of invisibility, the first two play a role in the description of the French preposition *derrière,* as the figure below illustrates.

Though they are located in two different areas of space, object A and object B are both said to be *derrière.* Principles of geometry show

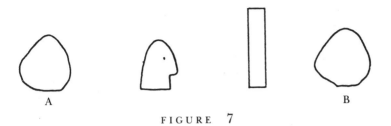

FIGURE 7

us no similarities shared by the area behind the speaker and the area hidden by the wall, and we are left with two independent meanings of the preposition *derrière*. Nevertheless, there is a connection between the two areas in figure 7: objects A and B, for different reasons, are both inaccessible to perception. In this shared imperceptibility we find the pragmatic bridge that connects both versions of the preposition *derrière*, motivating the choice of one single word to describe two different areas in space—a choice that otherwise would be judged arbitrary.

Accessibility to perception can involve different extensions in other languages. The meaning of the Cora particle *u* 'within' is based on an understanding of the common imperceptibility of objects located either outside the field of vision, or inside an object that itself is outside the field of vision, or inside any object.

FIGURE 8

Here object A, inside the box, and object B, outside the field of vision, and object C, behind the speaker, all may be qualified by this particle. Casad and Langacker (1982) justify the extension of the particle *u* to objects B and C in terms of the inaccessibility to perception shared by all three objects.

Thus, neither the extensions of the preposition *derrière* in French nor those of the particle *u* in Cora are arbitrary. Nevertheless, the two languages are free to choose the associations they will establish among the different causes of imperceptibility, and this choice in turn extends the networks of meaning in the respective lexicons. While French relies on the imperceptibility common to objects in back of the speaker and those hidden by another object, Cora exploits the similarity among objects located within an opaque object, outside the field of vision, or in back of the speaker.

Another consequence of accessibility to perception is illustrated in the distribution of the French prepositions *derrière* and *sous*. These two prepositions (see chapter 12) express imperceptibility along two different axes: along the horizontal axis for the preposition *derrière;* along the vertical axis for *sous*. However, the two prepositions coincide in the case of a vertical obstruction where the hiding object contacts the hidden object. Thus, if a map of Mexico hangs on my kitchen wall, I could say,

> (19) *il y a un coffre-fort sous la carte du Mexique*
> there is a safe under the map of Mexico

> (20) *il y a un coffre-fort derrière la carte du Mexique*
> there is a safe behind the map of Mexico

There are subtle yet systematic preferences, however, in the choice of *derrière* or *sous* when their domains coincide. For an object as thin as a map, I prefer (21) over (22); for a thicker object, such as a portrait of the pope, (23) seems better than (24).

> (21) *la mouche est sous la carte du Mexique*
> the fly is under the map of Mexico

> (22) *? la mouche est derrière la carte du Mexique*
> the fly is behind the map of Mexico

> (23) *la mouche est derrière le portrait du pape*
> the fly is behind the portrait of the pope

> (24) *? la mouche est sous le portrait du pape*
> the fly is under the portrait of the pope

We will see that this distribution is explained by an analysis in which the preposition *sous* is influenced not only by accessibility to perception but also by the bearer/burden relation (chapter 12).

1.3.4 Potential encounter

While the role of accessibility to perception is tied to our shared perceptual faculties, the role of potential encounter is explained by the use we make of space. In fact, all our actions can be expressed in terms of encounter, whether it be with our socks, our food, or the love of our life. Note, however, that although encounter implies movement, the inverse is not true. Movement, for example, plays an important role in the use of the verb *aller* 'to go', but this is not a sufficient condition for the use of the word. Such is my understanding of the contrast below.

(25) *le curé va à Rome*
the priest is going to Rome

(26) **le curé va*[8]
the priest goes

The unacceptability of (26) shows that *aller* is a verb of encounter rather than of movement. In fact, this verb is unacceptable if the second element of the encounter is not expressed. From the acceptability of sentence (27), we know that the verb *venir* 'to come' is superficially different from *aller*.

(27) *le curé vient*
the priest is coming

Although the place is not expressed in sentence (27), it is understood from the meaning of the verb *venir;* the place of encounter must be the place where the discourse is uttered.

I have demonstrated the connection between the use of *avant/ après* and potential encounter: the prepositional terms *a* and *b* are understood to be moving towards a sublexical (unexpressed) element, defined by the context, which I label the *pole* of the relation (Vandeloise 1984). This connection is suggested by the scene below and the examples in (28) and (29).

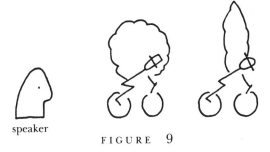

speaker

FIGURE   9

(28) *le curé est avant le ministre*
the priest is before the minister

(29) *le chêne est avant le peuplier*
the oak is before the poplar

The goal of the encounter in (28) is obvious: this is the destination of the two bikers. The situation may be schematized as $(a, b) \rightarrow P$. The biker closest to the pole is said to be *before* the second biker. In example (29), we can only speak of *encounter* if we imagine the potential movement of the speaker towards the trees. The tree closest to the speaker, in this case the oak, will be the first tree contacted along this imaginary path: the oak is thus *before* the poplar. The speaker's potential movement, which will be discussed in detail in chapter 10, may be schematized as follows:

P → (a, b).

Here the pole P of the encounter is the speaker. Examples (28) and (29) together may be expressed by the formula P ↔ (a, b), illustrating the relation between *avant/après* and the relative movement of the two entities. Either the terms *a* and *b* (as in [28]) or the pole (29) is mobile. This does not depend solely on physical movement, as the examples below illustrate.

(30) *l'automobiliste alla s'écraser contre le mur*
    the driver crashed into the wall

(31) *l'automobiliste vit le mur venir vers lui*
    the driver saw the wall coming towards him

Although the two utterances describe the same objective scene, the first expresses the movement of the car (car → wall). The second describes the scene from the point of view of the driver, contradicting the physical movement and choosing the wall as the mobile element (car ← wall).

Finally, potential movement implies the same relations as real movement. Even if the priest and the minister in figure 9 are resting for a moment against the oak and the poplar, they are still potential bikers as described in example (28). We see that the prepositions *avant /après* describe relative potential movement towards a pole.

1.3.5 General and lateral orientation

The symmetry and function of the human body clearly determine two privileged directions or axes, the frontal and lateral directions. These are illustrated below.

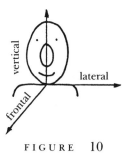

FIGURE   10

I have already pointed out that these notions only imperfectly characterize the prepositions *devant/derrière* and *à gauche/à droite*. They will be replaced (in chapters 7 and 8) with two family resemblance concepts: general and lateral orientation. The principal traits of general orientation include the line of sight and the direction of movement, as well as the frontal direction. This list is not exhaustive, however; if, as in figure 11, the king's mouth is located at the nape of his neck, we might perhaps say that the dish of game is *devant lui* 'in front of him.' In this case the organs of nutrition must be considered a feature of general orientation.

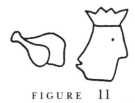

FIGURE 11

In conclusion, spatial prepositions are described by means of the following concepts:

localization;
concepts of naive physics such as the vertical axis, the bearer/
    burden relation, and the container/contained relation;
physical accessibility and accessibility to perception;
potential encounter;
general and lateral orientation.

Certain partisans of a more rigorous formulation of spatial relationships may be distressed by the naive and intuitive character of these concepts. To ward off such criticisms, I have attempted first to show the limitations of geometric and logical descriptions. Such descriptions pertain to the distribution of spatial prepositions but neglect their functions; they focus on consequences while ignoring causes. A statistical examination of the preposition *dans* will show us that its object is most often three-dimensional; if we then deduce a general rule from such a study, we are later astonished to find a one- or two-dimensional object as a counterexample. If we understand the function of this preposition, however, we know that its object must be a potential container; as long as the object satisfies this condition, the number of dimensions of the object is unimportant. The perceived arbitrariness of language is accentuated by a general misunderstanding of the functions of language and by an unwarranted dependence on the scientific rigor of formal languages. This exaggerates the arbitrariness of language, making the child's acquisition of language appear much more problematic than it perhaps is in reality.

2

The asymmetry of spatial relations

This chapter will present the different functions of prepositional subjects and objects, and the conditions they impose on the proper construction of spatial relations. I will then examine the nature of the relation between the object of the preposition and the speaker.

2.1 Target and landmark

It has been noted that the spatial relations *devant/derrière, à gauche/à droite,* etc., are not exact converse relations, since the following equations do not hold consistently:

$$a \text{ est devant } b = b \text{ est derrière } a$$
$$a \text{ est à gauche de } b = b \text{ est à droite de } a$$

The sentences below illustrate my point.

(1) *le bâton est devant la maison*
the stick is in front of the house

(2) *?la maison est derrière le bâton*[1]
the house is behind the stick

(3) *la cigarette est à gauche du fauteuil*
the cigarette is to the left of the armchair

(4) *?le fauteuil est à droite de la cigarette*
the armchair is to the right of the cigarette

Similarly, the relations *près/loin* are not always symmetrical, since the acceptability of *a est près de/loin de b* does not invariably imply the acceptability of *b est près de/loin de a.*

(5) *l'épingle est près du château*
the pin is near the castle

(6) *?le château est près de l'épingle*
the castle is near the pin

Why do we find sentences (2), (4), and (6) so bizarre? Because they violate a general principle of language when an object is located in space. The basis of this principle is extralinguistic: an object whose location is unknown cannot be situated without reference to an entity whose position is better known. The object to be located has been called, in the English literature, the *figure* (Talmy) or the *trajector* (Langacker), while the same authors call the corresponding reference point the *ground* or *landmark*.[2] I will call the object to be located the *target* (*cible*) and the object of reference the *landmark* (*site*). The positions of target and landmark are not left to chance in a spatial relationship; in well-formed utterances, the target always coincides with the subject of the relation, and the landmark corresponds with its object. The linguistic principle mentioned above may be expressed as follows:

subject of spatial relation = target
object of spatial relation = landmark

Sentences (2), (4), and (6) are unusual because they violate this principle. A misplaced walking stick may be located by reference to a house, but the inverse is not possible. An armchair may help me find my cigarette, but the opposite would be surprising, at the very least. And who would look for a pin in the grass in order to find the path to a castle, outside the pages of a detective novel? Any reversal of the order of target and landmark thus leads to unusual spatial relations.

What then are the characteristics of target and landmark? First, we can point out that the position of the target constitutes new information, while the position of the landmark repeats known information. Furthermore, although the target is small or difficult to perceive, the landmark is generally large and easy to distinguish. Finally, the target is usually mobile or potentially moveable, while the landmark is immobile and stable. The target and the landmark in example (7) exemplify the above qualities; sentence (8) is all the more unusual in contrast.

(7) *regarde l'étoile filante! Près du clocher*
look at the falling star! Near the church tower

(8) *?regarde le clocher! Près de l'étoile filante*
look at the church tower! Near the falling star

The falling star, fleeting and momentary, attracting the speaker's attention, is the ideal target, while the church tower, massive and immobile, shows all the characteristics of the ideal landmark. The target /landmark relation is not always so clear-cut, however.

(9) *le Cameroun est près de l'équateur*
Cameroon is near the equator

In example (9) the geographer must know the location of the landmark, even though the equator is nothing but an imaginary line compared with the stretch of land that constitutes the Federal Republic of Cameroon. Similarly we can accept sentence (10),

(10) *la grue est près des chalands*
the crane is near the barges

although the crane may well be immobile while the barges drift with the tides. Here the movement of the boats, fixed and predictable, provides an acceptable reference point. While it is easy enough to find counterexamples to the criteria large/small or mobile/immobile, it is difficult to imagine an example in which the location of the target would be known, but not that of the landmark: such an example would effectively say, "This object, whose position I can locate exactly, is situated next to this other object, located who-knows-where." The relation of new and given information is one essential characteristic of the target/landmark relation.

A lexically unexpressed, or sublexical, element may occasionally modify the acceptability of the target/landmark relationship. We see one example of this in comparing examples (11) and (12) with (13) and (14), below. As the first sentences indicate, a house may serve as landmark when we want to situate a signpost, but the inverse is difficult to imagine, without extenuating circumstances.

(11) *le poteau est près de la maison*
the signpost is near the house

(12) *?la maison est près du poteau*[3]
the house is near the signpost

Although a bus stop may be signalled by a signpost, the acceptability of sentence (14) contrasts with the strangeness of example (12).

(13) *l'arrêt du bus est près de la maison*
the bus stop is near the house

(14) *la maison est près de l'arrêt du bus*
the house is near the bus stop

The reason for this contrast follows from an element that is implicitly understood: the pedestrian's path between the house and the bus stop. Since the speaker is commonly identified with the landmark (see section 2.2), we interpret the first sentence by imagining a path leading from the house to the bus stop, whereas the second sentence suggests the opposite trajectory. Although both target and landmark are immobile in both examples, the acceptability of (14) is justified by the possibility of movement along a path.

Having introduced this qualification, I would like now to turn to an example proposed by Talmy (1980). Since a bicycle is smaller and less stable than a house, Talmy maintains that sentence (16) is less acceptable than sentence (15).

> (15) *la bicyclette est près de la maison*
> the bicycle is near the house

> (16) *?la maison est près de la bicyclette*
> the house is near the bicycle

Although it is true that contexts justifying (16) are far more unusual than those for (15), we can imagine a biker getting a flat tire in the rain, not far from his own house. It is evident that the target/landmark relationship is again justified by an implicit element: here, the path that the biker will follow, on foot, to his house.

Not all of the prepositions studied in this book will impose strict conditions on their subjects and objects. The prepositions *avant/après* are invariably converse, as the examples below illustrate.

> (17) *le banc est avant l'église*
> the bench is before the church

> (18) *l'église est après le banc*
> the church is after the bench

Similarly, the prepositions *au-dessus/en dessous* are inverse when the prepositions *sur/sous* cannot be substituted.

> (19) *le bombardier est au-dessus de l'usine*
> the bomber is above the factory

> (20) *l'usine est en dessous du bombardier*
> the factory is below the bomber

Note, however, that in each case a certain sublexical element independent of the landmark plays an important role in situating the target. In the case of the prepositions *avant/après*, this factor is movement (chapter 10); for the expressions *au-dessus/en dessous*, it is the vertical axis (chapter 6). Example (18), for example, is understood by reference to the potential path of the speaker from the bench to the church.

2.2 *The relation of landmark and speaker*

In the examples below, the linguistic description of the location of Paris becomes progressively more complicated.

(21) *Paris est près*
Paris is near

(22) *Paris est près de Saint-Denis*
Paris is near Saint-Denis

(23) *Paris est près par rapport à Saint-Denis*
Paris is nearby, judging from Saint-Denis

Nonetheless, if the utterance is pronounced in Saint-Denis, the three sentences probably describe identical objective scenes. In fact, the position of the speaker is the most likely landmark of example (21). The simplest linguistic description (i.e., example [21]) corresponds to the most egocentric location, in which the landmark is unexpressed. In contrast, in (23), the most complex description, the location of the speaker is described most completely. The landmark is introduced in this case by *par rapport à* 'with respect to', which is more marked (more infrequent and longer) than *de* in (22). I will suggest a basic state of language in which the landmark situating a target in space coincides with the position of the speaker. As the location becomes more objective and the landmark is differentiated from the speaker, the linguistic expression becomes more complex. Absolute objectivity, according to which the speaker is completely divorced from the landmark, demands the most extensive linguistic description. Natural language here approaches the goals of formal languages, which force speech as far as possible away from a dependence on speaker and context. We should not be surprised to find that the specific qualities of language are revealed when language distances itself from the rigor of formal logic, and not when it complies with this rigor. The *point de départ* of natural languages proceeds from an egocentric world view.

Between egocentrically situating the target by means of a sublexical landmark and situating it with respect to a landmark introduced by *de*, we find an intermediate stage: the nonegocentric interpretation of an unexpressed landmark. Although the most common interpretation of (21) focuses on the speaker, this reading is by no means the only possible reading: the unexpressed landmark may be any reference point specified by the linguistic or extralinguistic context. Imagine for example that the speaker of utterance (21), among a thousand possible interpretations, actually intends the sentence below.

(24) *Paris est près de Saint-Cloud*
Paris is near Saint-Cloud

What is the difference in the speaker's thought processes if he pronounces (or fails to pronounce) the landmark, when describing the same objective scene? Naturally, the speaker shows greater confidence in the interlocutor's ability to interpret the meaning of the utterance when the landmark is omitted. The interlocutor's clairvoyance is not the determining factor, however, and the omission of the landmark is equally likely in any case. The speaker chooses among several different strategies situating the landmark: omitting a nonegocentric landmark is one strategy falling midway between omitting an egocentric landmark and expressing a landmark introduced by the preposition *de.* The degree to which the speaker identifies with the landmark ultimately determines whether he chooses to express or omit this landmark. If the speaker identifies sufficiently with the landmark, it may be omitted; if not (as in the situation that presently interests us), I will argue that the landmark refers to the *virtual* position of the speaker. Here I postulate a mental movement of the speaker to the position of the unexpressed landmark (e.g., Saint-Cloud); this movement obeys the principle of transfer below.

> Transfer principle: The speaker has the ability to transfer mentally to any viewpoint that will be useful to the perspective from which he conceptualizes the objective scene.

The speaker can transfer to an infinite number of viewpoints, and conversation continues successfully as long as the addressee is able to follow the speaker's mental displacement. If this hypothesis is admitted, an unexpressed landmark always describes the speaker's position, but this position may be either real or virtual and determined by the transfer principle.[4]

When the landmark is lexically expressed and introduced by *de,* as in examples (22) and (24), it becomes a conscious landmark for the speaker. The separation between speaker and landmark is not complete, however, and the speaker will remember his former identification with the landmark. For the expressions *près de/loin de,* all the speaker has to do is transport himself to the place of the landmark; the problem is more complex, however, when we turn to other spatial expressions such as *devant/derrière* (chapter 7) and *à gauche/à droite* (chapter 8). In these cases the speaker must change not only location but orientation. In some instances we will see that the speaker organizes space in terms of the frontal *and* lateral orientation of the landmark to which he has transferred. This is one example of *total transfer,* in which the speaker adopts both the position and the orientation of the landmark. In other cases, if the speaker constructs space in terms of the lateral orientation of the landmark, he may continue to organize the world in terms of his own general orientation. I will refer to this as the *partial transfer* of the speaker to the position of the landmark.[5]

It has been suggested that when the landmark is unexpressed, the description of space is invariably egocentric, referring to the speaker's real or virtual position. When the landmark is introduced by the preposition *de,* the speaker is not entirely differentiated from the landmark, since certain qualities are shared by both speaker and landmark. The use of the expression *par rapport à* in (23) illustrates the maximum degree of detachment of speaker and landmark. The examples below illustrate my point.

> (25) *la table est à gauche de la chaise*
> the table is to the left of the chair

> (26) *la table est à gauche par rapport à la chaise*[6]
> the table is to the left with respect to the chair

Imagine that the speaker in the scenes below occupies the reader's position: example (25) describes figure 1 more accurately than it describes figure 2. In contrast, sentence (26) appropriately describes figure 2.

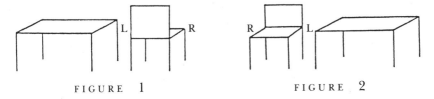

FIGURE 1   FIGURE 2

Why such a difference? In figure 1, the table is *left* if we take into consideration the speaker's lateral orientation, which is attributed to the chair. The separation of speaker and landmark is not complete. In figure 2, in contrast, the table is to the left judging from the intrinsic lateral orientation of the chair. Speaker and landmark are entirely independent in this case. The use of the expression *par rapport à* describes the complete detachment of speaker and landmark more precisely than the preposition *de* does. Instead, this latter, less marked preposition is used in situations where the landmark and speaker remain partially identified.

The following stages progress from the most egocentric cases of spatial description to those most independent of the speaker:

1. Unexpressed landmark referring to the real position of the speaker.

2. Unexpressed landmark referring to the virtual position of the speaker.

3. Lexically expressed landmark introduced by *de*, implying partial differentiation of speaker and landmark.

4. Lexically expressed landmark introduced by the expression *par rapport à*, implying total differentiation of speaker and landmark; the landmark here becomes a deliberately adopted point of reference.

Possibly the transition between phase 1 and 2 is more gradual than the above schema suggests; it is also possible that the speaker's awareness of separation from the landmark increases progressively. I do not wish to exclude the possibility that a speaker could leave the landmark unexpressed even while remaining mentally disassociated from it. For the majority of examples of an unexpressed landmark, however, the choice of this strategy is best explained by the speaker's identification with the landmark.

A series of examples will conclude this review of the connections between speaker and landmark: the following sentences illustrate the limits of the speaker's identification with the landmark. In the sentences below, the target of the prepositional phrase is the speaker himself.

> (27) *je suis au-dessus (de l'eau)*
> I am above (the water)

> (28) *je suis devant (l'arbre)*
> I am in front (of the tree)

Even though the landmark remains unexpressed in these examples, it is difficult to imagine the speaker setting up some mental identification with the landmark and then evaluating his own position from this perspective. These examples clearly demonstrate that the speaker need not identify even partially with a sublexical landmark. However, this does not contradict what has been argued above. The identification of speaker and landmark has been suggested only for the simplest usages of language; more complex linguistic forms will consequently force the separation of the two terms (speaker and landmark). It is interesting to note that sentences in which the speaker is identified with the target arise quite late in the child's acquisition of language. In this sense, examples (27) and (28) do not weaken the importance of the primitive relation between speaker and landmark.

2.3 Directional and functional prepositions

Spatial relations generally depend on two terms: the target and the landmark. The latter, we recall, is often identified with the position of the speaker. When landmark and speaker are distinct, can we then speak of three prepositional terms, speaker, target, and landmark? My response to this is no, when the relation remains independent of the position of the speaker, as in example (29), describing the scene in figure 3. The answer is yes, however, when the position of the speaker is crucial, as in (30), describing figure 4.

(29) *le chat est devant le fauteuil*
     the cat is in front of the armchair

(30) *la chaise est devant le fauteuil*
     the chair is in front of the armchair

FIGURE 3   FIGURE 4

The spatial preposition *devant* may depend on either two or three terms. I will discuss both versions of this preposition in chapters 7 and 9; the first interpretation is tied to the general orientation of the landmark, and the second is tied to the concept of access to perception. Another pair of three-term relations will be examined in chapter 10: *avant/après*, which depend on target and landmark but also on the pole, the second member of a potential encounter that is defined by the context of the utterance.

Three-term relations, such as the second version of *devant/derrière* and *avant/après*, do not have the same function as two-term relations such as *au-dessus/en dessous*, the first version of *devant/derrière*, and *à gauche/à droite*. These latter expressions generally characterize the position of the target with respect to the landmark along a specific axis: respectively, vertical, frontal, and lateral. Three-term relations, on the other hand, describe the manner in which the terms are spatially organized along any of these directions. The prepositions $devant_2$/$derrière_2$, linked to access to perception, indicate whether or not the target is perceptible to the speaker. The prepositions *avant/après* describe a potential contact that might occur along a vertical, frontal, or lateral axis. Interestingly, the bikers in the scene below may be described by sentence (31), but not by sentence (32).

(31) *le curé est avant le ministre*
the priest is in front of the minister

(32) **le curé est à droite du ministre*
the priest is to the right of the minister

FIGURE 5

In fact, the predominance of movement and potential contact in the above scene makes any lateral localization unusual.

I will call the first group of prepositions *directional* and the second group *functional*. It has already been pointed out that the first group consists of two-term prepositions, and the second group, three-term prepositions. We also find syntactic differences between the two types of prepositions. First, the landmarks of directional prepositions may be introduced by the preposition *de*, while those of functional prepositions may not.

(33) *l'aigle est au-dessus de la montagne*
the eagle is above the mountain

(34) **le peuplier est avant de le chêne*[7]
the poplar is ahead of the oak

Furthermore, directional and functional prepositions operate differently in comparative constructions. As the examples below illustrate, directional prepositions allow comparatives, while functional prepositions do not.

(35) *la voiture est plus à gauche que l'arbre*
the car is further to the left than the tree

(36) **la voiture est plus devant₂ que l'arbre*
the car is more before than the tree

(37) **la voiture est plus avant que l'arbre*
the car is more ahead than the tree

The use of the comparative is not perfectly acceptable for all directional prepositions however, and *plus haut* 'higher' is preferred over *plus au-dessus*.

One pair of directional prepositions, the first version of *devant/derrière*, behaves like the functional prepositions and may not be found in constructions with the preposition *de* or the comparative.

(38) *le fauteuil est devant₂ de la table*
the armchair is in front of the table

(39) *le fauteuil est plus devant₂ la table*
the armchair is more in front of the table

So the distinction between functional and directional prepositions is not perfectly clear-cut, and the two versions of *devant/derrière* add to this confusion. I have already sketched out (chapter 1) the reasons for the bisemy of this particular pair of prepositions. Since my analysis differs from the unified interpretation proposed for the English expressions *in front of/in back of*, I will return to this point in greater detail in chapter 9. Even if we cannot depend entirely on the distinction between functional and directional prepositions, this distinction may still help clarity the way spatial prepositions are put to use.

3

The representation of objects

In this chapter I will explore the various representations of the terms of a spatial relation. The criteria employed in this section are linguistic and aim at a unified description of spatial relations, minimizing the polysemy of these terms. Several alternative analyses will be presented, but it belongs to the field of psychology to make the final choice among these options.

Finally, I will examine the orientation of the objects of a spatial relation. As we will see, orientation may be either *intrinsic* or *contextual*.

3.1 The idealization of the terms of a spatial relation

Spatial relations would seem extravagantly complex if we failed to acknowledge that the terms juxtaposed in a spatial relation have different characteristics contributing to the variety of their uses. In fact, the objects located by spatial prepositions should not be forced into a particular mold; rather, they should be examined according to the perspective from which they are conceptualized.

A specific perspective will emphasize certain characteristics of an object, while ignoring others. The boundaries of certain objects are often indeterminate by their very nature; the exact line between the heel and the ankle, or the wrist and the arm, is relatively unimportant, given the adequacy of our general knowledge of these parts of the body.

Physical objects are not the only possible terms of a spatial relation; gases and liquids, other forms of matter, geographical entities, and even holes may play a part. It is not my purpose here to take up a psychological investigation of perception; I will discuss the various means by which our perception structures and recreates the world around us only when this is necessary for the interpretation of spatial prepositions.

The creative properties of perception can be understood if we return to the example of the table, first presented in chapter 1, figure 6. This piece of furniture must be conceptualized in two ways to explain the use of *en dessous* with one single usage rule: the table may be perceived as a global entity or only as a horizontal surface, as we see in examples (1) and (2).

> (1) *la chaise est en dessous de la table*$_1$
> the chair is under the table

(2) *le papier est en dessous de la table$_2$*
    the paper is under the table

If we fail to recognize the metonymy presented above, two different definitions of the expression *en dessous* will be needed, since the
chair is not lower than the lowest part of the table, although the paper
is. Here we must choose either a polysemic definition of the spatial
preposition *en dessous* or two different conceptions of the objects of this
preposition. Admittedly, the influence of language on a theory of perception is not unequivocal.

The analysis of the preposition *dans* will provide another example
of this interdependence. Before proposing a functional definition of
this preposition, I will evaluate the following topological definition,
formulated in terms of inclusion:

D$_1$: *a est dans b* if the limits of the landmark include the limits
of the target.

Topologically, a set A is included in a set B if all the points of A
coincide with points of B. Definition D$_1$ presents a problem for an
open container such as the glass in figure 1, described by sentence (3).

FIGURE 1

FIGURE 2

(3) *la mouche est dans le verre*
    the fly is in the glass

Although the fly is in the glass, it is not true that the fly is included
within the limits of the glass. This fact led me to postulate an imaginary horizontal plane closing off the container (Vandeloise 1979). If
we accept this hypothesis concerning the boundaries of a container,
the definition above applies without difficulty to example (3). This appears to be a natural solution and was proposed independently by
Vandeloise (1979) and Herskovits (1982). However, Herskovits points
out that the line closing an open container does not coincide with its
convex envelope.[1] Note that example (3) is not appropriate for figure
2, even though the fly is within the limits of the convex envelope of
the glass. This demonstrates that the imaginary closure proposed in

figure 1 may have unexpected repercussions. How can we allow for the imaginary line AB while excluding lines AC and BD? As we will see in chapter 13, our only recourse is to introduce the functional relation of container/contained, restricting the convex envelope of the glass to the containing part. Definition D_1, formulated in terms of boundaries and inclusion, leads us back to the function of the landmark of the spatial relation. A functional definition now is possible.

D: *a est dans b* if the landmark *b* (partially) contains the target *a*.

The extralinguistic container/contained relation, practiced by the child well before language is fully acquired, here receives its deserved position in our explanation of *dans*. This definition does away with the need for the closure suggested earlier. The psychological reality of this closure is no longer supported by linguistic evidence when we proceed from definition D_1 to definition D. The first definition gave a certain spatial character to the preposition *dans,* allowing the application of principles of geometry, since the definition emphasized the limits of the landmark. The second definition, emphasizing the function of the preposition, easily explains why the frothy head on the beer in figure 3 is still said to be *dans le verre* 'in the glass'. The speaker's everyday understanding of physics, capillary movement, and the properties of the foam suffice to explain how a glass can contain a liquid that extends beyond its limits.

FIGURE 3

Another example provides evidence of the interplay between definitions of a spatial relation and the way we conceptualize the objects participating in this relation. If we conceptualize a tree in its entirety, the example below clearly illustrates the partial inclusion of the target within the landmark.

(4) *l'arbre est dans la terre*
the tree is in the ground

If *the tree* refers not to the leaves and the trunk, but to the roots alone, example (4) describes the total inclusion of the target in the landmark. Such an analysis, naturally, offends our intuition; I point this out only to show the danger we run in exaggerating our idealization of the terms of a spatial relation.

Our freedom to mold and transform objective reality remains enormous, however. The idealization of an object[2] may be reduced by metonymy to one of its parts, as in the example of the table in (2). We might understand an object as an idealized contour, ignoring superfluous details, or as the nearest geometrical approximation. When measuring the height of a house, for example, we will probably ignore the chimney and the TV antenna. When we measure its width, we are likely to leave out the balcony and the porch roof. Irregular foundations will be assimilated to the shape of a rectangle or trapezoid. Finally, a spatial relation may represent an object by its horizontal or vertical projections. While the church is conceptualized as a volume in (5), it is represented by its horizontal projection and configured as a surface in (6).[3]

> (5) *le Saint-Esprit est au milieu de l'église*
> the Holy Spirit is in the middle of the church

> (6) *le curé est au milieu de l'église*
> the priest is in the middle of the church

In (7), the projection of the bird onto the field plays a role in the relation described.

> (7) *l'oiseau vole dans le pré*
> the bird flies in the field

Another option in this case would be to consider the surface of the field as a volume containing the air above it. In interpreting this sentence, we have a choice between idealizing the target (the bird) or the landmark (the field): it is psychology's role to explain this choice.

Among the various means of idealizing objects, Herskovits includes the reduction of the terms of the preposition *à* to a single point, and the closure of containers. I have argued above that the linguistic value of these idealizations depends largely on the definition we attribute to the prepositions *à* and *dans*.

3.2 Intrinsic orientation of objects

The top (*dessus*) of a bottle is its highest part, and the tail end (*arrière*) of a car is that part opposite the direction of its movement. Nevertheless, for an upturned bottle (figure 4) or a car backing up (figure 5), the top is the lower part of the bottle and the tail end of a car is located in the direction of its movement.

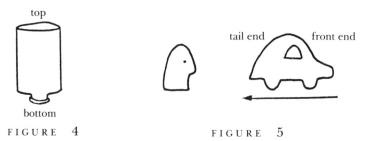

FIGURE 4   FIGURE 5

No one would want to accept two different versions of *dessus* or *arrière* in these cases. Instead, we note that one usage of these words corresponds to the normal use of the objects described, while the other usage describes an unusual, or less usual, situation. I prefer then to suggest a principle of fixation, formulated below.

> Fixation principle: An object may be described relative to its usual position, even if its actual position differs from the usual position at the moment of utterance.

The descriptions of the parts of the bottle and the car in figures 4 and 5 follow from this principle. When the fixation principle applies to an object along a single axis, the object is generally intrinsically oriented in this direction. Such is the case of the bottle, along a vertical axis, and of the car in terms of the direction of movement. The fixation principle does not invariably dictate the intrinsic orientation of an object, however. Imagine a couple, for example, who have the habit of turning the more leafy side of a fern towards the center of the room. If one member of this household accidentally orients the plant the wrong way, the other could easily remark,

> (8) *pourquoi as-tu mis le devant de la fougère en arrière*
> why did you put the front of the fern to the back

The fixation principle here plays a role in the private language of the couple, but this does not mean that the fern is intrinsically oriented in the frontal direction. In fact, the meaning of sentence (8) would probably remain opaque to a visitor in this house. For an object to be intrinsically oriented, it must almost always occupy the same position, and this must be recognized by nearly all the members of a single linguistic community. The fern satisfies the first of these conditions, but not the second.

An object is intrinsically oriented only if the parts orienting it are easily recognizable. This is generally the case for frontal or vertical directions but is more rarely the case for the lateral direction. Because of the symmetry along this axis, the fixation of *left* and *right* is rare. In fact, this is almost exclusively limited to humans and the vehicles we drive.

The fixation principle orients an object according to its usual position: this is the type of intrinsic orientation that has been noted by Bierwisch. A different type of intrinsic orientation, pointed out by Teller (1969), is anthropomorphic in character. Along the frontal direction, the most functional or most detailed side of an object will be labelled the *front*, by analogy with the human face; the opposing side will be called the *back*. Which type of orientation, positional or anthropomorphic, predominates? This is difficult to answer, since both are generally related. In fact, the functional traits of an object (anthropomorphic orientation) determine the position according to which the object is used (positional orientation): rather than being turned towards the wall, a chest of drawers is oriented to face its user, so that the user may more easily open its drawers.

Note, however, that the positional orientation along the frontal direction is reversed: the part of the object facing the speaker is called the *front*.

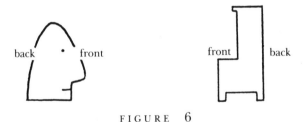

FIGURE   6

Later I will examine the similarity between this situation and the case of canonical interaction.

A certain category of objects, however, does not share the orientation observed above. These are objects such as telescopes, rifles, watering cans, garden hoses, etc. I will call these objects *projectors*, since they share the quality of provoking movement: that of the bullet in the case of the rifle, that of the water in the case of the hose. The functional part of such an object is called the *avant* (not *devant*), as opposed to the other part called the *arrière* (not *derrière*). Since positional orientation would predict the inverse, must we then conclude that it is the anthropomorphic character, rather than the position, of these objects that determines the naming of their parts? I don't believe so. I have already pointed out that we speak of the *avant* of a rifle, and not the *devant:* this distinction in terminology highlights the role played by movement in the orientation of these objects, as I will discuss in section 3.3.

Perhaps a more convincing argument for the importance of anthropomorphic orientation is illustrated by the lexical items used to designate parts of the body as well as parts of intrinsically oriented objects. In contrast to many native American languages (Casad 1982, Friedrich 1969), which almost exclusively make use of the parts of the body in their description of space, French seems rather impoverished in this type of vocabulary. We might note expressions such as *la face d'un timbre* 'the face of a stamp', *le dos du livre* 'the spine (back) of a book', *la tête du lit* 'the head of the bed', and *le pied du céleri* 'the root (foot) of the celery'. This shared vocabulary, illustrated in all the languages of the world, is doubtless a definitive argument in favor of anthropomorphic orientation.[4]

3.3 The contextual orientation of objects

The intrinsic orientation of an object is by definition independent of the position of the speaker. What of an object that has no intrinsic orientation along a frontal or lateral axis, such as a tree, for example? If we ask French speakers to point out the *avant* or the *devant* of such an object, they would doubtless respond that such a request makes no sense. If we force them to point out these parts of the object, *if such a part did exist,* all our informants would choose the part of the tree facing the speaker (figure 7). This type of orientation is not universal: Hill (1977) has pointed out that speakers of Hausa, a language spoken in western Africa, will orient the tree inversely (figure 8).

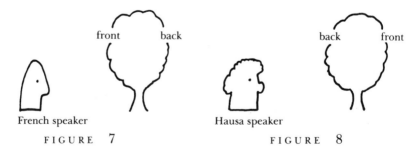

front   back   back   front

French speaker   Hausa speaker
FIGURE   7   FIGURE   8

As for lateral orientation, in contrast, both the French speaker and the Hausa speaker will directly attribute their own left and their own right to the tree, so that the total orientation of an object may be schematized as below in the two languages.

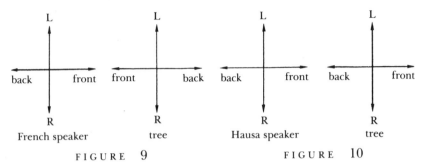

FIGURE 9   FIGURE 10

The first type of orientation is called *mirror-image,* and the second type is called *in tandem.*[5]

French, however, is not limited to a single strategy.[6] Although mirror-image contextual orientation is employed to determine the *devant/derrière* of an object that is not intrinsically oriented, tandem orientation may also be used to attribute the *avant/arrière* of a moving ball, such as in figure 11. The relation of *avant/arrière* to movement will be illustrated in more detail in chapter 10.

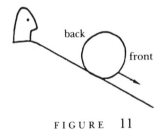

FIGURE 11

Projectors (hoses, rifles, etc.) are intrinsically oriented in tandem, most probably with regard to the movement of the projected object. The use of *l'avant* instead of *le devant* to qualify the positive side of such objects confirms this analysis. This explains why the class of projectors does not provide evidence in favor of the anthropomorphic origin of intrinsic frontal orientation. Because of their relation to movement these objects are oriented in tandem, not because of a preference for anthropomorphic over positional orientation.

One seductive explanation has been proposed by H. H. Clark (1973) to justify mirror-image orientation. The speaker, it is claimed, orients the object as an addressee in the position of *canonical encounter:* a short distance away, facing the speaker. If this were the only possible interpretation of events, this hypothesis would clearly delineate the ways we structure space. The paragraph above, however, cautions us to be more prudent. Language reveals our idealization of the terms of a spatial relation only by means of the specific definition of the preposition that relates these terms. In other words, in the relation R = *a is Prep b,* three interdependent parameters may be found: the idealizations of *a* and *b,* and the definition of *Prep.* The linguist is free to play with these variables to arrive at the most accurate interpretation of R. He may then offer a variety of possible solutions to the psychologist, but it is not the linguist's job to determine the most psychologically plausible solution. I will present another possible interpretation of mirror-image orientation below.

Clark himself recognized a problem with his solution. As the figures below illustrate, the distribution of *la droite* and *la gauche* differ depending on whether the speaker is facing an interlocutor (figure 12) or a contextually oriented object (figure 13).

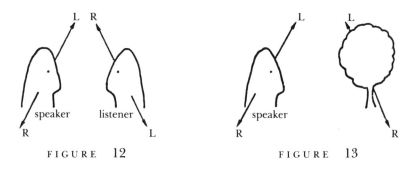

FIGURE 12   FIGURE 13

In fact, canonical interaction presents one of the rare cases in which the speaker reverses his lateral orientation rather than directly attributing it to the described object. Clark bases the direct attribution of contextual lateral orientation on the difficulties that are evident in the use of *la droite* and *la gauche.* The speaker is still able to point out his addressee's left shoulder and may even describe space by moving to the addressee's position, locating objects to the addressee's left or right. The intricate details of the use of left and right are not as complex as Clark would have us believe.

Child language acquisition poses another problem for the explanation of mirror-image orientation in terms of canonical encounter. Discussing the English words corresponding to the French *devant/der-*

rière, Clark (and others) claims that a target is located *in front of/in back of* the landmark if it is found on the front/back side of the landmark, which is oriented as a potential addressee—that is, in mirror image. If canonical encounter were the only intervening factor, we would expect to find that *in front of/in back of* would be acquired at the same time for every landmark; this is not the case, however. Miller and Johnson-Laird (1976) have found that children learn to use the relations *devant /derrière* with intrinsically oriented landmarks long before they use these relations with oriented landmarks. Thus children will say that the bench is *devant la maison* 'in front of the house' before they are able to say that it is *devant l'arbre* 'in front of the tree'. This evidence suggests that canonical encounter is not essential in the acquisition of the prepositions *devant/derrière*.

I would like to suggest another possible interpretation for mirror-image orientation. First, it seems wrong to consider frontal and lateral orientations globally, when our conception of space is in question. These different orientations are mastered by the child at different phases of language acquisition (Larendeau and Pinard 1968). Mirror-image orientation and tandem orientation may be useful descriptive tools, in the same way the dimensionality of the landmark is useful. The manner of orientation, however, is not necessarily more important than the dimension of the landmark. I propose considering stage by stage the child's acquisition of the ability to orient objects in space. Frontal orientation, evident at the earliest stage of development, is based on anthropomorphic principles (section 3.2) rather than positional ones. I deduce therefore that the earliest mode of orientation is anthropomorphic. This applies to the sides of an object that noticeably resemble the human frontal asymmetry. This includes all objects that are intrinsically oriented along a frontal direction (chairs, chests of drawers, etc.), but excludes objects that will later be contextually oriented (trees, spherical or square objects) and also excludes the lateral orientation of objects. The only objects intrinsically oriented along a lateral direction are certainly oriented anthropomorphically, since human beings and the vehicles we drive are included in this set. The anthropomorphic stage is followed by the positional stage, whereby objects that are insufficiently asymmetrical are oriented. Why does the observer's lateral orientation apply directly to the contextually oriented object even though the frontal orientation is reversed? Clark offers one plausible explanation of this phenomenon, by comparing this with canonical orientation. There is another possibility, however. Remembering that the intrinsically oriented object usually faces the speaker, we see that this type of interaction could later be generalized to objects that are contextually oriented. Here again, the linguistic use of the prepositions *devant/derrière* offers two solutions to the psychologist aiming to explain our perception of the world. It is probable that the two solutions, acting together, reinforce one another. However, the fact that children first learn to use prepositions such as *devant/derrière* with anthropomorphically oriented objects proves that canonical encounter is not as dominant a cognitive process as Clark would claim. Furthermore, I will show (chapter 9) that the role played by access to perception in the development of these prepositions has been too long neglected.

I would like to note, finally, that the speaker is not the only discourse participant who contextually orients an object. Any intrinsically oriented object in the context of the discourse may serve this purpose. Imagine a director asking an actor on stage to stand in front of a round table. The actor, it seems to me, could conceivably choose one of three positions, illustrated in figure 14.

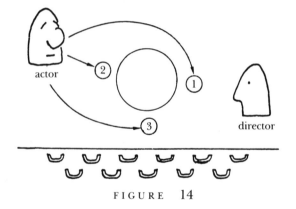

FIGURE 14

If he chooses position 1, the table is contextually oriented with respect to the director; in position 2, the actor himself orients the table. Finally, in position 3, the table is oriented with respect to the position of the audience.

4

Concepts involved in the description of spatial prepositions

In this chapter I will present the spatial prepositions studied in this book. I lay out the principles I have followed in collecting examples of these prepositions, and the concepts I have used to organize them.

The complexity of the actual distribution of spatial prepositions does not necessarily pose a synchronic problem for their acquisition. Diachronically, I will suggest that the symbolic association between signifier and signified must have been transparent at its origin. This original referent I call the *impetus* of a preposition. The evolution of a word's meaning from its impetus may often be anecdotal and accidental; the motivation of its present distribution may be lost and may appear synchronically arbitrary. In fact, in the case of spatial prepositions, I will show that the multiplicity of *usage rules* governing the prepositions, and the *selection restrictions* qualifying them, are systematically motivated. When the impetus corresponds to a global concept, its role is confirmed by evidence from language acquisition.

4.1 The corpus of the description

The expressions studied in this book are presented in the following order:

> *près/loin* 'near/far', *au-dessus/en dessous* 'above/below', *devant / derrière* 'in front of/behind', *à gauche/à droite* 'on the left/on the right', *avant/après* 'before/after', *à* 'at', *sur/sous* 'on/under', *dans /hors de* 'in/out'.

The examples of the uses of a preposition are interpreted liberally. I have allowed all the uses I have heard, whether these uses be particular to a region, allowed only by certain speakers, or even contested by some speakers. These departures from an accepted norm, frowned on in the name of linguistic purity, often shed light on the ways the meaning of a particular spatial preposition has developed. Among several examples heard in the region of Liège, I took note of an order a mother gave her barefoot child,

Sections 4.3 and 4.4 of this chapter are drawn from "Complex Primitives in Language Acquisition," *Belgian Journal of Linguistics* 2 (1987). Reproduced by permission of Editions de l'Université de Bruxelles, with assistance from the Linguistic Society of Belgium.

(1) *mets quelque chose dans tes pieds*
    put something in your feet

Utterances of this type, once singled out, are not admitted without embarrassment by their authors. Rather than reject them, however— and by what right? —I have always attempted to interpret them. Although the target of the preposition *dans* (see chapter 13) is usually the contained object, and the landmark the container, sentence (1) reverses this order in an interesting way, making a target of the slipper containing the foot. Only the most abstract signification of the preposition *dans,* the container/contained relation, motivates this example.

However liberal the selection of examples may be, I have covered only a small part of the uses of these spatial relations, and only the minutest part of the uses I have been fortunate to hear. As for the remainder of the examples presented here, I have trusted to my own native intuition.

No example in this study will be presented without reference to its extralinguistic context. The context is not restricted to the physical scene described by the speaker; I include also the social organization of the scene, and the perspective from which the scene is perceived. Langacker (1987a) has underscored the active role of the observer regarding the scene. A single physical reality may be conceptualized in many different ways. Each way of conceiving a scene may correspond to a different linguistic description. Thus, the sentences below share the same truth conditions but not the same meaning.

(2) *la statue est sur le piédestal*
    the statue is on the pedestal

(3) *le piédestal est sous la statue*
    the pedestal is under the statue

In fact, these sentences describe different images constructed from the same physical scene. In the first the statue is the target, while in the second it is the landmark. The same scene may be described from an infinite number of perspectives; I will present two of these aspects, described by the following sentences:

(4) *la statue est portée par le piédestal*
    the statue is borne by the pedestal

(5) *le piédestal porte la statue*
    the pedestal bears the statue

Active and passive voices here play roles parallel to the roles of the prepositions *sur/sous.*[1]

In order to be complete, each example in this work places a sentence in relation to a physical scene and includes the perspective according to which the scene is described. To facilitate the discussion, I will leave out perspective if this is obvious to the reader. Although our ability to shape physical reality is potentially unlimited, our understanding of this reality is essentially routine. By force of habit we often confuse physical reality with the most common idea we have of this reality. I will assume that my usual conception of a physical scene will coincide with my reader's interpretation, and will specify only perspectives that might appear unusual.

Objective scenes are generally illustrated by drawings in the text. Beyond the sketched environment, the context of an utterance includes our general knowledge of the world; obviously, this cannot be graphically represented in the text. For this reason I will ask the reader to attribute the normal function and the normal use to the illustrated objects unless otherwise instructed. The example below will illustrate the problem I have in mind here.

FIGURE 1   FIGURE 2

(6) *l'oiseau est à l'extérieur de la cage*
    the bird is outside the cage

(7) *? le couteau est à l'extérieur de la cage*
    the knife is outside the cage

The sentences and the sketches above point out that the object of the relation *à l'extérieur de* must be pragmatically related to its subject. Thus, example (7) is less acceptable than (6), since knives generally have less in common with cages than birds do. This knowledge results from our understanding of the ordinary world. This does not, however, exclude the possibility of an eccentric old man who keeps his birds in a drawer and his knives in a cage. If the above cage were his, the acceptability judgments of the sentences above would be reversed. However imaginative the reader will prove to be, I trust I will be spared this type of interpretation.

With rare exceptions, all the examples presented in this book are of the type *a Aux be Prep b*, where *a* and *b* are noun phrases obeying selection restrictions imposed by the preposition. I have chosen a neutral type of verb to minimalize the verb's influence on appropriate subjects and objects of the preposition.[2] I make no stylistic claims regarding these examples; occasionally I will phrase them paradoxically for the benefit of argument or illustration. Thus formulated, the examples remain acceptable, although I am entirely conscious of reducing their likelihood. Such examples will permit me to focus on the specific facts I wish to establish. For the same reasons, the examples will not be restricted to real-world contexts but will also include imaginary contexts whenever these elucidate the meaning of the word under investigation. In this way, we will not depend solely on our understanding of the world to interpret the acceptability of the prepositions we will study. Finally, I will consider only the most literal meaning of spatial relations, leaving aside figurative or metaphorical uses. In fact, I became interested in the linguistic description of space because the spatial domain allows for the most exact comparison between language and that which is expressed by language. Figurative uses of language do not provide this advantage.

For tactical purposes, in the hope of discovering unsuspected regularities or relations, I have tried to motivate *all* the uses of the spatial prepositions discussed in this book. This is not to say that I believe all the uses of these prepositions to be (ultimately) explainable. How then, without paradox, can we insist upon the creativity and the freedom of language, and at the same time claim to motivate all its possible divergences? In order to keep in mind these limitations, I will introduce the study of each preposition by quoting various uses, taken from literature or heard by myself, that defy any analysis.

4.2 Prepositional use

If we accept all the uses of a particular spatial relation, we also renounce the possibility of finding necessary and sufficient conditions determining its use. The reader should not expect to find classical categories[3] with well-defined boundaries in this book. According to a view of language employing the notion of classical categories, every object or relation is a member of a single lexical category; membership in a category is determined by necessary and sufficient conditions; boundaries are fixed and invariable; all members of a category have identical status. Rosch's work has shown, however, that languages do not function according to this type of categorization, but rather according to *natural categories,* which differ from classical categories in every way. A natural category has no well-defined boundary; there is no quality necessarily shared by each and every member of a category; boundaries are variable and may depend on modifications of the entire system; finally, not all the members of a category have the same status. Thus, there are certain uses of a word that may be more representative than others. The most representative use (or uses) is (are) considered prototypical. Since not all the uses of a preposition have the same status, I will attempt to organize the set of acceptable uses, in order ultimately to tease out one or more *usage rules* derived from a single impetus.

4.2.1 Questionable uses

All understandable uses of a spatial relation have been considered in the corpus of this work. Among the various uses, however, some are not understood without hesitation. The status of these questionable examples is unclear; they are most frequently understood by analogy with other, more representative uses. Once we allow a questionable use in our corpus, another even more questionable use may be suggested as a result. In this way, membership in a lexical category, instead of breaking off abruptly, decreases progressively, until it disappears altogether.

In the spatial domain particularly we find cases where an analogy with a representative use allows us to interpret a more questionable use. Point A in figure 3, for example, is clearly located in the upper part of the box. But what about point A'? and point A"? Their membership in the upper part of the box is progressively less obvious.

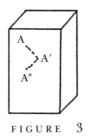

FIGURE 3

Because of this fuzzy area, it would be incorrect to identify *le haut* and *le bas* of the box with the upper and lower halves. This would imply, in fact, that there is a clear distinction between the two parts of the box, which does not correspond with reality. The distinctions between a representative use and questionable use will allow for a more appropriate explanation. Restricting this definition to the more representative uses, I identify *le haut* and *le bas* with the upper and lower parts of the box. I then extend this definition to the appropriate parts by means of a principle of proximity.

> Proximity principle: A point acquires the quality of another point as long as it is not closer to a third point bearing the contradictory quality.

A certain usage is less representative when a greater number of extensions are necessary to justify it. The proximity principle only applies to directional prepositions. Nominalizations such as *le dessus/le dessous* 'the top/the bottom' derive from the functional prepositions *sur /sous* (Vandeloise 1984) and may not be extended by the proximity principle. *Le dessus/le dessous* are restricted to the top/bottom parts of the box, while *le haut/le bas* are less clearly delimited.

The proximity principle only applies to a continuous volume. The separation between the two parts of the cupboard in the figure below prevents the proximity principle from applying. Examples illustrating spatial continuity are ideal for our study, since they clearly show when the extension of a word has progressed from its most representative to its most questionable uses.

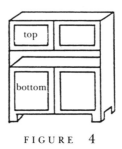

FIGURE 4

The same type of evolution is found in the domain of color terminology. Perhaps it is also found in other domains, from animate to inanimate, from vegetable to mineral, from imbecile to genius, etc. This progression occurs along several dimensions, however, and its exact details escape me.

The idea of questionable use must not be confused with that of *marginal use* in prototype theory. It is perhaps true that the penguin is not a typical bird, and it may occupy a marginal position in the category of *birds*. Nevertheless, taking into account the knowledge we have of penguins and birds in general, we will place the penguin in the category *bird* without the slightest hesitation. This use may be *mar-*

ginal, but never *questionable.*[4] This latter term could apply if an artist imagined some hybrid animal of unknown nature. Any attempt to categorize this fictional animal could be considered *questionable,* as long as common convention has not placed the animal in one or another category.

I do not consider errors and lapses to be questionable uses, if the intended meaning is clear from the discourse context. It is not unusual for someone to indicate the way to a pedestrian by pointing *left* but saying *right.* Even if the message is understood by means of the wave of the hand, we cannot consider this an understandable use of the word *right.*

4.2.2 Derived uses

I will limit the corpus of data by setting aside questionable uses of spatial prepositions, and replacing these with more explanatory representative uses. Another type of use, *derived use,* may also be set aside. A certain usage is derived if it can be deduced from another use of this word by the mechanical application of a general principle of the lexicon. The transfer principle and the fixation principle provide for such uses. In figure 5, the speaker will say that the cat is *à gauche* if he is speaking from his real position, but he will say it is *à droite* if he is speaking from the perspective of his addressee. The use of *à droite* is derived from the transfer principle and may be omitted from the corpus of this expression.

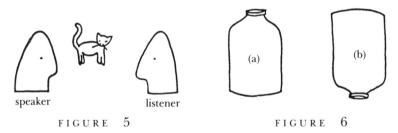

speaker   listener

FIGURE 5   FIGURE 6

In the same way, *le dessus* of the bottle is its upper part in figure 6a, but its lower half in figure 6b. The presence of both uses in the corpus of examples will complicate any attempt to define *le dessus* of the bottle. In fact, the second type of usage is derived from the first, by the fixation principle, and will therefore be omitted from the corpus.

If a questionable use is related to a representative use by the proximity principle, it might equally be considered an instance of a derived use. As I pointed out above, however, the relationship between ques-

tionable uses and the model they are based on is rarely this transparent.

Once questionable and derived uses have been eliminated from
our corpus, each spatial preposition is represented by its *normal use*.
This is the set of examples whose characteristics I will attempt to explain, and I will lay out the usage rules of each preposition in turn.

4.2.3 Characteristics

How can we describe the speaker's knowledge of the words he
uses? Two solutions may be proposed, at two ends of a continuum.

The first solution appeals to the capacity of memory to retain the
entire load of information in language acquisition: the speaker memorizes the list of uses of a word he has heard or uttered. He reproduces
the word when he recognizes a familiar context.

The second solution focuses on the similarities and regularities
perceived among different uses of one word. The speaker deduces a
minimum number of rules, one single rule by preference, which will
govern the usage of this word in the future.

The truth probably lies somewhere between these two ways of ac-
quiring a word, and the speaker's knowledge of each word has two
parts. On the one hand, he memorizes a list of uses; on the other
hand, he establishes a certain number of generalizations, which I will
term the *characteristics* of a word. I do not know the relative importance
of these two methods of acquisition. The degree of abstraction by
which these characteristics are perceived probably depends upon the
individual speaker. The list of characteristics may form an incomplete,
and sometimes contradictory, system of rules. The automatic use of
characteristics cannot lead to the appropriate use of a word without
drawing on additional knowledge.

If we ask a group of French speakers to define the meaning of the
prepositions *sur/sous* in the examples below, the spontaneous responses will illustrate what I mean by the characteristics of a word.

> (8) *la tasse est sur la table*
>   the cup is on the table
>
> (9) *la table est sous la nappe*
>   the table is under the tablecloth

Some speakers will point out that the cup/the table is above/below the
table/the tablecloth. Others will explain that the table is hidden by the
tablecloth. Still others will say that the cup and the table are in contact.

The characteristics of contact, access to perception, and order along a vertical axis do not all have equal status. When a characteristic describes at least one type of use that is not explained by the other characteristics, it will be called a *determining characteristic*. Contact alone is such a characteristic for the use of the preposition *sur*. The determining characteristics for the preposition *sous* are access to perception and vertical order. The descriptive qualities of the characteristics of *sur/sous* will be explored in chapter 12. We will see that all of these characteristics are either too general or not general enough, and they coincide in the descriptions of most of these prepositions. It seems that characteristics have only an approximate descriptive value: it is the linguist's part to elaborate these first generalizations and then look for the most appropriate usage rules. These rules will be considered in section 4.2.4.

First, however, I want to point out that the inadequacy of characteristics, the explicit knowledge the speaker has of the word, does not necessarily imply that a more elaborate, more structured, unconscious knowledge must exist, coinciding with some type of usage rule. Since the speaker's knowledge of a word has two parts, memory may easily supply information that a list of characteristics may lack.

4.2.4 Distributions and usage rules

Although characteristics represent the speaker's conscious knowledge of a word as much as possible, they are still far from ideal, if we as linguists hope to describe a language accurately. Here, in order of preference, are the conditions linguists would hope to find for the *usage rules* we attribute to a word.

1. A unique usage rule is a necessary and sufficient condition for the use of a word; that is, the rule is invariably satisfied when the word is employed and the word may be used only if the rule is satisfied.

2. A single usage rule is necessary but not sufficient. Outside the normal uses of a preposition, the usage rule also describes inappropriate uses. These uses must be eliminated by supplementary conditions, essentially selection restrictions bearing on the prepositional arguments. These restrictions will be considered reasonable if they are limited in number and if the concepts they introduce are pertinent to the description of the preposition. A restriction rejecting all landmarks with blue polka dots or crooked noses from the distribution of a particular preposition certainly cannot be called "reasonable."

3. A minimum number of sufficient rules in complementary distribution describe the distribution of the preposition. If many rules are required, this implies that none is necessary (none covers *all* the uses of a preposition). Nevertheless, taken together, these usage rules

are sufficient and occur in complementary distribution (that is, they do not overlap), together justifying a certain usage. *Complementary distribution* must here be understood in a restricted sense, taking into consideration the possibility that the same physical scene may be conceptualized according to different perspectives. Two rules in complementary distribution may apply to the same scene, as long as they describe the scene from different perspectives.

4. A minimum number of rules in complementary distribution (in the restricted sense), but not sufficient for set membership, define the distribution, and reasonable selection restrictions may apply. Since the rules are not sufficient in themselves, the inappropriate uses they allow must be eliminated by selection restrictions.

5. A minimum number of rules that are not in complementary distribution define the distribution of a preposition. The rules of a word overlap one another, so that a single use may be predicted by several rules simultaneously. If a rule is not required to justify at least one use, it must be eliminated in order to reduce the total number of usage rules.

As we move down this list of usage rules, the constraints on rules become less and less rigorous, and the rules resemble informal characteristics more and more. In the fifth type of usage rule, we recognize a particular type of characteristic: determining characteristics. Remember that there must be at least one use of a word that would not be described without a certain determining characteristic. These characteristics make up the minimum number of rules required for the description of a word. The five types of usage rules presented above form a perfect transition between the most formal usage rules—the necessary and sufficient conditions for use—and characteristics. Determining characteristics are the penultimate stage in this transition.

By their formulation, the majority of usage rules presented in this book fall into the first or second category. Such is the case, notably, for the usage rules proposed for the expressions *au-dessus/en dessous* and *à gauche/à droite,* described with respect to the vertical axis and lateral orientation, and for the prepositions *sur/sous* and *dans/hors de,* described by the bearer/burden and container/contained relations. It must be stressed, however, that the uniformity of this description is obtained at a price. We will see that lateral orientation and the bearer /burden relations are *global concepts,* which behave like family resemblance concepts and may be represented by different combinations of the traits that characterize them.

The prepositions *devant/derrière* are best described by two usage rules in complementary distribution. The second usage rule demands reasonable selection restrictions, notably in order to distinguish certain uses of *derrière* and *sous* (chapter 12). These usage rules belong to type 4 above.

The determining characteristics of the preposition *sous* (the fifth level of usage rules) are also presented in chapter 12. The synchronic description of this preposition is closest to the speaker's consciousness. Another analysis will be presented in terms of *logical diachrony* (section 4.2.5).

This completes our review of the different types of usage rules, and of the characteristics that will be employed in this description of spatial prepositions. In sum, usage rules offer a more structured description than characteristics, though the description may be more abstract. The search for usage rules will not be pursued as a purely formal exercise, however. This approach will illustrate the importance of concepts such as potential encounter in the distribution of the prepositions *avant/après*, for example, or in the container/contained and bearer/burden relations for the prepositions *dans/hors de* and *sur/sous*.

4.2.5 Logical diachrony and the impetus of a preposition

The signifier of every word is associated with a *complex category* (Langacker 1987a), which is represented by lists of characteristic uses and similarities relating these uses to different levels of abstraction. Usage rules represent the maximum degree of abstraction. Synchronically, the acquisition of complex categories may be partially explained by memory and therefore is not problematic.

In diachronic terms, however, it is indeed problematic that spatial prepositions have complex distributions. How can it be that a symbolic association has developed between a simple signifier and such a complex signified? It is unlikely that this association has developed simultaneously for all the nodes of the network representing the complex category. The child approaching a complex category enters through one door but cannot enter through all doors at the same time. The node by which we first approach this network of associations will be called the *impetus* of a word. However, certain lexical categories can be entered through different gateways by each individual. Such is the case, for example, with the word *dog*. The first referent you attach to this word may be closer to a basset, a bulldog, or a fox terrier, but the final knowledge you have of the category *dog* nevertheless does not vary from my own. Here there is no significant relationship between the impetus of the word and its final distribution, and this type of impetus is of little interest to a general theory of the lexicon.

For many other lexical categories, however, it seems that the networks of meaning are always entered through the same doorway. Specifically, if the acquisition of spatial vocabulary is tied to our extralinguistic knowledge of space, and if it is true that the acquisition of this knowledge is systematic and organized, it is likely that the impetus of a spatial term is identical for all the speakers of a single language. I will argue that at a certain time T_0, a transparent symbolic association is formed between the signifier of a word and its impetus.[5] The final distribution of a spatial term is acquired at a time following T_1 and is the result of a systematic development from the basis of the impetus. This development will allow us (1) to motivate the multiplicity of usage rules and characteristics, and (2) to motivate selection restrictions. Since this implies two different points in time that are not exactly situated in historical time, my analysis introduces the notion of an evolution in *logical diachrony:* the evolution from the impetus of the spatial word to its ultimate distribution.

4.3 Complex primitives and language acquisition

As I indicated in the preceding section, the majority of spatial prepositions addressed in this book will be described by a single usage rule formulated in terms of a global concept. My hypothesis is that each global concept is the impetus of a spatial preposition, governed by usage rules. The container/contained and bearer/burden relations, considered globally, are the primitives from which the lexical categories *dans* and *sur* are acquired. Eventually, the different aspects of these relations will be examined and analyzed separately by the speaker. Different aspects might individually motivate the various uses of a preposition. If the individual use comes too close to the global concept attached to a different preposition, some sort of arbitration becomes necessary; this is the case, for example, with the bearer/burden relation, which governs the preposition *sur.* Arbitration here occurs at the level of global concepts, as a certain amount of conventional knowledge intervenes in the most tangential cases. Different languages may make different judgments at these boundaries: this explains many of the difficulties encountered in mastering the prepositions of a foreign language, even if it is related to one's own.

Evidence from the literature on the acquisition of the English prepositions *in* and *on* appears compatible with this model. Studies on language acquisition often deal simultaneously with the acquisition of *in/dans, on sur,* and *under/sous.* In her second paper on these prepositions, E. Clark (1974) notes that *in* is acquired before *on*, and *on* before *under.* She thinks, however, that this ordering might be explained by *nonlinguistic strategies.* These strategies can be described by two ordered rules.

R$_1$: If the prepositional object is a container, put *x inside* it.

R$_2$: If the prepositional object is a supporting surface, put *x on* it.

According to these strategies, a young child will always put an object *in* a container, even if he is told to put the object *on* or *under* the container. As a consequence, the child will always succeed in the comprehension of *in* and fail in the comprehension of *on* and *under*, independently of his linguistic knowledge. Because of the second rule, the child will always put a toy *on* a horizontal surface. Therefore, he succeeds better in the comprehension of *on* than in the comprehension of *under*, but still for nonlinguistic reasons. "It is evident," writes Clark, "that the data are not a direct reflection of how well children of this age understand the spatial prepositions *in*, *on* and *under*. Instead, they appear to reflect the children's use of prior nonlinguistic strategies (*the child schema*) that are used in the virtual absence of comprehension" (1974, 169). Note that Clark does not wonder what would happen if a child were asked to put an object *in* an object with a salient horizontal surface. One might expect the child to put the object *on* the surface, being then credited with a better command of *on* than of *in*. This was the basis for a critique of Clark's position by Wilcox and Palermo (1974). These authors observed that children from two to three years of age have a tendency to place objects according to their canonical configurations. For example, they know that boats are usually located *under* bridges and not *on* them. Therefore, children are likely to overuse *under* if they are asked to put the boat *on* the bridge. According to Wilcox and Palermo, the reason Clark's subjects seemed to learn *in* before *on* is that the canonical relationships of the objects utilized in her experiments favored the preposition *in*. As a matter of fact, further data suggest that the command of *in* and *on* occurs almost simultaneously. Moreover, Bates and Learned's (1948) reports based on spontaneous verbalization by children between eighteen and forty-two months as well as a longitudinal study of a child by Tomasello (1987) seem to indicate that the use of *on* occurs slightly before the use of *in*. However, Clark's findings are confirmed by the results of Wilcox and Palermo's experiments with children too young to be aware of the canonical relationships between objects as well as with older children and a referent object designed to be contextually neutral. Bernstein's (1984) experiment with completely neutral and context-free objects also supports Clark's hypothesis.

From the preceding discussion it follows that the prepositions *in* and *on* are strongly related to containers and horizontal surfaces. Note that these notions differ in nature: while containers are functional, planes are geometric and mainly perceptual. I wonder whether it would be more difficult for a child to put a weathercock on a steeple than a cup on a table: if this is not the case, children might be sensitive to the functional nature of horizontal planes (they are ideal bearers) rather than to their two-dimensional aspect. Anyway, in order to compare the data on language acquisition with my description of *in* and *on* in adult language, I will interpret Clark's "non-linguistic strategies" as children's preferences first for containers, second for bearers.

Clark's experiments show that the child is sensitive to the functional notions of support and containment before he is able to connect these notions to the linguistic forms *in* and *on*. Now, why does Clark speak of *nonlinguistic strategies?* Probably because she assumes that the geometric approach is correct and, therefore, that support and containment are not the best concepts available for the description of *in* and *on* in adult language. But, in my analysis of these prepositions, the relationships container/contained and bearer/burden will turn out to be basic categories of adult language. If children's preferences are significantly related to basic categories of adult language, we will more accurately speak of a prelinguistic behavior.[6]

Now, is it possible that such data give us a clearer idea of the grasp that infants have of the relationship container/contained? The only precision one can get from Clark's paper is that her younger subjects (mean age twenty-one months) considered a box on its side, a tunnel, a truck, or a crib, as satisfactory containers even though containers with an upward opening elicited better responses than containers with an opening on the side. Experiments by Freeman, Lloyd, and Sinha (1980) with infants from twelve to fifteen months shed more light on the question. From that paper it appears that young children understand that the position of the container determines the position of the content. However, rather than referring to an abstract physical rule, the authors attribute this effect to the canonical position of the container. This conclusion is supported by the following experiment. The task assigned to the children was to locate a small object hidden behind a screen or a cup. Pieces of felt were glued either to the tops or bottoms of the cups, in order to provide a support for the small objects, which were moved with the cups during transportation. One small object was hidden behind one of two screens, another behind one of two inverted cups, and a third one behind one of two upright cups. Each pair was then transported, and the children had to relocate the small objects. The authors got a 5–5 pass-fail split with screens, a 9–1 pass-fail ratio with upright cups, and 1–9 pass-fail with inverted ones. Note that, from an experiment with upside-down houses, it appears that these results cannot be attributed to a general preference for containers with upward cavities. Freeman et al. conclude that "what dominates infants' performance is not the nature of the small objects but the nature of the location relations they enter into, not the rules governing the disappearance of objects so much as the characteristics of the things which seem to make objects disappear. . . . The effect may be named 'the canonicality effect': performance is affected by whether the experimenter uses the glass for its canonical purpose or misuses it" (1980, 259). Evidence for a strong tendency to look for a container in locative tasks is provided by the behavior of several children in Clark's (1974) experiments as well. Asked to put an object *on* an inverted glass, children turned the glass up and put the object inside it. One of the children went so far as to turn up the experimenter's glass. Other children who were asked to put an object *in* a plain cube tried to force it into the cube. Similarly in an experiment by S. Gillis (1982) testing the acquisition of the Dutch verbs *zetten* 'put vertically' and *leggen* 'put horizontally' a child refused to "leggen" an empty glass on a table because "it would spill out its content."

At this juncture, my discussion seems to lead to a peculiar conclusion: the knowledge of *in* and *on* by adults and children would be similar since both can be explained by the relationships container/contained and bearer/burden. This is obviously not the case. What I maintain, however, is that the first meaning attributed to *in* and *on* by the child sets up the complex concepts that regulate the intricate knowledge of these prepositions by adults; furthermore, it might act as a guide leading the child in his complete acquisition of *in* and *on*.

According to the above hypotheses, the distribution of *dans* and *sur* is basically motivated by the knowledge of some complex concepts (container/contained, bearer/burden) that derive from the first meanings that children attribute to these prepositions. While prepositions expressing such spatial relationships probably exist in all languages, detailed analyses show that there is room left for convention, that is, arbitrariness and cross-linguistic variations. This stems from two main facts: the existence of borderline situations and the overlapping of complex concepts.

For instance, slightly concave surfaces create borderline situations with respect to the relationships container/contained and bearer/burden. Languages cut this continuum at different points, that is, stipulate by convention that the former or latter relationship holds in such and such case. In examples from chapter 13, (10) and (11), semantic motivation does not compel us to use *dans* or *sur*.

(10) *le chien a des poils sur le dos*
the dog has hair on its back

(11) *le trésorier a des boutons dans le dos*
the treasurer has pimples on his back

Overlapping is due to the fact that many simple notions singled out in the analysis of spatial prepositions belong to several complex concepts. For instance, *contact* is involved in the analysis of the French prepositions *à, contre,* and *sur,* while *inaccessibility to perception* is involved in the analysis of *derrière₂* (see chapter 9) and *sous.*

Up to now, I have shown that convention tells us which preposition should be used when we are faced with a borderline situation or with an overlapping of (at least) two complex concepts. The whole picture of the prepositional system is still more complicated than it appears from the above considerations. Indeed, each preposition interacts not only with one other preposition but with many of them, if not with all the prepositions in the system. Furthermore, a language can express two related complex concepts by the same preposition while other languages analyze a complex concept further and split it up between two prepositions. That gives plenty of opportunities for convention to make a choice between two concepts whenever both of them might claim predominance. Simplistic as it may be, I believe that this interpretation of the prepositional system can explain the large part of motivation and of convention noticeable in the distribution of prepositions. Furthermore, it seems to be in keeping with the data from language acquisition. Indeed, it is consistent with my model that the motivations for the use of *dans* and *sur,* namely, the relationship container/contained and the relationship bearer/burden, directly derive from the first meanings attributed to these prepositions. Later on, children have to go into the intricacies of the interactions between prepositions. These interactions vary cross-linguistically. Whether children succeed in learning such conventions only by imitating adults or whether they get clues from the complex concept they have previously associated with the preposition is an interesting—and probably testable—question. It will be seen that complex concepts introduce in the description of prepositional uses a lot of simplifications and generalizations that cannot be due to pure chance.

So far two stages have been distinguished in the acquisition of prepositions: (1) the acquisition of the complex concepts motivating the distribution of prepositions; and (2) the analysis of these complex concepts into single features. At the second stage, the child has to learn the conventional decisions by which his language regulates the expression of the features common to different complex concepts. This model, however, is too simplistic in that it does not explain how the adequate linguistic form is matched to the complex concept it represents. Let us take the example of the form *in*. If it were directly matched to the relationship container/contained, the empirical consequence of the matching would be an almost immediate extension of the usage of *in* for all containers, since the child is able to recognize this relationship everywhere. However, a longitudinal study of a child by Gillis (1985) shows that the acquisition of *in* does not happen this way. Indeed, Gillis has noted that the child was able to use the Dutch preposition *in* for *boek in zak* 'book in bag' at 1 year, 9 months, and 12 days and *sleutel in auto* 'key in car' (speaking of a certain car) at 1 year, 9 months, and 21 days, but that it took as long as 29 days before he extended the use of *in* to other cars and 12 days more before he was able to use it when speaking of a small trunk. Gillis notes that "this abstract notion that permits us to make the link between *(book) in bag* and *(key) in car* makes it even more puzzling that the child does not use *in* in situations that need not imply such an abstract notion of containment (e.g., *book in bag* > *book in small trunk* seems to imply a less abstract notion of containment in comparison to *book in bag* > *(key) in car)*." My hypothesis would be that Gillis's subject, at this stage, has not made any generalization whatsoever and that his use of *in* is based on very precise memory instances in which he has heard *in* utilized by adults. In other words, the child has the complex concept of containment available, he knows the form *in,* but he does not make any direct connection between them because he believes that the meaning of *in* is far more specific than it really is. Only after applying *in* to many specific instances will he be able to match the form *in* to the relationship container/contained. Gillis's data unfortunately stop before this later stage, but my guess is that once this matching has taken place, a spurt must appear in the application of *in* to various containers.

A similar three-stage development of word acquisition has been assumed by Holzman (1981), who proposes a progression from holistic to featural mental processing. In the first stage of the development, the verbal concept presents itself as a set of *memories of instances.* Holzman quotes Schlesinger (1979), who claims that the child does not associate the word with a previously formed concept but that the concept develops as the word is associated with new instances. Such a process is certainly frequent in the acquisition of the lexicon. However, the acquisition of *in* seems to be different: indeed, the complex concept of containment is previously available, although the preposition needs to be associated with more instances before the matching takes place. At Holzman's second stage, the verbal concept presents itself as an *iconic abstraction:* "This stage differs from the first in that memories of separate instances have coalesced and in this sense, the concept has become an abstraction" (1981, 423). In my view, Holzman's second stage is necessary to warrant the association of a spatial preposition with the corresponding complex concept. Finally, at the third stage the verbal concept is understood as a *featural abstraction*, as is the case in my analysis of adult language, where a complex concept is eventually analyzed into several components. Similar pictures of the acquisition of verbal concepts appear elsewhere in the literature on child language. Sinha and Carabine, for example, note that "in the early stages of development the referential *function* of the utterance is insufficiently differentiated from its pragmatic content and the children are responding on the basis of their perception of the *overall* theme or frame of the linguistic interaction. The older children are beginning to acquire referential rules which enable them to make judgments about *particular attributes* of objects and object relations irrespective of the current framework of their use of the activity directed toward them" (emphasis mine; 1981, 118). Walkerdine and Sinha also propose an order of acquisition where "the older children are developmentally beginning to divorce themselves from the *functional* relation and to treat objects more on the basis of their *perceptual* properties" (1978, emphasis mine). This position is in keeping with Katherine Nelson's aphorism (1977): "Categories are formed on the basis of function and generalized on the basis of form." Note that besides the distinction between perceptual and functional concepts, I propose a distinction between complex and atomic concepts. Atomic concepts can be either functional or perceptual. Thus, in the relationship container/contained, the strength factor is mostly functional, whereas the inclusion factor is basically perceptual.

Smith's research on the contrast between holistic and differentiated perception of multidimensional stimuli (1979) provides important insights into the child's understanding of complex concepts. Studying developmental changes in the structures of categorization, Smith notes that young children's perceptions of complex stimuli are highly structured by holistic similarity, whereas older children's perceptions are structured by component dimensions. Young children seem predisposed to the global comprehension of perceptual concepts rather than to their analysis. This might also hold true for functional concepts such as the relationships container/contained and bearer/burden. The discrepancy between adult perception of color categories and their scientific classification along three axes (hue, brightness, and saturation) may also help us to understand what is going on in the global understanding of a multidimensional concept. Indeed, if color chips are ranked along the brightness and saturation axes, adults are unable to spontaneously disentangle these dimensions. Young children might react to complex concepts in the same way as adults react to the cluster saturation/brightness. Perceptual limitations alone cannot explain such reactions. Adults can be trained to distinguish brightness and saturation. Similarly, Smith has found that the attention that the younger children pay to the dimensional relations within a category increases under appropriate instructions, although they still have difficultly in ignoring holistic similarity relations.

4.4 Pragmatic bridges and language acquisition

A prerequisite for my analysis of spatial prepositions in adult language is that the uses of a preposition should be described by a unique rule whenever it is judged to be monosemic by native speakers. *Devant /derrière*, however, are often ambiguous. One reason for their ambiguity (chapter 3) is that the *intrinsic* general orientation of an object sometimes contrasts with its *contextual* general orientation provided by the speaker or by an intrinsically oriented object in the context. In chapter 9 I will provide independent reasons to add a second rule, D_2, involving the concept of access to perception.

D_2: *a est devant/derrière b* if the target/landmark is (potentially) the first (partial) obstacle to the perception of the landmark/target.

Furthermore, I will try to show how rule D_2 can be derived from D_1.

D_1: *a est devant/derrière b* if the target is located on the positive /negative side of the landmark's general orientation.

The argument runs as follows: as a consequence of our perceptual apparatus, we cannot see what is at our backs, that is, on the negative side of our frontal direction; on the other hand, we cannot see an object that lies on the positive side of our frontal direction but is hidden by another object; hence the connection, or pragmatic bridge, between rules D_1 and D_2 which is illustrated in chapter 9, figure 14. Yet one may doubt the psychological adequacy of this bridge, since it applies to the marked ("negative") term of the pair *devant/derrière*.

In fact, H. H. Clark's 1973 analysis predicts that the marked ("negative") preposition (i.e., *derrière*) is acquired after the unmarked ("positive") one (i.e., *devant*). This prediction clashes with the bridge illustrated in figure 14 (chapter 9). Indeed, according to this schema, *derrière$_2$* (which derives from *derrière$_1$*) should be acquired before *devant$_2$* (the concealing object being *devant$_2$* the rabbit in figure 14).

Fortunately for my analysis, the opinion of scholars in child language on the ordering of acquisition of *devant* and *derrière* has dramatically changed in the last years, and what could look like a handicap for the connection proposed in figure 14 turns out to be an advantage. Indeed, Cox (1979), Johnston and Slobin (1978), Tanz (1980), and Johnston (1984) have shown that *behind* is consistently learned simultaneously or before *in front of*. This point has been emphasized in a paper by Abkarian (1982), significantly entitled "More Negative Findings for Positive Prepositions." *Derrière*, therefore, seems to be a very reliable preposition for establishing the pragmatic bridge between rules D_1 and D_2.

The fact that children have easier access to *a is behind b* when *a* is completely hidden by *b* than when *a* is apparent would be consistent with rule D_2. Even though it was not carried out for that purpose, an experiment by Holzman (1981) provides a piece of evidence for this precedence. Holzman asked children to put an object *behind* a box with an opening in the front. She then removed the back side of the box in such a way that the object behind it became visible, and asked the children whether the object was *behind* the box (figure 7).

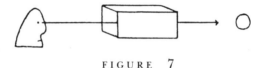

FIGURE 7

As is predicted by rule D_2, the errors in the second task increased by 43%. Another point worthy of attention is the way in which children can proceed from cases where *b* totally hides *a* to cases where there is only partial concealment. Indeed, when children have learned to say that an object *a* completely hidden by an object *b* is *behind* it, they still have to extend rule D_2 to partial inaccessibility to perception.

FIGURE 8

For example, even though most of the bottle in figure 8 remains apparent from the priest's point of view, it can be said to be *behind* the plate. There is an interesting connection between this use of *behind* and a surprising finding of Flavell, Shipstead, and Croft (1978). The authors tested three groups of children between the ages of 2½ and 3½. The child and the first experimenter were sitting side by side while a second experimenter faced them across the table. On each of four trials, the first experimenter held a screen in such a way that on the first trial (*All*) the screen completely blocked the child's view of a puppet and on the fourth (*None*) it completely blocked the second experimenter's view. On the second (*Top*) and the third (*Bottom*) trials, only the top and bottom thirds of the puppet were visible to the second experimenter. The child had to decide whether that experimenter saw the puppet or not. The correct answers, then, were *yes, yes, yes*, and *no*. The authors noted that correct answers (according to this pattern) decreased with age for the partial hiding conditions. Thus, while younger children decided that a partially visible puppet was visible to the experimenter, older children decided that it was hidden from him. Flavell et al. found "no convincing explanation for this peculiar result" (1978, 1210). It is worth noting, however, that by reacting to the partial concealment of the puppet instead of reacting to its partial visibility, children act in harmony with the expected extension of D_2. Indeed, the use of *derrière*/*devant* does not depend on the contrast *(partially) visible*/*completely hidden* but rather on the contrast *completely visible*/*(partially) hidden*. It is also worth noting that an apparently negative feature, viz. inaccessibility to perception, determines the acquisition of a preposition.

4.5 Review

The description of a preposition in this book will take the form shown in the diagram. The diagram serves essentially mnemonic purposes,

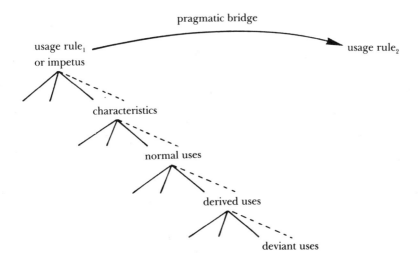

and it combines various notions. The speaker is psychologically conscious only of the various uses, the characteristics, and perhaps the concepts implied by the impulsions of the words he uses. The choice of usage rules is motivated by the linguist's aim, which is to capture the broadest generalizations and the greatest possible degree of abstraction in describing the use of a preposition. The choice is not self-evident, since two competing systems of usage rules may both fulfill this function satisfactorily.

Finally, logical diachrony is an attempt to find a unified description of each spatial preposition. Such a unified description seems neither motivated nor necessary in a synchronic description. There is, however, a time T_0 at which the symbolic association of the signifier and the signified must be transparent: this unique signified is what I term the *impetus* of a word.

PART TWO / SPATIAL PREPOSITIONS

5

The expressions près de/loin de *and accessibility*

*Toujours de retour sur les chemins du temps, nous n'avancerons ni
ne retarderons: tard est tôt, proche loin.*[1]

Maurice Blanchot,
L'Écriture du désastre

The expressions *près de/loin de*, independent of the notion of direction,
are without a doubt the simplest of the spatial relations. They are most
often described in terms of the distance between target and landmark,
a distance that is judged according to a certain norm. I will argue that
this norm depends largely on the access of the target/landmark to the
landmark/target. With the notion of accessibility I will be able to define the impetus of these expressions. One particular determining
characteristic, expressed in terms of distance, derives from this notion.
This will prove to be of further importance in our understanding of
the expressions *près de/loin de*.

This chapter concludes with a comparison of the expressions *près
de*, which is limited to spatial and temporal domains, and *proche de*,
which indicates proximity in every domain.

5.1 *The expressions* près de/loin de *and distance*

It is easy enough to see that it is impossible to define these expressions
in terms of absolute distance, where *près de* would refer to smaller distances than *loin de*. If any doubt remains, examples (1) and (2) should
convince the reader.

(1) *Jupiter est près de Saturne*
Jupiter is near Saturn

(2) *l'électron est loin de son noyau*
the electron is far from its nucleus

The expression *près de* in example (1) describes a greater distance between target and landmark than the expression *loin de* in example (2).

We can avoid this pitfall fairly easily by referring to a contextually
defined usual distance or *norm*, rather than defining these prepositions by any absolute distance. The usage rule of *près de/loin de* based
on this notion would then be the following:

P′/L′: *a est près de/loin de b* if the distance between target and landmark is lesser/greater than the norm.

It is more difficult, however, to specify the qualities of this norm: I will attempt to outline these difficulties in the following section. The principle characteristics of the norm relate to the accessibility of the target/landmark to the landmark/target.

5.2 Accessibility and the norm

Langacker (1987a) points out that the English expression *close to,* equivalent to the French *près de,* "permits apparently unlimited focal adjustments with respect to scale. The scale and the norm depend on the trajector of the relation." Although it is obvious that the size of the norm is proportional to the target, its dimension depends on other factors as well. Among these we note

1. *The dimension of the landmark.* We saw in chapter 2 that the landmark is rarely smaller than the target. In this respect, the dimensions of the target often determine the minimum norm of the relation. Although the norm rarely decreases with the size of the landmark, it may increase in proportion to the landmark. Thus, the distance between Jupiter and the landmark may be greater in example (3) than in example (1).

> (3) *Jupiter est près de la Voie lactée*
> Jupiter is near the Milky Way

2. *The speed of the target.* If the target is moving towards the landmark, the norm may increase with the speed of the target. In the examples below, the lake seems further from the antelope than from the tortoise.

> (4) *la tortue est loin du lac*
> the tortoise is far from the lake

> (5) *l'antilope est loin du lac*
> the antelope is far from the lake

If, on the other hand, the target is moving away from the landmark, the extent of the norm will diminish as speed decreases. In the hunting expeditions described in (6) and (7), the distance between the hunter and the tortoise may be greater than the distance between the hunter and the gazelle.

> (6) *la tortue est loin du chasseur*
> the tortoise is far from the hunter

(7) *la gazelle est loin du chasseur*
    the gazelle is far from the hunter

The distance between the tortoise and the hunter must be greater than the distance between the gazelle and the hunter, in order to make the hunter's access to the tortoise more difficult. In other words, if the target's speed makes its meeting with the landmark easier/more difficult, the normal distance increases/decreases.

3. *The speed of the landmark.* It is uncommon, in spatial relations, to find a landmark that is mobile with respect to the target. In the sentences below, however, the normal distance increases with the speed of the landmark.

(8) *le blessé est loin de l'hélicoptère*
    the wounded man is far from the helicopter

(9) *le blessé est loin du saint-bernard*
    the wounded man is far from the Saint Bernard

In the hunting scenes described in the following examples, the landmark is moving away from the target. The distance considered the norm between the two animals varies depending on the speed of the landmark: the distance between the fox and the rabbit is smaller than the distance between the fox and the hen.

(10) *le renard est près du lapin*
     the fox is near the rabbit

(11) *le renard est près de la poule*
     the fox is near the hen

Hence, we come to similar conclusions when we consider the relative speeds of the landmark and the target. If speed makes an encounter between these two entities easier/more difficult, the normal distance increases/diminishes. The notion of a norm is thus determined by the ease of access of the target/landmark to the landmark/target.

4. *The size of the speaker.* A water lily on the edge of a lake may seem *far* from the shore to a child, but *near* to his father. Once again, the ability to contact the target plays a role in determining the normal distance.

5. *The speed of the speaker.* A bar may seem *far* from the church if the speaker is on foot, but *near* if he is driving. Ease of access, more than distance, explains the choice of these expressions.

6. *The size and the speed of the addressee.* If the addressee is involved in situating the target, the speaker may describe the scene by consid-

ering his addressee's possible access to the target. Thus, a farm will be considered *near* a village if the addressee is a good hiker, but *far* if he is limping.

7. *Facility of access.* The normal distance increases/diminishes if the path to the meeting place of target and landmark is easy/difficult. The two houses in figure 1, at equal distances from the speaker, may in fact be judged *near* or *far* according to whether the speaker must walk up or walk down the hill.

> (12) *la maison rouge est loin*
> the red house is far

> (13) *la maison jaune est près*
> the yellow house is near

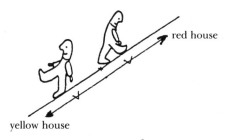

red house

yellow house

FIGURE 1

8. *Types of access.* While physical access is the principle factor in determining the norm, access to perception also plays a role. A mountain may be *near* if we are admiring its beauty from a hotel window, yet *far* if we intend to hike there. Here visual access is opposed to physical access. The wolves may seem *near* when we hear them howling in the woods, but luckily *far* enough away not to threaten our lives. In this example, auditory access and physical access are in opposition. Finally, a sailboat may be *far* to the naked eye, but *near* through binoculars. Two types of visual access contrast here. All these different types of access to the target change the value of the normal distance.[2]

5.3 The description of the expressions près de/loin de

The preceding paragraph clearly shows that the target's/landmark's access to the landmark/target[3] plays an important role in the use of the prepositions *près de/loin de*. The first definition P'/L', as a function of the normal distance, hides the role of distance behind the role of a specified norm. By this artifice, the definition of *près de/loin de* acquires a certain rigorous character so pleasing to lexicologists. I myself have succumbed to the charms of this analysis in the past (Vandeloise 1984). However, the role of accessibility in the distributions of the expressions *près de/loin de* seems too important to ignore.[4] Instead I propose the following usage rule for these expressions:

> P/L: *a est près de/loin de b* if the target/landmark is easily/not easily accessible to the landmark/target.

All the factors facilitating or complicating the meeting between target and landmark play a role in this definition. The principle factors are graphically laid out below.

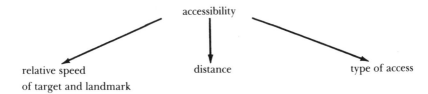

Among these factors, distance takes an important lead. Distance accounts for the rule P'/L', proposed above. As with all the factors determining ease of access, this rule constitutes a *characteristic* of the expressions *près de/loin de* in the theoretical framework employed here. Furthermore, examples (1) and (2) show that distance is a determining characteristic. In fact, for accessibility to play a determining role in sentence (1), exceptional circumstances would be demanded: for example, imagine a mad scientist on Saturn trying to attract Jupiter with a magnet. In most contexts, however, distance is essential in this type of objectively descriptive phrase, where the landmark is clearly detached from the speaker. Only distance can describe these sentences adequately.

To express this determining characteristic, rule P'/L' must be modified. We hope to avoid any reference to a norm of distance: this would only reintroduce all those factors determining access. However, only the dimensions of the target and the landmark play a role in determining the norm of sentences (1) and (2). These dimensions establish a *scale*, according to which the distance between target and landmark may be measured. I will modify rule P'/L' to express the determining characteristic P_1/L_1.

> P_1/L_1: *a est près de/loin de b* if the distance between the target and the landmark is small/large according to the scale determined by their dimensions.

Can this characteristic be seen as a usage rule? I demonstrated in chapter 4 that there is a continuum between the strictest rules and the weakest characteristics. A determining characteristic is, in fact, a usage rule that is relatively unencumbered by formal constraints.

Rule P/L is the impetus for the expressions *près de/loin de*, for the following reasons:

1. It motivates the characteristics of these expressions, in particular motivating the determining characteristic P_1/L_1.

2. It motivates the selection restrictions that must apply to the determining characteristic in order for it to be a sufficient condition.

Without this justification, the selection restrictions applying to the determining characteristic P_1/L_1 would be unreasonable.

5.4 A comparison of the expressions près de/proche de

In the examples presented up to this point, the expression *près de* demonstrates a spatial reference. However, this expression may also be used in a temporal sense.[5]

(14) *on est près de Noël*
    it's near Christmas

In the domains of color terminology (example [15]) or sentiment (example [16]), the expression *proche de* is generally preferred over *près de*.

(15) **le mauve est près du bleu*
    mauve is near blue

(16) **le ministre est près du curé*
    the minister is near the priest

(17) *le mauve est proche du bleu*
    mauve is close to blue

(18) *le ministre est proche du curé*
    the minister is close to the priest

Sentences (16) and (18) are intended to refer to the minister's friendship with the priest, and not his physical location.

The expressions *près de/proche de* differ essentially in their domains of application. Langacker (1987a) has noted a parallel situation for the English expressions *near/close to*. Because *proche de* applies to every domain, it is preferred over *près de* when we turn to investigate the impetus of the prepositions *avant/après* in chapter 10.

As sentences (19a) and (19b) illustrate, the adjective *lointain* stands in opposition to *proche*, but the expression *lointain de* cannot be used as the opposite of *proche de* (20) in the same way.

(19a) *le but est proche*
the goal is near

(b) *le but est lointain*
the goal is distant

(20a) *le docteur est proche du but*
the doctor is near the goal

(b) **le docteur est lointain du but*
the doctor is distant from the goal

6

Positions on the vertical axis

Il y a sept ans entre les deux premiers et le troisième. J'aurais préféré l'avoir au-dessus des deux autres.[1]

A mother in the Café de la Poste

In this chapter I will describe the characteristics of the vertical axis, its orientation, its direction, and its objective nature. This will be followed by a discussion of the prepositional expressions *au-dessus/en dessous*, which locate the target with respect to the landmark along this axis. Aside from historical considerations, the resemblance between *au-dessus/en dessous* and *sur/sous* is transparent to the speaker. For this reason, I will often refer to these latter prepositions, which will be studied in greater detail in chapter 12.

6.1 The vertical axis

The vertical axis is characterized by its orientation and its direction. It remains independent from the position of the speaker as long as the discourse involves only a limited portion of the terrestrial globe. This axis has no absolute origin.

6.1.1 Orientation and direction of the vertical axis

The vertical orientation is a family resemblance concept that will be illustrated below. It is parallel to

the position of a soldier saluting the flag,
the position of trees in a forest,
the direction of falling bodies,
the trajectory of missiles, etc.[2]

The positive direction of this axis extends from the earth to the sky, from roots to branches, from feet to head, from basement to attic, etc.

The reader might wonder why I describe the vertical direction by means of a list of traits, since gravity itself provides an economic—and some would say scientific—description of the facts. One of the goals of this book, however, is to describe the knowledge we, as speakers, have of our language. I would like to point out that expressions such as *au-dessus/en dessous* have been understood by French speakers long before the principles of gravity were discovered, and long before the child understands gravity's implications. While it may be true that the concepts of physics provide a metalanguage into which spoken language may be translated, these concepts often demand simplifications that exaggerate the importance of rules in the mastery of the lexicon, at the expense of memory and lists.

The following example demonstrates that gravity alone cannot adequately describe our understanding of the vertical axis. We need to transfer the speaker outside of a world where gravity holds, to an imaginary planet where smoke is blown out of chimneys with a bellows. Even if the houses float aloft in this weightless world, won't the speaker still be tempted to say that the smoke rises *above* the houses? While this use of the expression *au-dessus* is inexplicable in terms of gravity, it can be understood if we imagine all the chimneys the speaker has seen, with trails of smoke rising from them, deep in the woods. This forces us to integrate the direction of smoke, even on an airless day, among the traits characterizing the vertical axis. In this kind of extreme situation, one trait alone may motivate the use of the expressions *au-dessus /en dessous*.

Returning now to earth, we note that the vertical axis is a very coherent, united family resemblance concept, and it is rare—if not impossible—for its traits to contradict one another.[3] The usefulness of the family resemblance concept will appear more clearly in the description of general and lateral orientation (chapters 7 and 8).

6.1.2. The objective nature of the vertical axis

The vertical direction is generally independent of the position of the speaker.

The first limitation on the objective character of the vertical axis has to do with discourses referring to different parts of our planet. While example (1) describes the scene in figure 1, the expression *en dessous* is used with respect to the French vertical axis, while the use of the expression *au-dessus,* in the second part, refers to the African vertical.

> (1) *l'Afrique est en dessous de la France mais le sorcier est au-dessus de la montagne*
> Africa is below France but the sorcerer is above the mountain

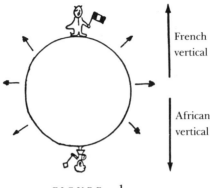

French
vertical

African
vertical

FIGURE   1

The description of the human body seems also to raise a doubt concerning the objectivity of the vertical axis. Couldn't we say of a gymnast walking on his hands, or a sunbather stretched out on the beach, that his head is *above* his feet, even if this is not the case along the vertical axis? This does not imply a reversal of the vertical axis, any more than a bottle turned upside down reverses the vertical axis. Rather, we see here an application of the fixation principle, where the body, like the bottle, is described by reference to its normal position, even if it occupies another position for a brief instant. What is more, this fixation is not imperative: in the examples of the gymnast and the sunbather, *au-dessus/en dessous* may also be used with respect to the normal orientation of the vertical axis. This is the case when we say that a thief hung by his feet in the air has his feet *above* his head.

In order to speak of a true reversal of the vertical axis motivated by an unusual orientation of the body, the new position must demand a different configuration of the parts of the body along the vertical axis, and also a new description of the elements of the exterior world. This seems to be Langacker's (1987a) intuition, when he affirms that a speaker walking on his hands could say sentence (2) as well as sentence (3).

(2) *the kite is above the house*

(3) *the house is above the kite*

Although certain English speakers share this intuition, I myself could not accept the French (4) corresponding to (3), even if I stood on my head.

(4) **la maison est au-dessus du cerf-volant*

An example adapted from Herskovits will illustrate how a horizontal speaker distinguishes between the position of his body and that of the external world. A sunbather, lying on the beach, could ask his neighbor,

> (5) *gratte-moi en dessous du genou*
> scratch me below the knee

But if there is a stone near the ticklish spot, and the speaker bent up his knees without changing his position otherwise, it would not be possible to say that the pebble is *en dessous de son genou* 'below his knee'. In other words, what holds true for the parts of the body no longer holds true when the target (here, the pebble) belongs to the external world. The above examples follow from the fixation principle, rather than from a reversal of the vertical axis based on the speaker's position.

In conclusion, the vertical axis remains objective as long as the discourse is restricted to a reasonable part of the terrestrial globe.

6.1.3 Origin of the vertical axis

It is possible that the examples below describe the same objective scene.

> (6) *l'oiseau est au-dessus (du haut) de mon nez*
> the bird is above (the top) of my nose

> (7) *l'oiseau est au-dessus*
> the bird is above

This is not to say that the line of sight obligatorily determines the position of the speaker along the vertical axis, or that an egocentric interpretation of (7) would be necessarily synonymous to (6). Example (7) could refer to the top of the speaker's head, as well as to his feet. In contrast to the expressions *à gauche/à droite* and *devant/derrière*, for which the speaker may generally be identified with a single point, the entire height of the speaker must be considered when the speaker locates a target with respect to himself along the vertical axis. We will see (chapters 7 and 8) that the expressions *devant/derrière* and *à gauche/à droite* generally depend on the position of the speaker. The objectivity of the vertical axis may explain why the egocentric uses of *au-dessus/en dessous* imply different landmarks on the speaker's body.

Example (7) could also refer to a landmark other than the speaker. In this case, the landmark is understood from the context of the discourse.

Figure 2 illustrates several possible interpretations of a sublexical

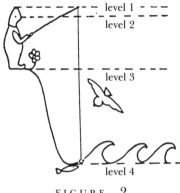

level 1
level 2
level 3
level 4

FIGURE 2

landmark: the top of the head, the line of sight, the level of the ground, and sea level. The flower is *en dessous* the two highest levels, but *au-dessus* the two lowest. The bird is *en dessous* the three highest levels, but *au-dessus* the fourth. There is no absolute origin along the vertical axis, that is, no level that is the lowest level absolutely. The fish in figure 2 demonstrates that sea level cannot be an absolute origin either: although the fish is *en dessous* the waves, it is still *au-dessus* the bottom of the sea.

6.1.4 Poles on the vertical axis

The vertical axis is an infinite straight line, parallel to a direction defined by a family resemblance concept that encompasses the alignment of a wall, a tree, and a proud man marching toward his destiny. This line may be travelled in both directions, and theologians will not be surprised when I describe the direction of the sky as *positive*, and the direction of the earth *negative*.

Two poles at the extremities of this axis are needed to define the positional adjectives *haut/bas*. I will call the positive, celestial pole H and the negative, terrestrial pole B. Using mathematical conventions, I could characterize these two poles by the coordinates ($+\infty$, $-\infty$). A comparison with an imaginary movement along the vertical axis will allow me to define these poles according to more plausible cognitive bases. With respect to this movement, pole B coincides with the origin of ascending movement, and pole H with its terminus. When the moving objects exceed the limits of the field of vision, as long as the direction of the movement is known[4] the points nearest pole H and pole B may be located, even if the poles themselves are invisible. If point A is closer to pole H/B than point C is, then A is higher/lower than C.

A comparison with the prepositions *avant/après* (chapter 10) will show why movement characterizes poles H and B more accurately than the notion of infinite coordinates does. In fact, we don't need to know whether the pole is located at a finite or infinite distance to determine which of the terms of the preposition is closer to/farther from the pole. If the moving objects leave the field of vision, only the axis and the trajectory of their movement is important. Similarly, an indefinite imaginary movement along the vertical axis allows us to establish a scale along this axis. I prefer the notion of an imaginary movement, whose axis and direction are known (though the extremities may not be [figure 4]), over and above the mathematical fiction of infinite distances as illustrated in figure 3.

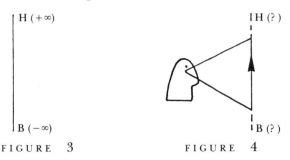

H ($+\infty$)	H (?)
B ($-\infty$)	B (?)
FIGURE 3	FIGURE 4

Once the poles H and B have been fixed, a usage rule of the positional adjectives *haut/bas* may be formulated.

H/B: *a est haut/bas* if the target is closer to pole H/B than it is to pole B/H.

In this positional definition of the adjectives *haut/bas* we recognize an application of the proximity principle, since the points closest to the poles are the very points to which the qualities *haut/bas* most clearly apply. They become less and less representative as they move away from the poles, and the central region of the vertical axis remains a vague area where such qualifications are uncertain.

As we will see in the definition of the prepositions *avant/après* (chapter 10), the word *plus* 'more' introduces an order whose domain is, here, the vertical axis. The adjectives *haut/bas* allow only one linguistically expressed argument: the target. This is not to say that the implicit landmark does not play a role in the expression, however. It is rare, if not impossible, for the adjectives *haut/bas* to situate a target in terms of the totality of the vertical axis. In general, the landmark sets the limits of this axis. The limits H′ and B′, the closest to the indeterminate poles H and B, play the role of the latter poles in the definition H/B. This is demonstrated by examples (8) and (9), describing the scenes below.

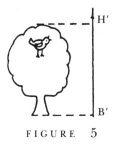

FIGURE 5

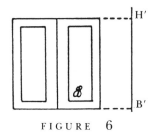

FIGURE 6

(8) *l'oiseau est haut*
the bird is high

(9) *la mouche est bas*
the fly is low

In figure 5, the summit of the tree determines the new pole H', and the ground sets the limits of pole B'. In figure 6, the top of the wardrobe sets the position of H' and the floor becomes pole B'.

6.2 *The expressions* au-dessus de/en dessous de

I will first present the characteristics of these expressions in terms of the arrangement of target and landmark on a vertical axis, and the type of contact permitted between the two. The dimensions of target and landmark are not restricted, as long as *au-dessus/en dessous* cannot be replaced by the expressions *sur/sous*. The expressions *au-dessus/en dessous* are generally converse.

Next I will show that order along the vertical axis plays an important role in the use of these expressions and constitutes the impetus explaining their behavior.

6.2.1 The characteristics of the expressions *au-dessus/en dessous*

Order along the vertical axis. The target of the expressions *au-dessus/en dessous* is generally higher/lower than the landmark. This order had long seemed a necessary condition for the use of these expressions, up until the day I heard myself say,

(10) *il y a un cafard en dessous du portrait du pape*
there is a bug under the portrait of the pope

We will soon understand how I was able to use *en dessous* in a situation where the target and the landmark were located at the same height off the ground. The expressions *au-dessus/en dessous* cannot actually reverse the order of target and landmark along the vertical axis, but the preposition *sur* occasionally can.

(11) *la mouche est sur le plafond*
the fly is on the ceiling

(12) **la mouche est au-dessus du plafond*
the fly is above the ceiling

The target and the landmark of the expressions *au-dessus/en dessous* must not simply be ordered with respect to the vertical direction: they must also be located on the same vertical axis. In fact, while example (13) describes figure 7, it cannot be understood to explain figure 8.

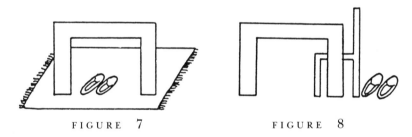

FIGURE 7   FIGURE 8

(13) *les pantoufles sont en dessous de la table*
the slippers are under the table

In consequence, horizontal projections of the target (a_h) and of the landmark (b_h) cannot be separated. The localization of the target and the landmark along the same vertical axis may be only approximate, however. The horizontal projections may intersect, as in example (14), describing the chair in figure 8. Finally, the horizontal projection of the target may contain that of the landmark, as example (15) illustrates, describing the rug in figure 7.

(14) *la chaise est en dessous de la table*
the chair is under the table

(15) *le tapis est en dessous de la table*
the rug is under the table

The horizontal projections of the target and landmark of these expressions may take the configurations shown in figure 9.

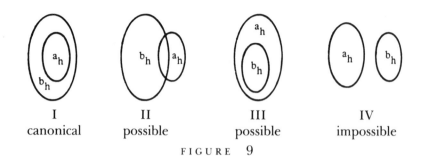

I	II	III	IV
canonical	possible	possible	impossible

FIGURE 9

The first characteristic of the expressions *au-dessus/en dessous* is best expressed with reference to a vertical axis, rather than with reference to the vertical direction in general.

> Characteristic A: *a est au-dessus/en dessous de b* if the target is higher/lower than the landmark on a vertical axis.

Contact. Since the target and the landmark of *au-dessus/en dessous* are ordered with respect to a single vertical axis, we have seen that their horizontal projections must intersect. As the examples below illustrate, this is not true for their vertical projections. Thus, sentence (16) is appropriate for figure 10 but not for figure 11.

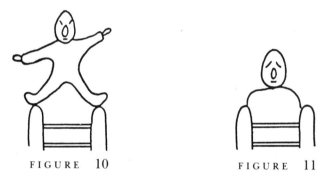

FIGURE 10   FIGURE 11

(16) *le président est au-dessus de l'échelle*
      the president is above the ladder

In the first scene, but not the second, the entire target is higher than the highest point of the landmark. Consequently, the intersection of the vertical projections of target and landmark here is null.

The second characteristic describes the contact between the vertical projections of the target and the landmark.

> Characteristic B: If *a est au-dessus/en dessous de b,* the intersection of their vertical projections is generally null.[5]

To sum up the behavior of *au-dessus/en dessous* relative to contact, recall that the intersection of the horizontal projections of the terms of *au-dessus/en dessous* may not be null.

The above characteristics do not describe all the details of the distribution of *au-dessus/en dessous*. In the first place, we do find canonical instances of the use of these expressions, as well as instances where this usage is more marginal. If, for example, we made a choice between the chair in figure 8 and the chair in the scene below, we would prefer to say of the latter that it is *en dessous de la table* 'below the table'. This choice is explained by characteristic A, which demands that the prepositional terms be located along a single vertical axis.

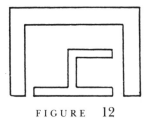

FIGURE   12

Figure 12 fits these demands more transparently than figure 8, but when we look at the vertical projections of the target and the landmark, the same preference is evident. As figure 10 illustrates, these projections may be tangential. Nevertheless, the use of the expression *au-dessus* is much less natural than the use of *sur* to describe the lamp in figure 13.

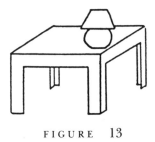

FIGURE   13

(17) *la lampe est sur la table*
      the lamp is on the table

(18) *?la lampe est au-dessus de la table*
      the lamp is above the table

This type of example improves when access to the target along the vertical axis is difficult. Thus, the president's balancing act on the ladder renders example (16) more acceptable. Similarly, we prefer (20) over (19) since cupboards are higher, and less accessible, than tables.

> (19) *la tasse est au-dessus de la table*
> the cup is above the table

> (20) *la tasse est au-dessus de l'armoire*
> the cup is above the cupboard

Sentence (19) itself is better understood coming from the mouth of the child in figure 14 than from his father. Since the child is small, his position with respect to the table parallels the position of his father with respect to the cupboard. Characteristic B is unable to explain these varying judgments.

FIGURE 14

In fact, there are counterexamples to characteristics A and B. The houses in figure 15 are not situated along the same vertical axis, and the intersection of their horizontal projections is null.

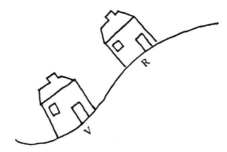

FIGURE 15

Furthermore, contrary to characteristic B, the intersection of their vertical projections is not null.

As illustrated by the example below, from Herskovits, the vertical projection of the landmark may in fact include the vertical projection of the target.

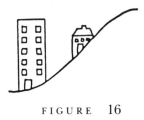

FIGURE 16

(21) *la chaumière est au-dessus de la tour*
     the cottage is above the high rise

I will attempt to remedy the inadequacies of these characteristics in section 6.2.2. Before proceeding, however, I will introduce the third characteristic of these expressions.

Symmetry of target and landmark. Among the prepositions studied in this work, only the expressions *au-dessus/en dessous* and *avant/après* respect the criterion of symmetry between target and landmark. These expressions are converse, with one exception: the equation

  a est au-dessus de b = b est en dessous de a

does not hold true when the prepositions *sur/sous* can be substituted for *au-dessus/en dessous*, and when the condition in section 2.1 on the target and landmark is violated. This is illustrated by examples (22) and (23).

  Sur and *au-dessus* are not interchangeable.

    (22a) *le parapluie est au-dessus de la tête du curé*
          the umbrella is above the priest's head

      (b) **le parapluie est sur la tête du curé*
          the umbrella is on the priest's head

      (c) *la tête du curé est en dessous du parapluie*
          the head of the priest is under the umbrella

  Sur and *au-dessus* are interchangeable.

    (23a) *la tasse est au-dessus de l'armoire*
          the cup is above the cupboard

(b) *la tasse est sur l'armoire*
   the cup is on the cupboard

(c) **l'armoire est en dessous de la tasse*
   the cupboard is under the cup

The differences in acceptability of the examples above will be explained in the next section.

6.2.2 The impetus and motivation of *au-dessus/en dessous*

The characteristics presented above do not have the status of usage rules. In particular, they are unable to explain the usage of *au-dessus* in example (21). Nevertheless, if we examine the information given by characteristics A and B, we arrive at a formula approaching the status of a usage rule.

aD_1/eD_1: *a est au-dessus/en dessous de b* if the lowest/highest point of the target is higher/lower than the highest/lowest point of the landmark along the same vertical axis.

In fact, this formula governs the immense majority of uses of *au-dessus/en dessous,* if we allow a certain leeway concerning the position of target and landmark along the vertical axis. However, exhaustiveness of description is one goal of this analysis, and we can make no claim to an exhaustive explanation unless a second usage rule is added to the first.

aD_2/eD_2: *a est au-dessus/en dessous de b* if the lowest/highest point of the target is higher/lower than the highest/lowest point of the landmark along a rising path.

Regarding this path, note that the vertical and horizontal projections of the situated objects (for example, the houses in figure 15), comply with characteristics A and B: the intersection of their projections along a plane perpendicular to the path is not null, although the projections of the houses are distinct. It will be possible to describe the expressions *au-dessus/en dessous* by two usage rules; the duality here is justified by the analogy existing between a vertical axis and an ascending path.

Another solution consists in looking for a single usage rule governing the expressions *au-dessus/en dessous* in two situations: when the prepositional terms are situated along a single vertical axis, and when they are located along an ascending path. Since these latter terms are situated on different vertical axes, this generalization will only obtain if we relinquish our desire to situate target and landmark along a single vertical axis. In this case we must formulate rule aD/eD in terms of the vertical direction in general.

> aD/eD: *a est au-dessus/en dessous de b* if the highest/lowest point of the target is higher/lower than the highest/lowest point of the landmark.

Since the positional adjectives *higher/lower* in this definition refer to the vertical direction in general (unless otherwise indicated), we do not need to introduce the factor of vertical direction into usage rule aD/eD.

This rule has the advantage of being exhaustive, but it is obviously too general and would allow a number of unacceptable uses of *au-dessus/en dessous*. I will demonstrate that it is possible to limit the applications of this rule by imposing the following selection restriction:

> Selection restriction: The relation of verticality between the target and the landmark of the expressions *au-dessus/en dessous* must be salient.

What does this mean? Even if the pairs of points (A, B) and (C, D) are situated along different vertical axes, as in figure 17, the relation of verticality between the points of the first pair is perceptually more salient than the same relation between the points of the second pair. This salience increases as the distance increases between the projections of the two points along a vertical axis, and diminishes with the distance between their projections on a horizontal axis. According to these formal factors, maximum salience is achieved by two points situated along the same vertical axis.

•A

                                                          C•

                                                                              •D
              •B

The salience of verticality, however, depends equally on functional or utilitarian factors. Because of these, the rule aD/eD and its selection restriction together form a system that describes the distribution of *au-dessus/en dessous* better than the two usage rules aD_1/eD_1 and aD_2/eD_2 do. The existence of an ascending path linking the target and the landmark reinforces the relation of verticality between them. In the descriptive system formed by rules aD_1/eD_1 and aD_2/eD_2, this fact was translated by an analogy between the vertical axis and the ascending path. However, there is a second functional factor that might accentuate the salience of verticality: the difficulty of gaining access to a target, due to its height. This factor explains the contrast between examples (19) and (20) and between the two utterances of (19) by the father and his child. These contrasts could not be motivated in the descriptive system formed by the two usage rules aD_1/eD_1 and aD_2/eD_2.

I will adopt usage rule aD/eD to describe the expressions *au-dessus /en dessous;* these expressions are ordered along a vertical axis. The salience of this order indirectly justifies the selection restriction applying to the rule. This salience also points up the contrast between *au-dessus/en dessous* and the positional adjectives *haut/bas:* these latter may apply to objects at different heights, even though the difference may be barely perceptible. Rule aD/eD allows a unified description of the expressions and motivates the selection restrictions holding for this rule; here we find the impetus for these expressions.

The expressions *au-dessus/en dessous* seem most appropriate when the prepositions *sur/sous* cannot be substituted in their place. In this case they are perfectly converse expressions. The explanation for this symmetry is that these expressions do not locate the target with respect to the landmark, but instead situate the two entities with respect to an objective given, that is, the vertical direction. We will see in chapter 10 that movement plays a similar role in the use of the prepositions *avant/après.*

Example (10) is the only sentence remaining to be explained. It seems that the expressions *au-dessus/en dessous,* because of their length, play an emphatic role when they are used in place of *sur/sous.* This emphasis might be responsible for the use of the expression *en dessous* rather than *sous* in (10).

The expressions *au-dessus/en dessous* have now been examined and described. In this description we may recognize a complex category[6] that has developed out of a unique impetus, whose central notions are *vertical direction* and *salience.* These are the notions motivating the behavior of *au-dessus/en dessous* with respect to contact. Other uses of these expressions serve the purpose of emphasizing the prepositions *sur/sous.*

7

The prepositions devant/derrière *and general orientation*

Les pieds devant moi, sous moi, derrière moi, ce sont les miens[1]

Marguerite Duras
La Vie tranquille

We will not be able to address all the uses of the prepositions *devant/ derrière* in this chapter; other cases will be studied in chapter 9.[2]

To begin, I will describe the canonical and marginal forms of a certain family resemblance concept: general orientation. The uses of *devant/derrière* studied in this chapter follow from this complex concept, rather than depending on the notion of the frontal direction. The relations between the speaker and the landmark of these prepositions will also be examined.

This chapter will conclude with a study of the expressions *en face de/dans le dos de*, expressions that better describe the frontal direction.

7.1 General orientation

The previous chapter demonstrated that the vertical axis is best described by a family resemblance concept, rather than by a single trait such as gravity. For this axis, few natural situations force us to acknowledge a family resemblance concept, since the various traits of the family resemblance describing *au-dessus/en dessous* generally coincide. However, the concept of a family resemblance will prove indispensable for a close examination of the prepositions *devant/derrière*, and will help us establish the contrast between these prepositions and the expressions *en face de/dans le dos de*.

I remind the reader of the definition of a *family resemblance concept*.

A family resemblance is a concept that is represented by different combinations of the traits characterizing it.[3]

As a corollary, if a word describes a family resemblance concept, the traits of the family are not in fact necessary and sufficient conditions for its use. A logical analysis cannot describe this type of relation satisfactorily: we cannot identify any implication such that, if one trait of the family resemblance is respected/not respected, the word will be appropriate/inappropriate.

Among the traits determining general orientation, I wish to stress the parallelism with

the frontal direction,

the direction of movement,

the line of sight,

the direction in which the other sensory organs are oriented (smell, hearing, etc.),

the directions of nutrition and defecation, etc.

Certain parts of the body, such as the forehead, the chin, the toes, the heart, etc., determine the positive direction of general orientation. The nape of the neck, the heels, the kidneys, etc., determine its negative direction. The direction of movement and the line of sight establish its positive direction; the direction of defecation, its negative direction. General orientation is thus directed from the kidneys to the stomach, the nape of the neck to the chin, etc.

Three of these traits are essential and will most particularly attract our attention: the line of sight, the direction of movement, and the frontal direction.

General orientation is a family resemblance concept comparable to the family resemblance concept of such prototypes as *climb*, presented by Fillmore (1982); these are concepts represented by several traits that coincide in the most representative situations. In fact, we almost always walk in the direction of our frontal orientation, looking straight ahead. This situation determines canonical general orientation.

What happens when one of the traits of general orientation conflicts with the others? I will present several examples of this possibility, beginning with the example of the crab, already discussed by Fillmore (1971).

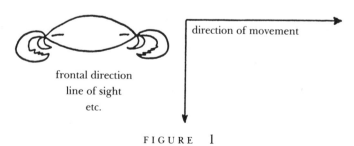

direction of movement

frontal direction
line of sight
etc.

FIGURE   1

The crab's direction of movement contrasts with the other traits of its general orientation; the sum of these remaining traits determine the crab's most canonical orientation.

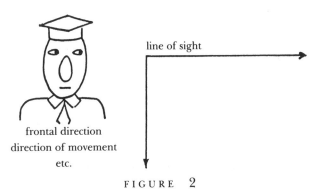

line of sight

frontal direction
direction of movement
etc.

FIGURE 2

In the second figure, the professor's gaze conflicts with the direction of the other traits, which together determine his canonical general orientation.

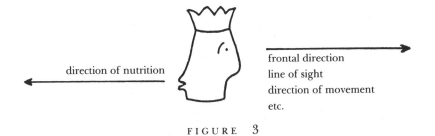

direction of nutrition

frontal direction
line of sight
direction of movement
etc.

FIGURE 3

Finally, as so often occurs in aristocratic families, the king in figure 3 is inbred and deformed, and his mouth is located at the nape of his neck. Again, the entire set of traits, and not the position of the mouth alone, determines the most canonical instance of general orientation. If we isolate each of the traits of general orientation one by one, we see that none is, individually, necessary and sufficient.

Figure 4 contrasts two traits of general orientation with the sum of the other traits, which again establish the most canonical general orientation.

There are contexts, however, in which one isolated trait may force a reading of a marginal general orientation. In such cases, the perspective according to which the scene is understood takes on excep-

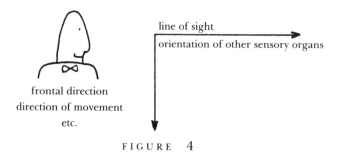

FIGURE 4

tional importance. The direction of the crab's movement could marginally determine its general orientation if the context of utterance gave this movement a crucial significance; the professor's gaze and his general orientation could coincide if the scene before him were of fascinating importance. Finally, if the king were a glutton facing an entire roast pig, the direction of nutrition could be invested with primary importance on its own.

One difficult question arises at this point: if a spatial preposition is motivated by a general orientation that is determined by a single trait, for example the line of sight, how can we be certain that the preposition describes a family resemblance characterized by this single trait? Perhaps, in contrast, it is motivated by the line of sight alone. The difference between canonical and marginal general orientation provides an answer to this question. Canonical orientation predominates in the majority of contexts and is indifferent to the direction taken, momentarily, by the line of sight. Only under particular circumstances does the line of sight take on the function of general orientation and the spatial relation it characterizes. Several examples of this phenomenon will be presented in the next section.

7.2 The prepositions devant/derrière and general orientation

I began this chapter with a few remarks on the intuitive and extralinguistic notion of general orientation. Since a family resemblance concept is complex, with a minimal logical organization, it should be used only as a last resort in linguistic description. I will demonstrate that general orientation is the *only* reasonable solution for describing the examples presented below. It is true that *frontal direction* (section 7.2.1) suffices to explain most of these examples. In less common contexts, however, certain uses of the prepositions *devant/derrière* are determined by the *line of sight* and the *direction of movement* (section 7.2.2). Other uses follow from more marginal concepts (section 7.2.3). I do not find it intuitively satisfying to continue multiplying the versions of *devant/derrière* each time a new concept motivates another usage;

rather, the various concepts intervene in the description of a spatial preposition, not independently, but only as traits of general orientation.

7.2.1 The prepositions *devant/derrière* and frontal direction

The uses of the prepositions *devant/derrière* may be classified according to the nature of their target and landmark.

The landmark is human.

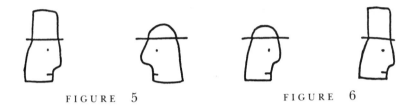

FIGURE 5   FIGURE 6

Figures 5 and 6 are described by sentences (1) and (2), respectively.

    (1) *le curé est devant le ministre*
        the priest is in front of the minister

    (2) *le curé est derrière le ministre*
        the priest is behind the minister

Depending on whether he is located on the positive or negative side of the frontal direction of the landmark, the priest is said to be *devant* or *derrière* the minister.

The landmark is intrinsically oriented.

FIGURE 7   FIGURE 8

Sentences (3) and (4) describe figures 7 and 8, respectively.

    (3) *le curé est devant la chaise*
        the priest is in front of the chair

    (4) *le curé est derrière la chaise*
        the priest is behind the chair

Whether the landmark is human or intrinsically oriented, we come to the same conclusions, expressed by usage rule D′₁.

D′₁: *a est devant/derrière b* if the target is located on the positive /negative side of the frontal direction of the landmark.

Another use of the preposition *devant* will also describe figure 8. This use will be included among the examples of the final group.

The landmark is not intrinsically oriented.

FIGURE 9   FIGURE 10

If there is no observer viewing the scene from a specific perspective (see chapter 9), example (5) may describe figure 9, but (6) is inappropriate for figure 10.

(5) *?le fauteuil est devant l'arbre*
the armchair is in front of the tree

(6) **le fauteuil est derrière l'arbre*
the armchair is behind the tree

Note that this type of utterance improves when the target is human, as in sentence (7) describing figure 11.

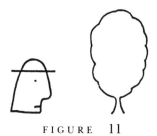

FIGURE 11

(7) *le curé est devant l'arbre*
the priest is in front of the tree

Although a wall is not intrinsically oriented, we can just as easily say,

(8) *je suis devant le mur*
I am in front of the wall

The uses illustrated by this group appear to be counterexamples to definition D′₁, since we cannot define the frontal direction of a landmark that is not oriented. However, while it is true that the landmarks in examples (5)–(8) are not intrinsically oriented, we have seen (chapter 3) that an intrinsically oriented target may contextually orient the landmark, by granting it the target's own orientation in reverse. The tree in sentences (5) and (7) is thus contextually oriented by the priest and, similarly, by the chair. The prepositions *devant/derrière* are distributed with respect to the frontal direction acquired by the landmark, and definition D′₁ remains viable.

Neither target nor landmark is intrinsically oriented.

FIGURE   12

With no observer to orient the scene appropriately, sentences (9) and (10) are impossible.

(9) **l'arbre est devant le rocher*
the tree is in front of the rock

(10) **le rocher est devant l'arbre*
the rock is in front of the tree

This follows from definition D′₁, since the landmark is not intrinsically oriented and in this case is not contextually oriented by the target.

Conflicts between intrinsic orientation and contextual orientation. The priest in figure 8 could in rare cases be considered *in front of* the chair, if the context favored this interpretation. If we ask the priest to stand in front of a chair that is accessible from all sides, figure 13 illustrates his probable movement. However, if a table prevents the priest from standing in this location, the position illustrated in figure 14 will be his second choice.

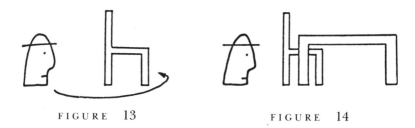

FIGURE 13   FIGURE 14

The difference between figures 13 and 14 can be explained by a conflict between the intrinsic and contextual orientations of the landmark. The priest's initial movement demonstrates that intrinsic orientation generally takes precedence over contextual orientation, although this may not be absolute. The priest will probably choose the position imposed by contextual orientation only if the table prevents him from moving in front of the chair. The predominance of intrinsic orientation is illustrated again by the scenes below.

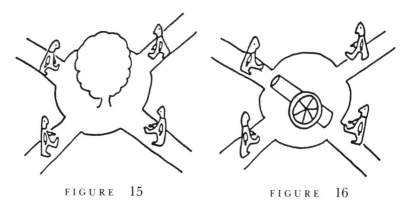

FIGURE 15   FIGURE 16

(11) *les présidents sont devant l'arbre*
the presidents are in front of the tree

(12) *? les présidents sont devant le canon*
the presidents are in front of the cannon

The first utterance is appropriate since the tree is not intrinsically oriented, and each president can orient the tree contextually in front of himself. But the plural of the second utterance is questionable, since the cannon is intrinsically oriented, and only one of the presidents may properly be considered *in front of* the cannon.

Although example (3) may describe figure 7 as well as figure 8, the ambiguity of this utterance is entirely covered by usage rule D'_1. In fact, this rule describes the use of *devant/derrière* as a function of the frontal direction of the landmark. The ambiguity has to do with which means of orientation is dominant: the interpretation illustrated by figure 7 corresponds with the chair's intrinsic orientation, while figure 8 corresponds to its contextual orientation.

Remember now that intrinsic orientation (chapter 3) is probably anthropomorphic in nature. Contextual orientation, on the other hand, has been associated with canonical encounter by H. Clark. The priest's positions in figures 13 and 14 demonstrate that intrinsic orientation is more basic than contextual orientation. Evidence from first language acquisition confirms this: Miller and Johnson-Laird (1976) have shown that children learn the use of the prepositions *in front of/ behind* earlier for intrinsically oriented landmarks than for other landmarks. This suggests that we orient the objects around us anthropomorphically, long before canonical encounter comes into play. It is possible that contextual orientation could be an extension of anthropomorphic orientation as much as it is a consequence of canonical encounter, since anthropomorphically oriented objects such as cupboards, typewriters, etc., are generally turned to face us. A linguistic analysis of *devant/derrière* allows both interpretations.

7.2.2 The correspondence of line of sight and direction of movement with *devant/derrière*

In the examples below, the line of sight and the movement of the landmark do not play primary roles; this argues for a definition of these prepositions in terms of the frontal direction. Figure 17 is described better by sentence (13) (frontal direction) than by (14) (direction of movement). Similarly, example (15) (frontal direction) describes figure 18 better than (16) (line of sight) does.

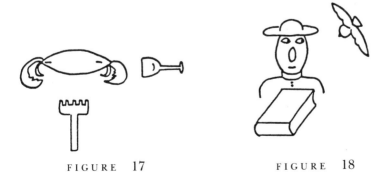

FIGURE 17   FIGURE 18

(13) *le râteau est devant le crabe*
the rake is in front of the crab

(14) *?la pelle est devant le crabe*
the shovel is in front of the crab

(15) *la bible est devant le curé*
the Bible is in front of the priest

(16) *?le Saint-Esprit est devant le curé*
the Holy Spirit is in front of the priest

An extension of usage rule D$'_1$ will be needed to explain the following scenes; here context lends importance to the direction of movement (figure 19) and to the line of sight (figure 20).

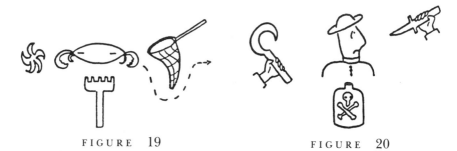

FIGURE   19   FIGURE   20

(17) *le filet est devant le crabe*
the net is in front of the crab

(18) *le couteau est devant le curé*
the knife is in front of the priest

The acceptability of examples (17) and (18) contrasts with the strangeness of sentences (14) and (16). The direction of movement and the line of sight do not always motivate the use of *devant/derrière*. A particular trait must be emphasized by the context of the utterance: in the cases of the crab and the priest, the net and the knife lend dramatic importance to the context. Furthermore, the use of *devant* to describe movement, in figure 19, does not necessarily motivate the use of the opposite preposition *derrière* to describe the opposite direction. Thus the sentence below is inappropriate.

(19) **l'étoile de mer est derrière le crabe*
the starfish is behind the crab

In fact, if the direction of movement in this situation is important enough to justify example (17), this is due to the possibility that the crab might be captured, and the starfish does not feature in this drama significantly. If, on the other hand, the crab is lucky enough to avoid the trap and continue along his way, as in figure 19, example (20) would be possible.

> (20) *le filet était devant le crabe mais maintenant le danger est derrière lui*
> the net was in front of the crab but now the danger is behind him

We have already seen that direction of movement and line of sight need particular contexts if they are to motivate the use of the prepositions *devant/derrière*. We see now that it is not always possible to use *devant/derrière* for the same situations. Instead, context may be important only for one pole of the relation, leaving the second pole inapplicable. We will see that the selection restrictions limiting the use of *devant/derrière* are determined, not directly by the direction of movement or the line of sight, but by the capacity of these traits to establish a marginal general orientation.

7.2.3 From frontal direction to general orientation

Another example will demonstrate that the line of sight and the direction of movement are not the only traits capable of determining the use of *devant* when they contrast with the frontal direction. Returning to the deformed king in figure 3, we might say that he is *in front of* a dish of game, even if this feast is located on the negative side of the frontal direction.

> (21) *le gibier est devant le roi*
> the game is in front of the king

FIGURE 21

In this situation the gluttonous king's direction of nutrition determines the use of *devant,* at least for a certain time. The direction of nutrition is one trait of general orientation, along with the line of sight and the direction of movement. Any trait of this family resemblance concept may determine the use of *devant/derrière* in the appropriate circumstances. However, no one would want to propose a new usage rule for these prepositions based on the location of a deformed king's mouth, or any other trait of general orientation that is only momentarily dominant.

It should be clear that the prepositions *devant/derrière* do not depend on several different notions (the frontal direction, the line of sight, the direction of movement, and the position of the nutritive organs). Rather, these prepositions depend on a single family resemblance concept encompassing these traits: general orientation. In most contexts, the frontal direction represents the usual, canonical general orientation, and it is the most stable characteristic of this family resemblance concept. The more variable traits, such as the line of sight and the direction of movement, individually motivate the use of *devant/derrière* only when unusual circumstances give them sufficient importance. In such cases a marginal general orientation is determined by a more salient trait. Canonical uses of the prepositions *devant/derrière* are related to canonical general orientation; marginal uses are related to a marginal general orientation. The rule D'_1 may now be reformulated in terms of general orientation.

D_1: *a est devant/derrière b* if the target is located on the positive/negative side of the landmark's general orientation.

The examples below illustrate another advantage of this formulation. One aspect of the scenes in figures 19–21 has been described by examples (17), (18), and (21). In these examples, the use of the preposition was attributed to the direction of movement, the line of sight, and the position of the mouth (or the marginal general orientation). A different aspect of these scenes is described by the utterances in (22)–(24); here the preposition *devant* is attributed specifically to the frontal direction (or the most canonical general orientation).

> (22) *le râteau est devant le crabe*
> the rake is in front of the crab

> (23) *le poison est devant le curé*
> the poison is in front of the priest

> (24) *le couteau est devant le roi*
> the knife is in front of the king

However, the conjunction of these sentences with examples (17), (18), and (21) to describe the scenes in figures 19–21 is impossible.

> (25) **le filet et le râteau sont devant le crabe*
> the net and the rake are in front of the crab

(26) *le poison et le couteau sont devant le curé*
    the poison and the knife are in front of the priest

(27) *le gibier et le couteau sont devant le roi*
    the game and the knife are in front of the king

If the first uses of *devant* are motivated by the frontal direction and the second uses are motivated by the direction of movement, the line of sight, and the position of the mouth, respectively, an arbitrary restriction is needed to rule out sentences (25)–(27). If, on the other hand, the first uses of *devant* are motivated by canonical general orientation and the second uses by marginal general orientation, then we can account for the impossibility of sentences (25)–(27): a single landmark may have a canonical general orientation *or* a marginal general orientation, but not both at the same time. The ungrammaticality of (25)–(27) follows from this observation.

7.3 *The prepositional terms of the relations* devant/derrière

This section will demonstrate that the uses of *devant/derrière* studied in this chapter only depend directly on the prepositional terms. Following this, the relation between the speaker and the landmark of these prepositions will be discussed in greater detail.

In examples (28) and (29), the speaker is the target and the landmark of the relation, respectively.

(28) *je suis devant l'arbre*
    I am in front of the tree

(29) *l'arbre est devant moi*
    the tree is in front of me

These sentences depend on two terms: the speaker, who is identified with the target/landmark of the relation, and the landmark/target. Examples (30) and (31) might seem to illustrate three-term relations, encompassing the speaker, the target, and the landmark.

(30) *le curé est devant l'église*
    the priest is in front of the church

(31) *le curé est devant l'arbre*
    the priest is in front of the tree

However, inasmuch as example (30) is independent of the position of the speaker and depends only on the intrinsic general orientation of the landmark, we may consider this example to illustrate a two-term relation, counting the target and the landmark. According to the most common interpretation, if the landmark in (31) is not intrinsically oriented, it must be contextually oriented by the target. Here again, the relation is independent of the speaker's position, and depends only on the target and the landmark. The uses of *devant/derrière* studied in this chapter depend on only two prepositional terms. These uses are independent of the position of the speaker, as long as the speaker is not identified with either landmark or target. The uses of *devant/derrière* in this chapter contrast with the uses of these prepositions that will be presented in chapter 9.

It was pointed out in chapter 2 that the simplest spatial relations, those in which the second term remains unexpressed, are generally egocentric. However, when the landmark of *devant/derrière* is expressed, the relation is independent of the speaker's position as long as the speaker is not identified with any of the terms of the preposition. To generalize this description, we might consider the speaker's position as a free parameter that may be transferred to the location of the landmark of the preposition. In positing such a transfer, we claim that the landmark of these prepositions will always be identified with the speaker, whether this identification be real or virtual. Such a claim will doubtless prove too strong for sentence (28): does the speaker really transfer himself to the location of the tree to judge his own position? Sentences in which the speaker is the target of the spatial relation, however, appear quite late in first language acquisition. The identification of the speaker with the landmark probably plays an important role in the use of *devant/derrière* before this stage.

Evidence for this identification is found in cases where the landmark of the relation is intrinsically oriented. The speaker will, in fact, describe the scene in figure 22 by the utterance in (32).

FIGURE 22

(32) *le chat est devant toi et la souris est à gauche (*à droite)*
the cat is in front of you and the mouse is to the left
(*to the right)

In this example, it is clear that the speaker is adopting the position of the landmark, that is, the addressee, to situate the mouse laterally.

We find a similar situation for an intrinsically oriented inanimate land-mark. This is the case in (33), describing figure 23.

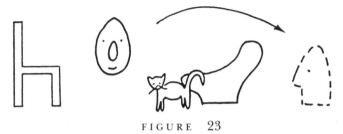

FIGURE 23

(33) *la chaise est devant le fauteuil et le chat est à gauche (*à droite)*
the chair is in front of the armchair and the cat is to the left (*to the right)

If the speaker considered his real position, he would situate the cat in front of himself; if he adopted the position of the target he would locate the cat to the right. In (33), however, the speaker has situated the cat on the left: this demonstrates the speaker's transference to the position of the landmark, as figure 23 illustrates.

When the landmark is contextually oriented, the speaker does not transfer to the landmark's position. Figure 24 is described by example (34).

FIGURE 24

(34) *le chat est devant l'arbre et la souris est à droite (*à gauche)*
the cat is in front of the tree and the mouse is to the right (*to the left)

Here the orientation of the mouse on the lateral axis demonstrates that the scene is described from the cat's position, and not from the position of the tree. On the one hand, the tree may be oriented by analogy with the anthropomorphic orientation of intrinsically oriented objects; on the other hand, it may be oriented by analogy with canonical encounter. In any case we recognize a certain humanization in the orientation of the tree.

There is always a connection between the speaker and the landmark of the prepositions *devant/derrière*. This connection is especially evident when the landmark is intrinsically oriented. In this case we can postulate a transfer of the speaker to the landmark's position, since the speaker can be understood to situate the other elements of the scene from the landmark's position. The connection between speaker and landmark is weaker in the case of a landmark that is not intrinsically oriented. In this case the speaker-landmark relation is limited to the anthropomorphization of the landmark.

7.4 The expressions en face de/dans le dos de and frontal direction

The principal traits of general orientation include the frontal direction, the line of sight, and the direction of movement. One of these traits in isolation may determine a marginal general orientation if the context makes this trait stand out over the others. The single trait could then momentarily motivate the use of *devant/derrière*. Furthermore, each one of these traits may be described by spatial relations particular to it alone. I will demonstrate in chapter 9 that line of sight and access to perception are expressed by a second version of *devant/ derrière*. The direction of movement and the contact potentially resulting from this movement are characterized by the prepositions *avant/ après*, as we will see in chapter 10. In this section, I will compare the prepositions *devant/derrière* with the expressions *en face de/dans le dos de*. I will show that the latter expressions more particularly describe the frontal direction.

As figure 25 illustrates, the target of *devant/derrière* may be located anywhere within the field of vision. In contrast, the target of the expressions *en face de/dans le dos de* must be located within a relatively narrow band along the axis of the frontal direction.

> (35) *le lapin est en face de (devant) l'abbesse*
> the rabbit is in front of (before) the abbess

> (36) *les chats sont devant (*en face de) l'abbesse*
> the cats are before (in front of) the abbess

I will focus particularly on the part of the field of vision where *en face de/dans le dos de* and *devant/derrière* coincide. The substitutions *de-*

FIGURE   25

vant/en face de and *derrière/dans le dos de* are possible only if general orientation and frontal direction coincide.

7.4.1 The expression *dans le dos de*

The use of this expression in French is fairly restricted. Its compositional character is strongly felt, so much so that this expression is absolutely unacceptable when the preposition *derrière* describes a marginal general orientation that is distinct from the frontal direction, as in figure 20.

    (37) *la faucille est derrière le curé*
           the sickle is behind the priest

    (38) **la faucille est dans le dos du curé*
           the sickle is in back of the priest

    The expression *dans le dos de*, strictly speaking, locates the target in the negative part of the axis describing the landmark's frontal direction.

7.4.2 The expression *en face de*

The back is a part of the body relating exclusively to the axis of the frontal direction. Because of its mobility, the face is less restricted than the back. However, the substitution of the expression *en face de* for the preposition *devant* is questionable in the case of figure 20.

    (39) *le couteau est devant le curé*
           the knife is before the priest

    (40) *?le couteau est en face du curé*
           the knife is in front of the priest

    If a marginal general orientation is determined by movement, the preposition *devant* may not be replaced with the expression *en face de*.

In contrast to example (17), repeated here, sentence (41) cannot describe figure 19.

> (17) *le filet est devant le crabe*
>   the net is before the crab

> (41) **le filet est en face du crabe*
>   the net is in front of the crab

The preposition *devant* and the expression *en face de* may occur together in a single sentence, with contrasting meanings.

> (42) *le crabe regardait la mer en face de lui sans voir le filet devant ses pattes*
>   the crab looked at the sea in front of him, without seeing the net before his claws

Thus, the expression *dans le dos de* strictly characterizes the negative side of the landmark's frontal direction, and the expression *en face de* describes its positive side. The usage rule of these expressions may be expressed as follows:

F/D: *a est en face de/dans le dos de b* if the target is located on the positive/negative side of the frontal direction of the landmark.[4]

This single usage rule may be equated with the impetus of these expressions. The expression *en face de* often becomes more specific when it is used with a human target and landmark: example (43) describes figure 26 more appropriately than figure 27.

FIGURE 26

FIGURE 27

> (43) *le curé est en face du ministre*
>   the priest is facing the minister

The meaning of sentence (43) may be confused with that of (44).

> (44) *le curé et le ministre sont face à face*
>   the priest and the minister are face to face

One condition for the use of *en face de/dans le dos de* follows directly from their impetus: their landmark must have a frontal direction.

Thus, although the (a) examples below are acceptable, the (b) examples are meaningless, since neither the ball nor the tree is an intrinsically oriented object.

(45a) *l'arbre est en face du banc*
the tree is in front of the bench

(b) **le banc est en face de l'arbre*
the bench is in front of the tree

(46a) *la balle est dans le dos du pêcheur*
the ball is in back of the fisherman

(b) **pêcheur est dans le dos de la balle*
the fisherman is in back of the ball

Once again, an object that is not intrinsically oriented may acquire a contextual orientation. Thus, example (45b) is not acceptable for figure 28 but is acceptable for figure 29.

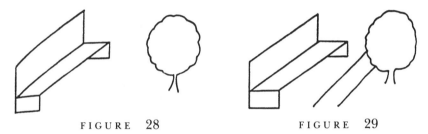

FIGURE 28   FIGURE 29

When a path is added to the picture, the bench and the tree in figure 29 suddenly take on a contextual orientation. This orientation is not explained by canonical encounter. Instead, the bench and the tree are oriented towards the path by analogy with the arrangement of houses on a street. I have already demonstrated (chapter 3) that no single linguistic fact will make the connection between canonical encounter and contextual orientation a necessary one. The examples above demonstrate that canonical encounter is not the only possible origin of contextual orientation.

Sentence (45b) and figure 29 illustrate an interesting development of the meaning of *en face de*. Actually, this expression is similar to the English preposition *across* in this sentence. The schemas in figures 30–32 show the positions that could be considered *en face* 'facing' each other in the geometrical figures of an oval, a rectangle, and a circle.

The following points are considered *en face:* the intersections *a* and *b* of an oval with all the parallel lines at its width, and with the

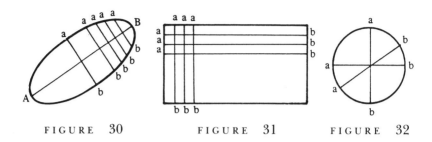

FIGURE 30   FIGURE 31   FIGURE 32

extremities A and B of its length; the intersections *a* and *b* of a rectangle with the parallel lines of its four sides; the intersections of the perimeter of the circle with its diameters. In each of these cases, the geometrical form contextually orients the landmark of the expression *en face de*.

8

The expressions à gauche/à droite *and lateral orientation*

Lateral orientation is a family resemblance concept that has two principal traits: lateral direction and the axis perpendicular to general orientation. I will demonstrate that the concept of lateral orientation describes the expressions *à gauche/à droite* better than any other definition that could make use of the line of sight or the lateral direction alone.

Once we have established the lateral orientation, the two poles of this orientation, *la gauche* 'left' and *la droite* 'right', will be defined in terms of a family resemblance concept.

I will conclude this chapter by illustrating the relation between the speaker and the landmark of the expressions *à gauche/à droite*.

8.1 The advantages of the lateral direction over the line of sight

The lateral direction, as developed here, is essentially characterized by the line of the shoulders. In this section I will demonstrate that the lateral fields containing the points situated *à gauche* and *à droite* are best described by the lateral direction, rather than by the line of sight. To be honest, I have previously defended the opposite point of view (Vandeloise 1979); Klein (1980) has recently proposed a definition of the expressions *à gauche/à droite* that also makes use of the line of sight. A comparison of these alternative solutions will permit me to trace the arguments leading me to change my position. If the speaker is the landmark, possible usage rules are the following:

G'_1/D'_1: *a est à gauche/à droite* if it is located to the left/right side of the line of sight of the speaker.[1]

G'_2/D'_2: *a est à gauche/à droite* if it is closer to the speaker's left/right shoulder than to his right/left shoulder.

These rules are illustrated by examples (1) and (2), describing figure 1.

(1) *le chat est à gauche du curé*
the cat is to the left of the priest

(2) *le lapin est à droite du curé*
the rabbit is to the right of the priest

FIGURE 1

We will see, below, how the left-hand side is distinguished from the right-hand side. At this point we are concerned with understanding the differing implications of the two rules above.

At first sight, definitions G'_1/D'_1 and G'_2/D'_2 make the same predictions. They determine the use of the expressions *à gauche/à droite* in the examples (1) and (2) equally well. I will present two reasons for preferring the second definition to the first.

In contrast to the prepositions *devant/derrière*, the expressions *à gauche/à droite* allow comparatives.

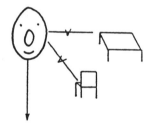

FIGURE 2

(3) *la table est plus devant que la chaise*
    the table is more in front than the chair

(4) *la table est plus à gauche que la chaise*
    the table is more to the left than the chair

Sentence (4) describes figure 2, in which the table and the chair are at equal distances from the speaker. The distance of the furniture from the speaker does not determine which object is furthest to the left. Only the proximity of the furniture to the line passing across the shoulder motivates this comparative. In fact, the angle formed by the line joining the object and the speaker and the line of the speaker's shoulders is the important factor here: the smaller this angle, the more representative the situation is of the expression *à gauche/à droite*. Definition G'_2/D'_2 thus presents the advantage of defining the expressions *à gauche/à droite* by means of their most characteristic elements.

To remedy this shortcoming, definition G'_1/D'_1 could be reformulated in the following way:

G''_1/D''_1: *a est à gauche/à droite* if it is closer to the left/right extremity of the speaker's visual field than to the right/left extremity.

However, this revised definition is not ideal: the shoulders, which are ideally representative of the left and the right, remain outside the speaker's visual field.

The object located outside the speaker's field of vision offers another argument in favor of the second definition G'_2/D'_2. In fact, in figure 3 the priest could say (5), even if he is unable to see either the cat or the rabbit.

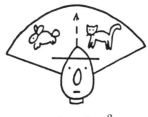

FIGURE 3   FIGURE 4

(5) *le lapin est à droite*
     the rabbit is on the right

(6) *le chat est à gauche*
     the cat is on the left

Examples (5) and (6) are directly explained by definition G'_2/D'_2. Since neither the cat nor the rabbit are within the speaker's field of vision, definition G'_1/D'_1 demands a transfer on the part of the speaker. The most natural transfer, in which the speaker turns around, is illustrated by figure 4. If the priest adopts this position and applies the expressions *à gauche/à droite* according to definition G'_1/D'_1, he will say, wrongly,

(7) **le lapin est à gauche*
     the rabbit is to the left

(8) *le chat est à droite
 the cat is to the right

Another transfer, in which the priest walks backwards until both cat and rabbit are within his field of vision, is suggested by figure 3.[2] This movement would enable the priest to see the animals, and definition G'_1/D'_1 would locate them laterally in the appropriate manner. However, at the end of this chapter we will see that mental transfers generally occur along the most probable potential physical path. If a wild animal attacked a hunter from behind, it seems clear that a defensive movement in the direction of the arrow in figure 3 is improbable.

Klein (1980) has pointed out the problem that objects in back of the speaker represent for a definition of à gauche/à droite in terms of the line of sight. He dismisses this problem because left and right do not seem to be well defined in this area, according to his view. I disagree. For the two reasons above, I prefer to define the expressions à gauche/à droite as a function of the lateral direction, rather than in terms of the line of sight.

8.2 The advantages of lateral orientation over lateral direction

In this section I will show that definition G'_2/D'_2 itself does not satisfactorily describe the expressions à gauche/à droite. Only lateral orientation, a family resemblance concept, accurately characterizes these expressions; the lateral direction, represented by the line of the shoulders, is only one of the traits of this family resemblance concept.

The first argument for the concept of lateral orientation is the same argument that led Klein (1980) and myself (1979) to define the expressions à gauche/à droite in terms of the line of sight. Two scenes from chapter 7 are reproduced below: utterance (9) is in fact appropriate to describe figure 5.

FIGURE 5   FIGURE 6

(9) le poison est à droite du curé
 the poison is to the right of the priest

The usage rule G'_1/D'_1 correctly explains this use of the expression *à droite* with regard to the line of sight, whereas definition G'_2/D'_2 fails in this respect. The scene illustrated in figure 6, in contrast, demonstrates that the direction of movement also may participate in a definition of the expressions *à gauche/à droite.*

    (10) *le râteau est à droite du crabe*
        the rake is on the right of the crab

Although examples (9) and (10) are made possible because the contexts emphasize the line of sight (in figure 5) and the direction of movement (in figure 6), examples (11) and (12) remain the most likely means of characterizing another aspect of these two scenes.

    (11) *le couteau est à gauche du curé*
        the knife is to the left of the priest

    (12) *le filet est à gauche du crabe*
        the net is to the left of the crab

These sentences can be explained only by usage rule G'_2/D'_2, which has been established as a function of the lateral direction. As in the case of the prepositions *devant/derrière*, at least three notions are needed to define *à gauche/à droite:* lateral direction, the line of sight, and the direction of movement.

As examples (13) and (15) illustrate, lateral direction is dominant when the preposition *devant* describes the canonical general orientation; when this preposition describes the marginal general orientation, the use of *à droite* is determined by the line of sight (14) or by movement (16).

    (13) *le poison est devant le curé et la faucille est à droite*
        the poison is in front of the priest and the sickle is on
        the right

    (14) *le couteau est devant le curé et le poison est à droite*
        the knife is in front of the priest and the poison is on the
        right

    (15) *le râteau est devant le crabe et l'étoile de mer est à droite*
        the rake is in front of the crab and the starfish is on the
        right

    (16) *le filet est devant le crabe et le râteau est à droite*
        the net is in front of the crab and the rake is on the right

Lateral direction corresponds with canonical general orientation; the direction of movement and the horizontal line perpendicular to the line of sight correspond with marginal general orientation.

Finally, as we have seen for the prepositions *devant/derrière,* the conjunction of canonical and marginal uses of the expressions *à gauche/à droite* is impossible.

(17) *la faucille et le poison sont à droite*
the sickle and the poison are on the right

(18) *l'étoile de mer et le râteau sont à droite*
the starfish and the rake are on the right

All of these examples show that the expressions *à gauche/à droite* are governed by a family resemblance concept, lateral orientation. Among its traits, this family resemblance concept includes the lateral direction represented by the line of the shoulders. The line of sight and the direction of movement participate only indirectly in the family resemblance concept. In figures 5 and 6, we note that both are perpendicular to the marginal general orientation. The lateral direction, on the other hand, is always perpendicular to the canonical general orientation. Canonical general orientation corresponds to canonical lateral orientation, sharing every trait (examples [13] and [15]). A marginal general orientation corresponds to a marginal lateral orientation, which is distinguished from the lateral direction ([14] and [16]).

I will return to the example of the deformed king to illustrate that the line of sight and the direction of movement are not the only traits distinguishing lateral orientation from the lateral direction. Since the dish of fowl in figure 7 is marginally in front of the king, the glass of wine cannot be to his right, as we would otherwise suppose from the most canonical general orientation. Instead the wine must be on the king's left, based on the line perpendicular to his marginal general orientation.

FIGURE 7

The examples above have established that the expressions *à gauche/à droite* are best explained by the concept of lateral orientation, rather than lateral direction. When the speaker is the landmark, the usage rule governing these expressions is expressed as follows:

a est à gauche/à droite if it is on the left/right side of the lateral orientation of the speaker.

If the landmark is not the speaker, this rule must be written more generally.

G/D: *a est à gauche/à droite de b* if the target is located on the left/right side of the lateral orientation of the landmark.

We will see in section 8.4 that lateral orientation may be either intrinsic or imposed on the landmark by the speaker. The principal traits of this orientation are as follows:

it is parallel to the lateral direction, and

it is perpendicular to general orientation.

The lateral direction may be represented by different traits, such as the line parallel to the shoulders, the line parallel to the eyebrows, etc.

Because of the last trait of lateral orientation mentioned above, we concur with Fillmore (1971) that the lateral orientation of an object commonly follows from its general orientation. In figure 8, it appears nevertheless that the lateral orientation of a two-handled basket is more salient than its general orientation. As inverse dependency of the general and lateral orientations can be illustrated here.

FIGURE   8

The example of the basket demonstrates how mental transfers are modelled on the most probable potential physical paths. If the basket is presented perpendicular to the speaker, as in figure 9, the speaker will not be able to indicate which handle is left and which is right.

FIGURE   9

Imagine now that the speaker stands with his right shoulder to the wall, so that only one potential physical path will allow him to pick up the basket: he will put his left hand on handle 2, his right hand on handle 1. Imagining this movement, the speaker will call handle 2 the *left* and handle 1 the *right*. On the other hand, if the wall is on the speaker's left-hand side, preventing him from turning in this direction, his left hand will grasp handle 1, his right reaching for handle 2: the speaker's notions of left and right are now reversed.

The following example illustrates the importance of the potential physical path. In figure 10, the torsos of the priest and the minister are turned toward the reader, but the priest is looking to the left, while the minister looks to the right. If the lines of sight determine marginal general orientation, the two men are looking along the same axis, but in opposite directions, as the schema in figure 11 illustrates.

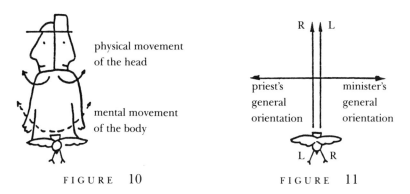

FIGURE 10

FIGURE 11

The corresponding marginal lateral orientations likewise will indicate the same horizontal axis, but opposite directions. The priest and the minister may utter sentences (19) and (20), respectively.

(19) *la colombe est à gauche*
the dove is on the left

(20) *la colombe est à droite*
the dove is on the right

Here, left and right are attributed by means of a mental movement of the torso—the orientation of the torso imitates the movement of the head—to the left of the page for the priest, to the right for the minister. With this movement, the priest turns his left shoulder to the dove; the minister turns his right.

8.3 La gauche/la droite

The argument for usage rule G/D, describing the expressions *à gauche /à droite* in terms of left and right, may seem circular. Essentially, this allows us to divide our field of vision into two parts. The child is conscious of these two zones before he is able to name them adequately, and in the early stages of learning, the terms may be systematically reversed.[3] Which is *la gauche?* Which is *la droite?*

To answer this, I must return once more to the notion of a family resemblance concept. Among the traits characterizing *la gauche*, we find

the position of the heart,
the position of the watch,
the position of the least agile hand,
the position of the hemisphere of the brain specialized in language, etc.[4]

Among the traits characterizing *la droite*, we find

the position of the most adept hand,
the position of the hemisphere of the brain specialized in music, etc.

The best way to establish the need for a family resemblance concept is to show that no single trait is a sufficient condition for the use of *gauche /droite*.

Examples (21–(24) demonstrate this point.

(21) *le curé a le coeur du côté droit*
the priest has his heart on the right side

(22) *le ministre porte sa montre au bras droit*
the minister wears his watch on his right arm

(23) *le professeur écrit de la main gauche*
the professor writes with his left hand

(24) *une lésion dans l'hémisphère droit du cerveau a rendu le colonel aphasique*
a lesion in the right hemisphere has made the colonel aphasic

From these examples we conclude that the people described in these utterances are not physically normal, or do not share our habits; we do not conclude that the speaker is using the expressions *à gauche/ à droite* inappropriately.

8.4 The prepositional terms of à gauche/à droite

In this section I will examine the relation between the speaker's lateral orientation and that of the landmark. I will conclude that the expressions *à gauche/à droite* depend directly on two terms: the target and the landmark, laterally oriented by the speaker.

When the target is located with respect to the intrinsic lateral orientation of the landmark, it is clear that the expressions *à gauche/à droite* depend on two terms only. Landmarks that are intrinsically oriented along the lateral direction are rare and almost exclusively limited to humans. According to the priest's lateral orientation, figure 12 will be described by examples (25) and (26).

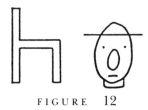

FIGURE   12

(25) *la chaise est à droite du curé*
the chair is to the right of the priest

(26) *la chaise est à la droite du curé*
the chair is on the priest's right

Example (26) unambiguously demonstrates that the target is located laterally by reference to the intrinsic lateral orientation of the landmark.

Although landmarks that are *directly oriented* along the lateral axis are rare, a landmark that is intrinsically oriented along the frontal direction may be *indirectly oriented* along its lateral direction. This is the case of the cupboard in figure 13, described by examples (27) and (28).

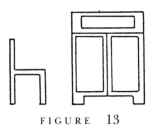

FIGURE   13

(27) *la chaise est à droite de l'armoire*
the chair is to the right of the cupboard

(28) *la chaise est à la droite de l'armoire*
    the chair is on the cupboard's right-hand side

The definite article (*à la droite*) in sentence (28) shows unambiguously that the target is situated with respect to the intrinsic lateral orientation of the landmark.

A speaker could also describe the scenes in figures 12 and 13 in terms of his own lateral orientation. For example, situated in the position of the reader, the speaker could utter sentences (29) and (30), instead of (25) and (27).

(29) *la chaise est à gauche du curé*
    the chair is to the left of the priest

(30) *la chaise est à gauche de l'armoire*
    the chair is to the left of the cupboard

If the landmark is not intrinsically laterally oriented, directly or indirectly, the only possible lateral localization is in terms of the speaker. In these cases, the lateral orientation of the speaker must be transferred[5] to the landmark. This confirms the connection between the speaker and the landmark of spatial relations, a connection proposed in chapter 2.

Figures 14 and 15 described by sentences (31) and (32), respectively.

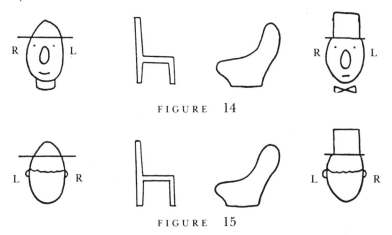

FIGURE 14

FIGURE 15

(31) *la chaise est à droite du fauteuil*
    the chair is to the right of the armchair

(32) *la chaise est à gauche du fauteuil*
    the chair is to the left of the armchair

The unusual aspect of these examples is that the sentences apply correctly to the scenes they describe, either when spoken by the priest, located in the left-hand corner of the page (with respect to the target and the landmark), or when pronounced by the minister, located at the right-hand side of the page. The intrinsic orientations of the chair and the armchair are obviously not factors here. How can we explain this overlap? It is useless to posit a hypothesis directly based on the lateral orientation of the priest or the minister. If the chair is closer to the right-hand shoulder of the minister than to his left, then this cannot be true for the priest, who nevertheless may also describe the scene with sentence (31). Must we conclude that this utterance is independent of the speaker's position? Figure 15 presents the opposite approach: if the priest and the minister turn their backs to the reader, example (32) best describes the position of the chair for both speakers. My informants' reactions, when I ask them to turn their backs and locate the chair, is worthy of note. First, they spontaneously pronounce sentence (32). Noting then that this differs from sentence (31), they are astonished, since their own position with respect to the chair and the armchair has not changed. Sometimes they want to change their minds, but then confirm their earlier impression reluctantly, as if they had been victims of a bad joke. In fact, they are troubled by an unexpected manifestation of a commonly used cognitive strategy, which has become unconscious. Here it is.

It is clear that the position of the landmark is the point of reference for locating the position of the chair in examples (31) and (32). In this sense, it is introduced by the preposition *de*. The location of the priest and the minister with respect to the furniture is unimportant. The lateral alignment of the two speakers is the important factor, as the difference between figures 14 and 15 illustrates: not their lateral direction *from their own position*, as we have seen above, but their lateral direction *transferred to the position of the landmark*.

The scenes above illustrate a partial connection between the landmark and the speaker. Since this identification is complete in the simplest spatial descriptions, the phenomenon described above could illustrate one stage in the transference of the speaker to the landmark. This stage would fall midway between the most egocentric description of space and its most objective description. The attribution of the speaker's lateral orientation to the landmark conforms partially to the transfer principle presented in chapter 2.

> Transfer principle: The speaker has the ability to transfer mentally to any viewpoint that will be useful to the perspective from which he conceptualizes the objective scene.

Nevertheless, this transfer is only partial, since the qualities transferred by the speaker are determined by the perspective imposed by *à gauche/à droite*. It includes only the lateral direction of the speaker.

The relations *devant/derrière*, studied in chapter 7, depend on two prepositional terms, the target and the landmark. This is also the case for *à gauche/à droite* when the landmark is intrinsically oriented along the lateral axis, whether directly (as in figure 12) or indirectly (as in figure 13). The difference lies in whether or not the landmark is contextually oriented. Nonetheless, the speaker's role in these prepositional phrases is only partial and indirect: only the speaker's lateral orientation is transferred to the landmark. In this sense, the relations *à gauche/à droite* depend on target and landmark only, although the landmark may be laterally oriented by the speaker.

In summary, we have distinguished two different types of transfer involved in the expressions *à gauche/à droite*.

1. A general transfer, shared by all the directional relations studied thus far, where the speaker transfers to the position of the landmark. Forgetting his own lateral orientation, the speaker adopts the landmark's orientation, while retaining his own frontal orientation.

2. A strategy unique to the expressions *à gauche/à droite*, where the speaker lends his lateral orientation to the landmark without adopting the landmark's frontal orientation.

This discussion of the expressions *à gauche/à droite* concludes our review of the directional expressions in French. These are repeated here:

along the vertical axis: *au-dessus/en dessous;*
along the frontal direction: *devant/derrière, en face de/dans le dos de;* and
along the lateral axis: *à gauche/à droite.*

Although we have made use of simple directional parameters, the importance of certain more complex concepts has been established.

1. *General orientation* is a family resemblance concept whose principal traits are the frontal direction, the line of sight, and the direction of movement. This concept is needed to explain the use of the prepositions *devant/derrière* adequately. These expressions contrast with *en face de/dans le dos de*, which more strictly apply to the frontal direction alone.

2. *Lateral orientation* is a family resemblance concept whose principal traits include the lateral direction, characterized by the line of the shoulders, and the line perpendicular to general orientation. This concept provides a complete explanation of the use of the expressions *à gauche/à droite.*

9

The prepositions devant/derrière *and access to perception*

> *Lorsque nous aimons une chose qui nous est semblable (par-devant), nous nous efforçons (par-derrière) autant qu'il nous est possible (par-devant) de faire qu'elle nous aime en retour (par-derrière).*[1]

Pierre Mac Orlan
La Maison du retour écoeurant

I will begin this chapter with an example of the use of the prepositions *devant/derrière* that cannot be explained by the usage rule formulated in chapter 7; the new data presented here make a second usage rule necessary.

I then will propose a single usage rule that is made possible by the concept of canonical encounter. Clark and other anglophone linguists have proposed canonical encounter to describe the English expressions *in front of/in back of*. I will discuss the limitations of this solution and suggest a second usage rule, related to access to perception. This second usage rule completes the synchronic description of the prepositions *devant/derrière*.[2]

One of the main hypotheses of this book is that there is a transparent relationship between the original signifier and signified of a spatial preposition. The first usage rule of *devant/derrière*, related to general orientation, is the impetus of these prepositions. This rule is related to the second usage rule by a pragmatic bridge: the fact that an object located in back of the speaker and an object hidden by another object are both inaccessible to perception.

9.1 Bisemy of the prepositions devant/derrière

A *bisemic* word is governed by two usage rules. The prepositions *devant /derrière* illustrate an ambiguity that calls for two usage rules. This ambiguity is particularly striking in the case of example (1), which may describe figures 1 and 2, although the positions of the two chairs are reversed in the two scenes.

FIGURE 1   FIGURE 2

(1) *le fauteuil est devant la chaise*
   the armchair is in front of the chair

The use of *devant* to describe figure 1 derives from the general orientation of the chair (*devant₁*). This use is independent of the speaker's position, though I have included the speaker in the drawing in order to accentuate the similarities and contrasts between the two scenes. On the other hand, when example (1) describes figure 2, its acceptability crucially depends on the position of the speaker. However, it was pointed out in chapter 4 that the ambiguity of a word should be established in terms of its normal uses. No general principle of the lexicon, such as the transfer principle or the fixation principle, can motivate the different interpretations of sentence (1). Although none of the principles presented in chapter 4 can explain the connection between the scenes in (1) and (2), H. H. Clark has proposed a cognitive principle unifying the descriptions of the two scenes. This principle, canonical encounter, was introduced in section 3.3. Clark's proposal is discussed below in detail.

9.2 A unified description of the English expressions in front of/in back of

The unified description covering the uses of *in front of/in back of* depends on the frontal direction of the speaker when the speaker is equated with the landmark. When speaker and landmark are distinct, it depends on the frontal direction of the landmark, oriented in mirror image by the speaker. This type of orientation is a simplified version of contextual orientation, which is not exclusively determined by canonical encounter. Thus, the way houses are generally oriented along a street also explains the use of *en face de* (section 7.4.2) for a bench and a tree along a pathway, although this use would be questionable otherwise.

If landmarks can be oriented by canonical encounter, a unified explanation of *in front of/in back of* is possible. This usage rule is the following:

   a is in front of/in back of b if the target is located on the positive/ negative side of the frontal direction of the landmark.

This rule correctly predicts the uses of the prepositions *devant/ derrière* in sentences (2)–(5), describing figure 3.

(2) *A est derrière (le locuteur)*
   A is in back (of the speaker)

(3) *B est devant (le locuteur)*
   B is in front (of the speaker)

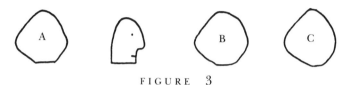

FIGURE 3

(4) *B est devant C*
     B is in front of C

(5) *C est derrière B*
     C is in back of B

The unified explanation is factually correct, if we exclude intrinsically oriented landmarks. The effects of intrinsic orientation are illustrated in figure 1, described by the utterance in (1).

Miller and Johnson-Laird, whose analysis of *in front of/in back of* is otherwise similar to Clark's analysis, point out, "One might expect children to master the apparently simpler deictic system before the intrinsic system, but evidence for *front* and *back* does not support that expectation" (1976, 402). If the use of *in front of/in back of* is mastered first for intrinsically oriented landmarks, these landmarks must play a primary role in the use of the expressions. It is probable that, in the adult linguistic system, when the landmark's contextual orientation conflicts with its intrinsic orientation, the latter generally holds. This was illustrated in chapter 7, where we saw the position chosen by the priest in figures 13 and 14.

How can a unified interpretation resolve the ambiguity of example (1)? In the first reading, we see the landmark's intrinsic orientation; in the second, its contextual orientation is understood. Note that, in figure 2, mirror-image orientation corresponds with the intrinsic orientation of the chair. Sentence (1) is explained by a single rule based on the frontal direction of the landmark, context alone determining whether this orientation is intrinsic or contextual. Since the landmark's intrinsic orientation usually has priority, it seems suspicious that we should need to refer to contextual orientation to explain figure 2. This reversal in priority is even more surprising since it only occurs in specific situations: those in which the speaker, the landmark, and the target are aligned in a straight line, so that one of the terms of *devant/derrière* hides the other.

Rather than resolving the conflict between intrinsic and contextual orientation with a single rule, I will account for the two interpretations of sentence (1) with two different usage rules. The first, related to the landmark's general orientation, has already been discussed. In section 9.3 several arguments will be presented to show that the second usage rule brings in the factor of access to perception.

A comparison of the French prepositions *devant/derrière* with the English expressions *in front of/in back of* evidently presupposes their equivalence. This fact is generally admitted. However, in contrast to the French prepositions, the English expressions refer to two parts of the body, rendering the frontal orientation of the landmark particularly salient. In this they are parallel to the French expressions *en face de/dans le dos de*. I have wondered whether the preposition *behind*, which does not refer to any part of the body, contrasts with the expression *in back of*. I have not explored this question systematically, but I have collected a few remarks that suggest that the first could more easily express inaccessibility to perception than the second. The expression *in back of* would approximate my first version of *derrière*, and the preposition *behind* would correlate with my second version.

9.3 *The second usage rule of the prepositions* devant/derrière

In order to distinguish the uses of *devant₁/derrière₁* (see chapter 7) from the uses considered in this chapter, I will label the latter *devant₂/derrière₂*.

My claim here is that the uses of these prepositions are best explained in terms of access to perception, rather than in terms of canonical encounter. The first argument for this analysis is offered by example (6) and figures 4 and 5.

FIGURE 4   FIGURE 5

(6) *le lapin est derrière l'arbre*
    the rabbit is behind the tree

Example (6) appropriately describes figure 4, in which the speaker, the target, and the landmark are aligned. The unified interpretation presented above accounts for this situation, since the speaker orients the rabbit towards himself as if it were a potential interlocutor. However, this fails to take into account the rabbit's intrinsic orientation, which is an important factor in the use of *devant/derrière*. Furthermore, the presence of the tree between the two potential inter-locutors seems to hinder "canonical" communication. In figure 5, the tree has been moved slightly to the right of the page, facilitating con-versation; following the basic rules of politeness, the rabbit is turned to face its presumed interlocutor. Paradoxically for the unified inter-pretation, sentence (6) is much less appropriate for the scene in figure 5, although this scene has been altered specifically to conform to the demands of this analysis.

This confirms the existence of two versions of *devant/derrière*. For the uses labelled *devant₁/derrière₁*, the target may be located anywhere with respect to the landmark, as the schema in figure 6 illustrates. For the second version of *devant/derrière*, the target and the landmark must be aligned as in figure 7. Example (7), but not (8), describes figure 7 appropriately.

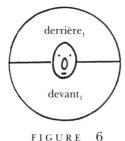

FIGURE 6

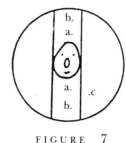

FIGURE 7

(7) *a est devant b*
   a is in front of b

(8) **a est devant c*
   a is in front of c

The unified rule cannot explain the contrast between the schemas in figures 6 and 7. Furthermore, the unacceptable example conforms to the logic of the rule more than the acceptable sentence does. Ac-cording to my interpretation, the use of *devant* in sentence (7) de-mands a new usage rule. Since the alignment of speaker, target, and landmark has the necessary consequence of rendering the landmark or the target inaccessible to perception, I will appeal to this concept to explain the second version of the prepositions *devant/derrière*.

Another example will raise a doubt concerning the explanatory value of canonical encounter for certain uses of *devant/derrière*. This example confirms the existence of two versions of these prepositions.

H. H. Clark describes the characteristic principle of canonical encounter in the following terms: "its most important property is that they [the speaker and his addressee] will be facing each other a short distance apart" (1973, 34).

The rabbit in figure 4 has, by its intrinsic orientation, already contradicted the main criterion of this argument. Figures 8 and 9 below, described by sentence (9), cast a doubt on its second part.

FIGURE 8   FIGURE 9

(9) *la tente est devant l'arbre*
    the tent is in front of the tree

For a speaker in the reader's position, this sentence is appropriate for figure 8, in which the tent is close to the tree, but not for figure 9, in which the tent is further away from the tree. The contrast confirms the unified explanation. This is true, however, only for a certain subset of the uses of *devant*. Example (9) is in fact appropriate for figure 9 only if the speaker is located in the position of the priest, oriented along the same axis as the target and the landmark. The first version of the prepositions *devant/derrière* is exemplified by (9), uttered from the reader's position; the second version comes into play when the sentence is uttered from the position of the priest. For the first version, the acceptability/unacceptability of (9) varies as the distance from the tree to the tent varies. Between these two extremes is an area of indecision, where acceptability judgments are hesitant and contradictory. The contrast between figures 8 and 9 is explained by the variation of one parameter within a single usage rule: as the distance between the tree and the tent increases, the tent is less and less able to orient the landmark contextually, as the prepositions $devant_1/derrière_1$ require.

When the priest is brought into the scene in figure 9, we find a contrast that can only be explained by a new usage rule. Because of the alignment of speaker, target, and landmark, access to perception will be a factor here. As in figure 4, one prepositional term prevents the speaker from perceiving the second term clearly. The distance between the presumed interlocutors ceases to be important in this instance.

The data assembled by Hill in several articles on Hausa provide me with another argument establishing the relation between access to perception and frontal orientation in that language. The prepositions *gaya/baya* correspond to the French prepositions *devant/derrière*. Hill notes that the speaker and the landmark of *gaya/baya* are not oriented in mirror image, but in tandem (see section 3.3), yet this strategy is reversed in one specific instance: when the target hides the landmark. It is clear that a description of these prepositions should include two usage rules, one of which must refer to access to perception.

The need for a second usage rule governing *devant/derrière* seems to be established by this point. This usage rule is formulated as follows:

D'_2: *a est devant₂/derrière₂ b* if the target hides/is hidden by the landmark.

A certain number of modifications must be added to this rule. First, the following examples illustrate that sight is not the only sense of perception to play a role in judging whether the target and landmark are accessible to perception. The scene in figure 10 is poorly described by example (10).

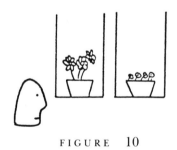

FIGURE   10

(10) *les marguerites sont devant les violettes*
      the daisies are in front of the violets

In terms of sight, the target and the landmark are in fact equally perceptible to the speaker. However, example (11) seems to be preferred to describe this scene.

(11) *je ne sens pas les violettes parce que les marguerites sont devant*
      I can't smell the violets because the daisies are in front of them

In this example, the domain of sight is replaced by that of the sense of smell. Because the strong perfume of the daisies prevents the speaker from perceiving the smell of the violets, example (11) is acceptable. The contrast between examples (10) and (11) places sight and smell in opposition. I could contrast all of the five senses in the same way, but I will refer only to one final example to demonstrate the role of the auditory sense. If the churches of Saint-Servais and Saint-Jacques are both visible to the speaker, example (12) is inappropriate. Example (13), in contrast, is acceptable if the two churches ring their bells at the same time, and the sound of the church bells of the first church covers the music of the second.

(12) *l'église Saint-Servais est devant l'église Saint-Jacques*
the Church of Saint-Servais is in front of the Church of Saint-Jacques

(13) *je n'entends pas sonner Saint-Jacques car Saint-Servais est devant*
I can't hear the bells of Saint-Jacques because Saint-Servais is in front

Of the five senses, note that the sense of touch contributes to the confusion between perception and movement.[3] In fact, we can see or smell a rose at a distance, but we cannot touch it. If the flower is out of reach, the action of reaching necessarily implies a movement. The role of touch appears in figure 11, described by example (14).

FIGURE 11

(14) *la rivière est devant l'arbre*
the river is in front of the tree

Although the river does not prevent the speaker from seeing the tree, it does prevent him from touching the tree without getting his feet wet.

A second modification must be made to definition D'_2. The landmark/target of the prepositions *devant/derrière* does not have to be totally obscured by the target/landmark, as sentence (15) demonstrates, describing figure 12.

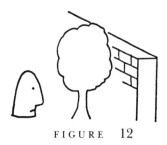

FIGURE   12

(15) *l'arbre est devant le mur*
      the tree is in front of the wall

Although the tree does not hide the wall entirely from sight, example (15) is in fact acceptable.

One final modification should be added to definition D'_2 to explain why sentence (16) cannot apply to the boulder in figure 13.

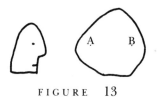

FIGURE   13

(16) **A est devant B*
      A is in front of B

While it is true that the information value of this utterance is slight, the sentence cannot be ruled out for this reason alone. Example (17), which is just as uninteresting as (16), is in fact more acceptable.

(17) *A est avant B*
      A is before B

The important issue here, it seems to me, is that the target/landmark of *devant/derrière* must be the first visible object preventing the perception of the landmark/target. In figure 13, the first obstacle to perceiving point B is not point A, but the surface of the boulder. However, this condition, which rejects example (16), is too strong, since it would also reject (18). In fact, (18) is perfectly acceptable.

(18) *l'estomac est devant le foie*
    the stomach is in front of the liver

In this case the first part of the body hiding the liver is the skin of the abdomen, and not the stomach itself. The possibility of surgery, or the transparency of the body under X-rays, makes example (18) possible, however. As long as the target/landmark of the prepositions *devant/ derrière* is potentially the first object blocking perception of the landmark/target, the situation is acceptable. Point A fails to comply with this condition in example (16).

Taking into account the above restrictions, definition D$'_2$ may be rewritten.

D$_2$: *a est devant/derrière b* if the target/landmark is (potentially) the first (partial) obstacle to the perception of the landmark/ target.

The existence of two versions of the prepositions *devant/derrière* seems to be well established by this point. One is tied to the general orientation of the landmark, while the second is related to access to perception. The first is independent of the position of the speaker when the speaker is not one of the terms of the preposition; the second crucially depends on the speaker's position. Although the prepositions *devant$_1$/derrière$_1$* depend on only two terms, the target and the landmark (generally the speaker), the prepositions *devant$_2$/derrière$_2$* depend on three terms: the target, the landmark, and the speaker. The diagram summarizes the relations between the two versions of *devant/derrière*.

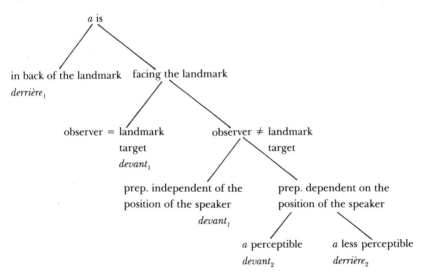

9.4 *The impetus of the prepositions* devant/derrière

One fundamental hypothesis of this book is that at the origin of each spatial preposition there was a transparent and unambiguous correspondence between the signifier and the signified. Do certain synchronic considerations allow us to determine the impetus of the prepositions *devant/derrière* from one of the two usage rules?

We should note first of all that rule D_1 is simpler than rule D_2 in that it implies only two terms. Furthermore, for the preposition *devant*, rule D_2 is an elaboration of rule D_1. In fact, it is impossible for a target to be located *devant$_2$* a landmark without also being *devant$_1$*.

The relation between *devant$_1$* and *devant$_2$* clearly demonstrates that rule D_1 must be selected as the impetus of the prepositions *devant/derrière*. The meaning of *derrière$_2$* is derived from the meaning of *derrière$_1$* in the following way:

1. At the first stage of the logical evolution of the word, the preposition *derrière* designates something in back of the speaker.

2. Because of human nature, most objects located behind our backs are not perceptible.

3. There are other objects, located in front of us, that escape our perception: objects hidden by other objects. This similarity establishes a pragmatic bridge between the two regions of space illustrated below.

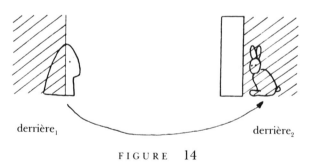

derrière$_1$ derrière$_2$

FIGURE 14

Both areas are described by the preposition *derrière*.

The pragmatic bridge extending the meaning of *derrière* is forgotten, and two usage rules become necessary to describe the synchronic use of these prepositions. However, it is possible that the acquisition of the two uses of *derrière* is facilitated by a partial consciousness of this pragmatic relation.[4]

To establish which usage rule is more salient in the speaker's mind, we might examine an object that is simultaneously in back of the speaker and perceptible. Will we say this object is *devant*, thus establishing the superiority of access to perception, or *derrière*, retaining the importance of general orientation? This type of situation may be artificially created with the help of a mirror. What will I say if I look into a mirror at the cupboard located behind my back? Example (19) seems the most probable to me.

    (19) *l'armoire est derrière moi*
         the cupboard is behind me

    The hierarchy between the two rules could also be tested by someone speaking with his eyes closed. Will he say that the tree in figure 15 is *devant lui* (general orientation) or *derrière lui* (access to perception)? The first choice is by far the more probable.

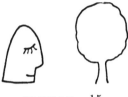

FIGURE   15

    These tests seem to establish the primacy of the first usage rule over the second usage rule as the impetus of the prepositions *devant/derrière*. The evidence that these examples bring to bear on the question does not entirely convince me, however. Rather than demonstrating a preference between the two usage rules, perhaps these examples simply reflect the speaker's preference for the usual view of the world, instead of the less familiar view of the world when it is perceived through a mirror or with closed eyes.

10

The prepositions avant/après *and order in potential encounter*

J'avance à reculons.[1]

Bertolucci

Last Tango in Paris

Three usage rules for the prepositions *avant/après* will be compared in this chapter. The first, expressed in terms of order along a scale, will allow us to explore the distribution of these prepositions. While this rule is concise and exhaustive, it has the disadvantage of explaining an intuitively simple preposition by a complex notion. This would be a major fault in a book claiming to describe spatial prepositions in terms of basic cognitive concepts.

While the notion of order is inevitable in the definition of these prepositions, it must be made explicit. A second usage rule will add precision to the first, drawing on the relative movement between the prepositional terms, and a pole defined by the context of the utterance. The influence of movement on the prepositions *avant/après* is dramatically illustrated by figure 1, described by examples (1) and (2).

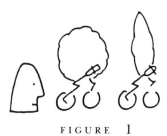

FIGURE 1

(1) *le curé est avant le ministre*
the priest is before the minister

(2) *le peuplier est après le chêne*
the poplar is after the oak

This chapter is a revised and extended version of an article that appeared in *Recherches linguistiques* (1985).

Although the two bikers and the two trees are schematically aligned, they are described by opposite prepositions. The bikers' movement $(a, b) \rightarrow P$ towards their goal (the pole in sentence [1]) is obvious. As for example (2), I will demonstrate the possibility of a potential movement $P \rightarrow (a, b)$. Here the speaker, the pole of the relation, moves towards the two trees.

The formula $P \leftrightarrow (a, b)$ summarizes these two movements. It leads us to the final definition of the prepositions *avant/après* in terms of potential encounter, a fundamental notion in the organization of space. I will return later to illustrate the advantages of this final definition.

The importance of movement and potential encounter in the use of *avant/après* explains why time plays an important role in these constructions. Time is not a sufficient criterion, however, and fails to motivate the total distribution of these prepositions.

The expressions *en avant/en arrière* will be discussed in the last section. I will conclude this chapter by comparing the distributions of the prepositions *avant/après* and *devant/derrière*.

10.1 The prepositions avant / après *and order along a scale*

One usage rule for the prepositions *avant/après* may be formulated as follows:

A_1: *a est avant/après b if a is mth/nth and if b is nth/mth in an ordered relation, and* m < n.

Order is specified in a *domain* if, for each pair (a, b), there is a *scale of comparison* R such that $R(a, b)$ or $R(b, a)$. I will turn now to examine the domains covered by *avant/après* and the principle scales of comparison defined in these domains.

10.1.1 Domains of the prepositions *avant/après*

In the examples below, these prepositions are used in several different domains: time, space, numbers, the alphabet, and competitions.

(3) *mars est avant juin*
March is before June

(4) *Rome est avant La Mecque*
Rome is before Mecca

(5) *1 est avant 3*
1 is before 3

(6) *a est avant b*
   a is before *b*

(7) *miss Californie est avant miss Salvador*
   Miss California is before Miss El Salvador

We could try to choose the primary domain of *avant/après* from among these examples. The uses of these prepositions in other domains then would be metaphorical. On the other hand, we might look for a more abstract quality, shared by all uses of *avant/après* in all their domains. Figure 2, described by examples (8) and (9), demonstrates that the second alternative is needed.

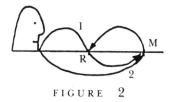

FIGURE   2

(8) *Rome est avant La Mecque*
   Rome is before Mecca

(9) *La Mecque est avant Rome*
   Mecca is before Rome[2]

If the spatial domain alone is considered, the spatial uses of *avant /après* in sentences (8) and (9) will be contradictory. Only the notion of order can reconcile these two readings. These examples are explained by reference to two different scales of comparison: path 1 for the first utterance, path 2 for the second utterance.

The prepositions *avant/après* will be defined in terms of the order established by each domain.

10.1.2 Scales of comparison

In the spatial domain

The most common scales of comparison in space are *path* and *line of sight*. Figure 2 illustrates how different paths may indicate different uses of the prepositions *avant/après*. The function of the line of sight in the use of these prepositions is illustrated by figure 3, described by example (10).

(10) *le poteau rouge est avant le poteau jaune*
      the red telephone pole is before the yellow telephone
      pole

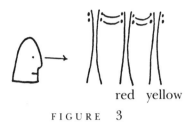

red   yellow

FIGURE   3

Although path and line of sight are the most natural scales of comparison in space, the prepositions *avant/après* apply also to more sophisticated scales of comparison. Variables other than distance may come into play. I will restrict myself to one example here, that of a sailboat race in the Pacific Ocean, illustrated by figure 4.

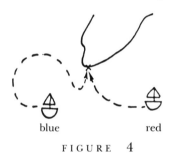

blue   red

FIGURE   4

In terms of any scale of distance, it is obvious that the blue boat is *avant* the red boat. But a knowledgeable journalist, aware of the prevailing winds, the currents, and the tides, will not judge the race based on distance alone. Taking into consideration certain supplementary factors, this journalist might report that the red boat is *avant* the blue boat. This judgment will be based on a pragmatic scale of comparison that considers not only distance, but also a range of atmospheric conditions. The list of scales of comparison in space is potentially infinite, and each discourse situation will set up the scales needed for its own purposes.

In the temporal domain

The progression of time from the creation of the world to the Last Judgment determines the most common scale of comparison in this domain. The use of the verb *avancer* 'to advance' in sentence (11) implies a different scale, however.

> (11) *tous les jours, le lever du soleil avance de deux minutes*
> every day, sunrise advances by two minutes

This utterance is understood in terms of time projected onto a scale of twenty-four hours, and not in terms of time's eternal progression.

In the abstract domains

The entire set of cardinal numbers is generally ordered by the relation > (greater than). The alphabet establishes a scale of comparison within the set of letters used in our writing system. The sets of letters and numbers constitute what I call *neutral orders,* in that the relation *p est avant q* does not imply that the first unit is preferred over the second. Contests or competitions, on the other hand, are *orders of value.* A competitor is judged to be better if he is placed ahead of another. The scale of comparison depends on the judgment of the speaker.

10.2 The prepositions avant / après *and relative movement*

In this section I present a definition of the prepositions *avant/après* in terms of the pole, as follows:

> A'_2: *a est avant/après b* if the target is closer to/farther from the pole than the landmark is.

The use of the comparative construction in this rule demonstrates that it is still necessary to refer to an ordered relation. In this definition, the pole provisionally represents a free parameter that will be set for each of the following cases (see section 10.2.1):

1. The two terms of the relation are static.
2. One term of the relation is static.
3. The two terms of the relation are mobile.

As we will see, the position of the pole in the spatial domain is either initial or final. This is also the case in other domains of the prepositions *avant/après* (see section 10.2.2).

It is clear that in the third case the pole is at the endpoint of the movement $[(a, b) \rightarrow P]$. In section 10.2.3 I will demonstrate the potential movement $P \rightarrow (a, b)$ of the pole in cases 2 and 3. The free parameter in definition A'_2 will be specified in terms of potential movement. The rule is rewritten as follows:

> A_2: *a est avant/après b* if the target is closer to/farther from the pole than the landmark is, when both terms are involved in a potential relative movement with the pole.

Time is a necessary factor in movement and thus plays a primary role in the distribution of the prepositions *avant/après*. I will demonstrate, however, that time alone cannot entirely motivate this distribution.

10.2.1 The position of the poles in the spatial domain

The two terms of the relation are static

The principal scales of comparison here are path and the line of sight. The two scales set up the same rules for the uses of *avant/après* when the objects are located in front of the speaker. In these cases, the pole is at the origin of the line of sight or the path. For points located in back of the observer, however, the two scales of comparison demand different uses of the prepositions *avant/après*, as figure 5 illustrates. This scene is described by examples (12)–(14).

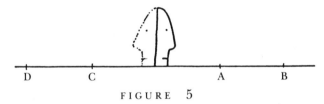

FIGURE 5

(12) *A est avant B*
A is before B

(13) *C est avant D*
C is before D

(14) *C est après D*
C is after D

Sentence (13) must be interpreted according to the order determined by the line of sight: although the observer is facing A, he is speaking as though he were looking toward C, in the position indicated by the dotted line. The pole remains at the origin of the line of sight. In example (14), the observer is speaking as though he were at the origin of the path. In both cases, the pole is at the origin of the scale of comparison.

One term of the relation is static

Figure 6 is described by the utterances in examples (15) and (16).

(15) *l'auto est avant l'arbre*
the car is before the tree

(16) *l'arbre est après l'auto*
the tree is after the car

FIGURE 6

In order for A′₂ to describe these sentences correctly, the pole must be located at the origin of the scale of comparison. Whether both terms are static or only one is, the pole must be at the origin of the scale.

The two terms of the relation are mobile

This time the pole is located at the end of the scale of comparison, as example (17) illustrates, describing figure 7.

FIGURE 7

(17) *le curé est avant le ministre*
the priest is before the minister

Thus we find two types of orders in space: *static orders,* in which at least one of the terms is immobile, and *dynamic orders,* in which the two terms are mobile. The first type has an initial pole, while the second has a final pole. This duality, as we will see, is repeated in other domains where the prepositions *avant/après* may apply.

10.2.2 Orders in other domains

Examples (18) and (19) illustrate that temporal poles are normally at the origin of the scale of comparison.

(18) *Jules César est né avant Napoléon*
Julius Caesar was born before Napoleon

(19) *Dieu créa l'homme avant la femme*
God created man before woman

The following example demonstrates a final pole on the temporal axis. In the sentences below, the verb *avancer* may be paraphrased as *(faire) avoir lieu avant* '(make something) take place before'.[3]

(20) *le ministre avance la réunion*
the minister is moving up the meeting

(21) *la montre du curé avance*
the priest's watch is fast

Imagine that four o'clock is the time originally set for the meeting, and also the present time. As the schema below illustrates, although the time of the new meeting moves backwards on the temporal axis, the time indicated by the fast watch, in contrast, moves ahead.

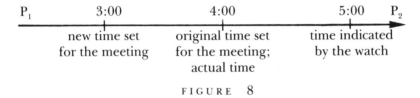

FIGURE 8

For definition A$'_2$ to apply to this paradigm, two different poles must be allowed along the temporal axis. The first, corresponding to example (20), is at the origin, as we find in instances of static orders in space. The different times of the meeting are metaphorically considered as immobile points along the temporal axis. In (21), in contrast, the pole is final, as we find in the dynamic spatial orders. Now the normal time and the time indicated by the watch are interpreted as mobile objects following each other along the temporal axis.

Among the abstract orders, neutral orders, such as the numbers and the alphabet, clearly have their pole at the origin of the scale of comparison.

(22) *1 est avant 2*
1 is before 2

(23) *a est avant b*
a is before *b*

Orders of value on the other hand demonstrate a final pole. The football team with the most points, the star with the greatest number of "star qualities," the candidate with the most votes, these are all placed *before* their competitors. The neutral orders seem then to assimilate metaphorically to the static orders, while the orders of value behave like dynamic orders.

The position of the poles for the different orders is summarized in the table.

Order	Scale of Comparison	Position of Pole
Spatial domain		
Static order	line of sight or path	initial
Dynamic order	path	final
Temporal domain		
Static order	flow of time	initial
Dynamic order	flow of time	final
Abstract domain		
Neutral order	relation <, alphabet	initial
Order of value	speaker's judgment	final

10.2.3 The potential movement of the initial pole

The unified character of definition A'_2 is misleading. It appears unified because we have appealed to the artifice of a pole that may designate both the origin and the terminus of the scale of comparison. Now we must establish the link between the initial pole and the final pole. I will demonstrate that in both cases the pole acts as the second element in relative movement with the terms of the prepositions *avant/après*.

This point is evident when we look at the dynamic orders, where the two prepositional terms are moving towards the final pole. The possibility that the pole is potentially mobile in the case of the static orders will be demonstrated by the following argument:

1. If the static pole is a potentially mobile object, the use of the prepositions *avant/après* must be the same, regardless of whether the speaker is moving or immobile. I will review the scenes described in section 10.2.1, this time presenting examples in which the speaker is mobile. The description the mobile speaker offers will be identical to the descriptions used by the immobile speaker.

2. Since the use of the prepositions *avant/après* is identical whether the speaker is mobile or immobile, I am free to attribute a potential movement to the immobile pole, as long as no counterexample invalidates my hypothesis. I will, however, present some positive evidence arguing for the movement of the initial pole.

10.2.3.1 Compatibility of static orders with a pole in potential movement

Here I return to the examples in section 10.2.1, introducing a mobile speaker.

The two terms of the relation are immobile. This time, the speaker is walking along a path and realizes he has forgotten his crown at the foot of an oak tree. As an immobile speaker he will describe the objects in front of him. The alternative pictured in figure 5 is available when the speaker describes objects behind him. This is illustrated in figure 9, described by examples (24) and (25).

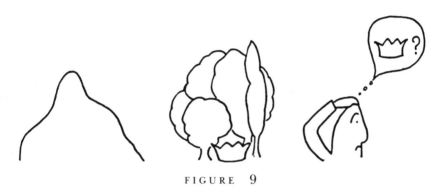

FIGURE 9

(24) *heureusement que les arbres sont avant la montagne*
luckily the trees are before the mountain

(25) *vous souvenez-vous, duchesse, des arbres après la montagne*
Duchess, do you remember the trees after the mountain

As we saw in section 10.2.1, these utterances rely on different scales of comparison. The first depends on the line of sight or the possible path of the speaker retracing his steps to retrieve the crown. The second option is tied to the direction of the path itself, as followed by the speaker in the course of his hike. In both cases, the pole is at the origin of the scale of comparison.

One term of the relation is immobile. Figure 10, in which the target and the speaker are travelling along the same path, may be described by the examples below.

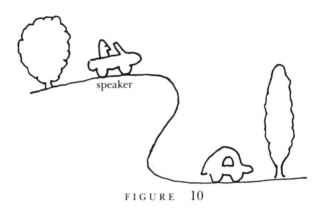

FIGURE   10

(26) *la voiture est avant le peuplier*
the car is before the poplar

(27) *le peuplier est après la voiture*
the poplar is after the car

This scene would be described in the same way by an immobile speaker.

A comparison of examples (28) and (29) is particularly interesting.

(28) *le chêne est avant le peuplier*
the oak is before the poplar

(29) **le chêne est après le peuplier*
the oak is after the poplar

The first sentence is explained by reference to the linear progression of the path. In contrast, the use of the preposition *après* must be motivated by the line of sight. However, it is impossible for the speaker to see both trees at the same time. Utterance (29) is therefore impossible. Since the direction of movement and the line of sight generally coincide, the two notions are often difficult to isolate. When the target and the landmark are not simultaneously visible, the preposition *après* is unacceptable; this confirms the connection between this use of *après* and the line of sight.

Both terms of the relation are mobile. Example (17) still describes figure 7 appropriately if the speaker follows the minister and the priest on a bicycle. Here again, a mobile speaker uses the prepositions *avant/après* in the same way an immobile speaker would.

All the situations described in section 10.2.1 have now been reviewed. Whether the speaker is mobile or immobile, the use of the prepositions *avant/après* remains the same, with one exception: if the speed of the speaker is significantly greater than the speed of the target or the landmark, then a dynamic order may become static. This phenomenon is dramatically illustrated by figure 11, which examples (30) and (31) describe.

FIGURE 11

(30) *la tortue est avant l'escargot*
the tortoise is before the snail

(31) *l'escargot est avant la tortue*
the snail is before the tortoise

In example (30), the order is dynamic, and pole P_1 is final. In (31), the pedestrian's potential speed makes the speed of the tortoise and the snail negligible by comparison, so much so that the order becomes a static one. Pole P_2 of this scale of order is initial.

With this single exception, the prepositions *avant/après* are used identically by a mobile and an immobile speaker; this is the basis of my claim that the immobile speaker is at least potentially mobile. I will turn now to show that this hypothesis is not only possible but desirable.

10.2.3.2 Proof of potential movement in the static scales of order

To demonstrate the importance of movement in the static orders, I will present two inappropriate usages of the prepositions *avant/après,* which become possible if a static element of the context is replaced by a potentially mobile element.

For a speaker in the position of the reader, example (32) is appropriate only for figure 13.

FIGURE 12   FIGURE 13

> (32) *le chat est avant le lapin*
> the cat is before the rabbit

Even if the tree is immobile and the car is parked, only the potentially mobile object can function as the pole in example (32).

The importance of potential movement in the static relations is confirmed by a second example. If the speaker is once again in the reader's position, example (33) describes figure 15, but not figure 14.

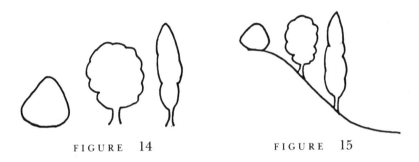

FIGURE 14   FIGURE 15

> (33) *le chêne est avant le peuplier*
> the oak is before the poplar

Due to the slope of the terrain and the risk of an avalanche, a potential for movement is introduced into the scene, transforming the boulder of the second scene into a possible pole. Since this potential is not a factor in the first scene, the boulder in that case cannot play such a role.

Since a potentially mobile object—and only a potentially mobile object—may function as a pole in the static relations of order, we must consider the speaker in figure 1 in terms of his mobility. Looking at the oak and the poplar, the speaker imagines a possible movement towards the trees. In sum, the movement $(a, b) \rightarrow$ P of the dynamic orders corresponds to the movement P $\rightarrow (a, b)$ of the static orders.

Note that the movement of the terms of a dynamic order may be only potential, just as the pole of the static orders may be only potentially mobile. Sentence (34) then correctly describes figures 16, even if the priest and the minister are immobile.

FIGURE 16

(34) *le curé est avant le ministre*
the priest is before the minister

Both are in position, waiting for the starting gun to fire, before dashing to the finish line. This explains why the preposition *avant* is chosen with respect to the final pole of the dynamic orders, and not with respect to the initial pole of the static orders.

To conclude this discussion, static and dynamic orders are both represented by a single formula P $\leftrightarrow$ (*a, b*), in which the movement of pole P as well as the movement of the terms *a* and *b* may be potential.

The prepositions *avant/après* are converse relations, even more obviously than the expressions *au-dessus/en dessous*. In fact, if *a est avant b*, we may always deduce that *b est après a*. The expressions *au-dessus/en dessous* are converse in being tied to the objective reality of the vertical axis. The converse uses of the prepositions *avant/après* can be explained by their relation to movement. The asymmetry of target and landmark is particularly salient for the prepositions *devant /derrière* and *à gauche/à droite,* since their landmark is generally equated with the speaker.

10.2.4 The prepositions *avant/après* and time

The relation of the prepositions *avant/après* to movement explains why time plays an important role here. Although it is a necessary condition, it is not sufficient for the use of these prepositions. We can examine figures 12 and 14 as long as we like, but examples (32) and (33) will remain inappropriate as long as a potentially mobile object does not feature in the scene.

Another example will illustrate that time alone cannot describe all the uses of the prepositions *avant/après*. Imagine a race between a bishop and an attorney general. The latter, a faster runner, allows the man of the cloth several minutes' head start but will still be the first to cross the finish line. A minute before the attorney general passes the bishop, the race will still be described by sentence (35).

(35) *l'évêque est avant le procureur général*
the bishop is before the attorney general

How can this example be motivated by the notion of time? If we consider the length of time passed since each runner took off, the attorney general should erroneously be said to be *before* the bishop, since he has run for a shorter length of time than the bishop. The same reasoning applies if we count the time separating the runners from the finish line. Only the physical distance separating the sprinters from their goal can accurately motivate the use of *avant* in example (35).

Time is a necessary condition in the use of the prepositions *avant* /*après* and plays an increasingly important role. This evolution is particularly interesting when we consider the English prepositions *before*/ *behind*. As their etymology indicates, these two prepositions were originally exclusively spatial. The preposition *before* has today become essentially temporal, while the converse preposition *behind* has retained its spatial use. Two new pairs of converse spatial relations have come into English as a result: *before*/*after* 'avant/après' and *in front of*/*behind* 'devant/derrière'.[4]

10.3 Potential encounter

The formula P ↔ (*a*, *b*) suggests that the pole and the terms of *avant*/ *après* will approach each other and potentially meet; one or the other participant may play the active role in this situation. The pole is then the second element of the encounter and may be omitted from the final definition of these prepositions.

> A₃: *a est avant/après b* if the target is closer to/farther from the second element of the potential encounter than the landmark is.

I have purposely avoided including the expressions *près de*/*loin de*, which essentially call to mind the spatial domain (see chapter 5). Each type of encounter determines the scale of comparison by which the expressions *plus proche*/*plus éloigné* 'closer/farther' must be understood. In the temporal domain, for example, these will be synonymous with *plus tôt*/*plus tard* 'earlier/later'.

At this level of abstraction the description of *avant/après* is in fact a unified description. The single description was only artificially achieved by definition A₂, which used the notion of initial and final poles to camouflage the differences between the two types of use presented in figure 1. In determining which of the two elements of the potential encounter is active or passive, definition A₃ refers only secondarily to the distinction between these two types. The concept of order motivates the uses of *avant/après* when there is a potential for an encounter, no matter which member of the encounter is active.

Definition A₃ directly explains why these prepositions cannot apply to the scene in figure 17.

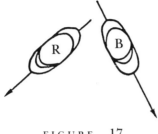

(36) *l'auto rouge est avant l'auto bleue*
       the red car is before the blue car

(37) *l'auto bleue est avant l'auto rouge*
       the blue car is before the red car

Since the two cars are heading in different directions, they cannot be moving toward a common meeting point. In contrast, if the trajectories of the two cars intersect, the prepositions *avant/après* may apply.

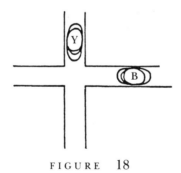

FIGURE   18

(38) *la voiture jaune est avant la voiture bleue*
       the yellow car is before the blue car

Example (38) is explained by means of the intersection, the potential meeting point of the two cars. The vehicle closest to this point is *avant* the vehicle farther away. More generally, if the mobile objects of a dynamic order have different trajectories, the pole is found at the intersection of these paths; this is the only point all the mobile objects will contact.

Definition A_3 thus correctly explains the contrast between figures 17 and 18. It provides a unified account of all the natural usages of the prepositions *avant/après*. The concept of potential encounter is introduced by this definition and will be particularly useful in our understanding of space. Here we see that an exhaustive study of the most complex distributions may sometimes be explained by basic cognitive concepts.

10.4 The expressions en avant/en arrière

Up to this point, only the preposition *après* has been placed in opposition to *avant*. Once nominalized, *avant* is also opposed to *arrière*. I will describe the uses of this word before turning to a close study of the expressions *en avant/en arrière*.

10.4.1 Arrière

The first difference between the words *arrière* and *après* is syntactic. The latter may be either a preposition or an adverb, but never a noun. *Arrière*, on the other hand, is generally a noun, but never a preposition. It is most often used in the expressions *en arrière/à l'arrière* 'in back/in the back'. It may also be used as an interjection.

The second difference between *après* and *arrière* concerns the domains of their use. While the prepositions *avant/après* are in opposition in every domain, *arrière* is restricted exclusively to the spatial domain. Here we can focus on one property specific to this domain, to shed some light on the meaning of this word: there is no single point from which the entire spatial domain will be perceived. The totality of the temporal domain may be metaphorically perceived from its origin; the set of positive numbers may be perceived from the origin of zero; etc. The spatial domain has no origin, however. Wherever the speaker may be, half the universe is always behind him. The word *arrière* applies exactly to the part of space that cannot be seen. Although the contrast *avant/après* is described in terms of the second member of a potential encounter, the contrast *avant/arrière* is better expressed by the contrast seen/not seen, as figure 19 illustrates.

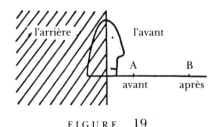

FIGURE   19

10.4.2 The expressions *en avant/en arrière*

So far I have not attempted to analyze the preposition *en;* as a result, I cannot decide to what extent the expressions *en avant/en arrière* are compositional. They will be studied here as unanalyzed phrases.

Examples (39)–(41) introduce a discussion of these expressions.

> (39) *le curé marche en avant*
> the priest is walking forward

> (40) *le curé est assis en avant*
> the priest is sitting facing forward

> (41) **la maison est en avant*
> the house is forward

Although example (39) is more natural than (40), both are acceptable, in contrast to (41). How is this contrast motivated? In (40), even if the priest is momentarily sitting to eat or to pray, he is a potentially mobile object and will soon go on his way. This is evidently not the case for the house in example (41). For these expressions, as for the prepositions *avant/après*, a potentially mobile object may behave as if it were indeed a mobile object. Unlike the house in (41), however, this object may not be perpetually static. In contrast, the subject of *avant/après* may be static. Figure 20, described by examples (42)–(45), confirms the contrast between the pairs *avant/en avant* and *après/en arrière*.

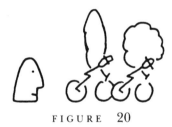

FIGURE 20

> (42) *le curé est avant le ministre*
> the priest is before the minister

> (43) *le curé est en avant*
> the priest is (moving) ahead

> (44) *le peuplier est avant le chêne*
> the poplar is before the oak

> (45) **le peuplier est en avant*
> the poplar is (moving) ahead

Example (45), but not (44), is rendered unacceptable by the inherent immobility of its target.

The target of the expressions *en avant/en arrière* must therefore be potentially active in the encounter. The landmark of these expressions is always sublexical and may be deduced from the context. In figure 21, described by example (46), the speaker is the landmark of the relation.

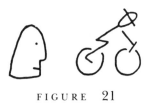

FIGURE 21

(46) *le curé est en avant*
      the priest is ahead

If the priest is participating in a bike race, the landmark implied by sentence (46) will probably be the group of bikers still behind him. The utterance would be true only if no biker were ahead of the priest. However, the priest could be part of a small group leading the race; in this case, even if a few bikers were in front of the priest, sentence (46) would still be acceptable.

The expressions *en avant/en arrière* are governed by the following usage rule:

> *a est en avant/en arrière* if it is among the nearest/farthest active elements from the second member of a potential encounter.

The definition of *en avant/en arrière* differs essentially from the definition of *avant/après* by the introduction of the word *active*. While *avant/après* describe the two movements P → (a, b) and (a, b) → P, the expressions *en avant/en arrière* only describe the movement (a, [b]) → P, in which the landmark is in brackets to show that it is sublexical.

10.5 *The distributions of* avant/après *and* devant/derrière

The distribution of the first version of the *devant/derrière* was explained by general orientation, while a second version of these prepositions was motivated by access to perception. We have established the relation of *avant/après* to the concept of potential encounter, which necessarily implies movement. Since general orientation is a family resemblance concept whose traits include the line of sight and the direction of movement, it follows that certain uses of *devant/derrière* and *avant/après* must be difficult to distinguish. Remember that a family resemblance concept may be represented by different combinations of traits, and even by a single trait if the context of the utterance emphasizes a particular trait over the others. The direction of movement and the line of sight figure among the traits capable of determining a marginal general orientation. Because of this confusion, the empirical value of my analysis may be tested. A summary is diagramed in the schema.

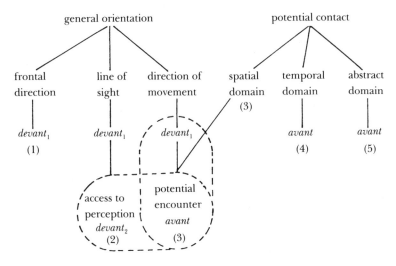

Since movement is a trait of general orientation and a cause of potential encounter at the same time, it may motivate both *devant₁* and *avant*. The line of sight generally coincides with the direction of movement, causing confusion in the distributions of *devant₂* and *avant*. Finally, the line of sight, a trait of general orientation, may motivate both versions of the prepositions *devant/derrière*. Here, if the uses of *devant₁/derrière₁* and *devant₂/derrière₂* are not distinguished by the number of their terms, we have a case of total confusion. The overlap of the prepositions *avant/après* and the two versions of *devant/derrière* is limited to the two zones enclosed by a dotted line in the schema.

I will demonstrate that these ambiguous zones are not due to a faulty analysis; rather, they correspond to circumstances where the distribution of *avant/après* and *devant/derrière* actually do overlap. Two prepositions are not necessarily synonymous simply because they can be used to describe the same situation: each preposition presents a different aspect of the same objective scene. The meaning of a word cannot be entirely explained by its role in the truth value of the sentence; we will draw on examples highlighting the perspective of the scene to illustrate this point.

To establish the empirical value of the schema, I will first present situations where *avant/après* and *devant/derrière* both apply. I will then introduce circumstances in which these prepositions contrast in acceptability. Both overlap and divergence may be explained by the usage rules I have already proposed.

Coincidence of the prepositions avant/après *and* devant/derrière. Examples (47)–(50) describe the figures below.

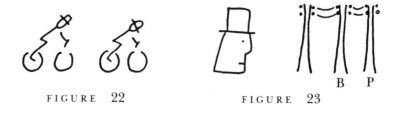

FIGURE 22   FIGURE 23

(47) *le curé est avant le ministre*
      the priest is before the minister

(48) *le curé est devant₁ le ministre*
      the priest is in front of the minister

(49) *le poteau bleu est devant₂ le poteau rose*
      the blue pole is in front of the pink pole

(50) *le poteau bleu est avant le poteau rose*
      the blue pole is before the pink pole

Since figure 22 allows both mobile *and* oriented prepositional terms, it may be described by example (47) as well as example (48): the prepositions *avant* and *devant₁* are simultaneously acceptable. Figure 23 may also be understood according to two different perspectives: on the one hand, the blue pole hides the pink pole, on the other hand, the minister may imagine a movement towards the poles. Both *devant₂* (example [49]) and *avant* (example [50]) may be employed in these circumstances.

Figures 22 and 23 illustrate the overlapping domains of the prepositions *devant₁/avant* and *devant₂/avant*. Each preposition emphasizes different aspects of the scenes. The sentences below, describing figure 22, point up these differences.

(51) *le curé est avant le ministre et il ne sera pas en retard*
the priest is before the minister and he will not be late

(52) *le curé est devant le ministre et il ne sera pas en retard*
the priest is in front of the minister and he will not be late

(53) *le curé est devant le ministre et il a un trou dans sa soutane*
the priest is in front of the minister and he has a hole in his cassock

(54) *le curé est avant le ministre et il a un trou dans sa soutane*
the priest is before the minister and he has a hole in his cassock

Although examples (51)–(54) all adequately describe figure 22, example (51) is preferred over (52), and (53) is preferred over (54). In fact, the second clause in examples (51) and (52) emphasizes movement, and the preposition *avant* is preferred for this very reason. In contrast, the second clause in examples (53) and (54) emphasizes access to perception, and the preposition *devant* is preferred. If the speaker's perspective determines the acceptability of examples (51) and (52), on the one hand, and (53) and (54) on the other, it is likely that the choice of preposition similarly indicates different perspectives in examples (47) and (48), and (49) and (50).

Differences in the uses of avant/après *and* devant/derrière. These prepositions are interchangeable in only a limited number of circumstances. This substitution is clearly impossible in examples (55)–(58).

(55) *le visage de l'ambassadeur est devant₁ (*avant) moi*
the ambassador's face is in front of (before) me

(56) *Rome est avant (*devant₂) La Mecque*
Rome is before (in front of) Mecca

(57) *lundi est avant (*devant) mardi*
Monday is before (in front of) Tuesday

(58) *le colonel met l'armée avant (*devant) l'école*
the colonel places the army before (in front of) education

Under normal circumstances, example (55) emphasizes the canonical orientation of the landmark, rather than movement. Therefore, the preposition *devant₁* is chosen (branch [1] in the schema above). In example (56), the choice lies between the prepositions *avant* and *devant₂*. There is no normal situation in which Rome may hide Mecca from perception. The path between the two cities motivates the use of *avant* in this example (branch [3] of the schema). Finally, examples (57) and (58) describe temporal and abstract orders, which may be described only by the preposition *avant* (branches [4] and [5]).

This section has reviewed cases of overlap and contrast between the prepositions *avant/après* and *devant/derrière*. Even when these prepositions may apply to the same situation, we have seen that the choice of different prepositions illustrates different aspects of the situation.

The nominalizations of these prepositions[5] also emphasize the fact that *devant/derrière* are associated with the landmark's general orientation, while *avant/après* are related to movement. Remember, for example (see chapter 3), that projecting objects have an *avant* but no *devant*.

(59) *l'avant (*le devant) du fusil est tourné vers le curé*
       the front of the rifle is pointed at the priest

This choice seems to be motivated by the movement of the projectile (the bullet, in the case of the gun).

On the other hand, the *avant* of a mobile object may differ from its *devant*. This contrast is illustrated by sentence (60).

(60) *la portière avant (*devant) de la voiture est sur le côté*
       the front door of the car is on the side

The choice of *avant* is motivated here by the car's direction of movement. Since the preposition *devant* describes the general orientation of the landmark, it is incompatible with a target situated on the side.

In conclusion, even though general orientation, the line of sight, and the direction of movement often coincide, the evidence presented above suggests we should associate the first two of these concepts with the prepositions *devant/derrière*, and the last with *avant/après*. When these concepts coincide, the speaker may choose between overlapping prepositions, but each preposition will present a different aspect of the objective scene.

11

The preposition à *and localization*

The relation *x est à y* has often been defined by two formal properties: the spatial co-occurrence of the prepositional terms *x* and *y*, and the unidimensionality of the prepositional object *y*. In describing the distribution of *à*, these properties constitute the ideal conditions for situating *x* with respect to *y*. The functional notion of localization, fundamental in our interaction with the world, is the determining factor in the distribution of the spatial uses of *à* and its prepositional terms. We will see that the asymmetry of the target and the landmark is respected for the preposition *à*, whose spatial uses obey the following rule:

A$_1$: *x est à y* if *y* localizes *x*.

When a landmark calls to mind certain social rituals, the preposition *à* may exceed the limits of its purely spatial role: in such cases, I will argue that it indicates that the target is associated with a routine evoked by the landmark. The knowledge of this routine must be shared by the discourse participants for the meaning of the preposition to be understood. These derived usages are defined by rule A$_2$.

A$_2$: *x est à y* if the positions of *x* and *y* are associated in a routine evoked by *y*.

The routine imposes supplementary constraints on the target and the landmark in these instances.

11.1 The formal properties of the preposition à

"*Dans* is the three-dimensional spatial preposition, understood not only as a surface but with everything that fills it. *Sur* is the two-dimensional spatial preposition, perceived in all its nakedness and not only as a horizontal surface: this is the preposition of adherence." Here Gougenheim (1949) relates the meanings of the prepositions *dans* and *sur* to the dimensions of the prepositional object. Although this association was criticized by Dauzat (1950), it has been taken up independently by numerous English-speaking linguists (see chapter

This chapter was previously published in *Cahiers de lexicologie* 53 (1988). Reproduced by permission. For other work on the preposition *à*, see Vandeloise (1989).

1). In an article on the relation between the linguistic description of space and the child's conceptualization of it, H. H. Clark (1973) has proposed a direct relation between the prepositions *in, on,* and *at* and the number of dimensions of the prepositional object. The dimensionality of the prepositional object also plays a role in the "core meanings" of Herskovits (1982). According to her analysis, the prepositional object of *in* has one, two, or three dimensions, while the prepositional object of *on* is a flat surface or a line, and the object of *at* has less than three dimensions. Herskovits notes that, in the most frequent uses of *at,* the prepositional object is conceptualized as a single point.[1]

In any case, I do not believe that the number of the object's dimensions significantly characterizes the preposition *à.* H. H. Clark's position regarding the unidimensionality of the prepositional object of *à* is motivated by a functional concept: the target is situated with respect to a landmark. Anyone who has ever been to pick up a friend at the airport or the train station without specifying the meeting place has undoubtedly wished that the prepositional object of *à* (*at the airport, at the train station*) were indeed unidimensional. Because of its function as a reference point, the prepositional object of *à* is conceptualized as a single point, regardless of its actual physical dimensions.

A second formal aspect of the meaning of *à* is the *coincidence* of its target and landmark. According to the core meaning proposed by Herskovits, the prepositional subject must coincide with the prepositional object or be included within the object. Examples (1)–(4) illustrate that the spatial configurations of the prepositional terms of *à* cannot explain the constraints weighing on the choice of its prepositional object.

(1a) *l'empereur est à la fenêtre*
the emperor is at the window

(b) **l'impératrice est à l'arbre*
the empress is at the tree

(2a) *l'empereur est à la plage*
the emperor is at the beach

(b) **la cafetière est à la table*
the coffeepot is at the table

(3a) *l'empereur est à son établi*
the emperor is at his workbench

(b) **la chaise est à la table*
the chair is at the table

(4a) *l'impératrice est à l'église*
the empress is at church

(b) **l'impératrice est à la hutte*
the empress is at the shack

The acceptable (a) examples illustrate all the possible topological configurations of two objects: respectively, *proximity, contact, partial inclusion,*[2] and *total inclusion.* Note, however, that although the (a) examples describe the same types of configurations as the (b), the first are acceptable, while the second are not. It should be clear that these contrasts cannot be explained by reference to the topological relations between the terms of the preposition.

The preposition *à* may be used to express relations other than spatial coincidence; in fact, it expresses this relation inadequately. The examples of two identical pieces of paper and two points superposed clearly demonstrate my point. As examples (5) and (6) illustrate, the preposition *sur* more appropriately expresses spatial coincidence, while the preposition *à* is unacceptable.

(5) *le point est sur (*au) le point*
the point is on (at) the point

(6) *la feuille est sur (*à) la feuille*
the page is on (at) the page

Another problem: spatial coincidence is a perfect example of a symmetrical relation and contradicts the essentially asymmetrical character of the preposition *à*. When the prepositional terms of *près de* are of similar size, it is possible to invert them: both *la cuiller est près de la tasse* 'the spoon is near the cup' and *la tasse est près de la cuiller* 'the cup is near the spoon' are acceptable. The terms of the preposition *à*, on the other hand, may not be reversed in this manner. Furthermore, the relation *a est devant b* has a converse relation *b est derrière a*, but the preposition *à* has no converse relation R such that, if *x est à y*, then *y est Rx*. We could account for this asymmetry if *à* functioned to situate a target with respect to a characteristic landmark (the intrinsic asymmetry of this particular relation will be established in section 11.2); we cannot explain this asymmetry, however, if *à* only expresses the coincidence of its terms. Explanations of the preposition *à* have relied on the notion of spatial coincidence specifically because it corresponds to the function of localizing a target by means of a landmark. Since the two elements have different requirements, however, they cannot coincide absolutely, as we will see.

11.2 The preposition à and localization

In this section I will show that the preposition *à* maximizes the asymmetry between its terms (section 11.2.1), since it functions essentially to locate the target with respect to the landmark. I will then examine the influence of the distance between speaker and target on the use of the preposition *à* (section 11.2.2). Finally, section 11.2.3 will describe the localization of the target with respect to a part of the landmark.

11.2.1 Target and landmark of the preposition *à*

If the prepositional subject or object is not representative of the ideal target or landmark, the utterance is unacceptable. This type of anomaly is illustrated by examples (1)–(4) in chapter 2. This section will focus on three factors determining the contrasts between target and landmark; size, movement, and the position of target and landmark in the shared knowledge of the discourse participants.

11.2.1.1 Relative size of target and landmark

Spatial relations are more or less tolerant regarding the relative sizes of the target and the landmark. In this respect, *avant/après* and *au-dessus/en dessous* are among the least constraining. The preposition *à*, however, tends to maximize the asymmetry between target and landmark. In contrast to the examples we have seen of *près de* and *devant*, the terms of *à* are never of equal size.

> (7) *la cuiller est près de la fourchette*
> the spoon is near the fork

> (8) *la cuiller est devant la fourchette*
> the spoon is in front of the fork

> (9) **la cuiller est à la fourchette*
> the spoon is at the fork

Furthermore, two neighboring towns may be described by example (10) but not by example (11).

> (10) *Evanston est près de Wilmette*
> Evanston is near Wilmette

> (11) **Evanston est à Wilmette*
> Evanston is at Wilmette[3]

In contrast, note the acceptability of example (12).

> (12) *Evanston est à Chicago*
> Evanston is at Chicago

Since Chicago is larger than Evanston, the relative sizes conform to the ideal between target and landmark.[4]

Although the landmark must be large enough to be easily distinguishable, it must also be limited enough to determine the search domain unequivocally. The appropriate size depends on the distance between the place of utterance and the landmark. The point of view adopted by the speaker to conceptualize the landmark also determines the landmark's possible size. This is illustrated by examples (13) and (14): although they may be uttered in the same location, only (13) is acceptable.

> (13) *New-York est aux États-Unis*
> New York is in the United States

> (14) **New-York est au fleuve Hudson*
> New York is at the Hudson River

Since the Hudson River is, in a sense, larger than New York, it respects the first constraint on targets and landmarks: landmark > target. Although the river is smaller than the total area of the United States, however, we might expect it to specify the search domain just as well as the larger geographical area. This contrast may be explained by the linear character of the river. The speaker's point of view in conceptualizing the river is an alternative explanation: distant targets are often situated by reference to several nested locations. These lead the speaker closer and closer to the target, using landmarks that are increasingly precise and restricted in area. While the United States may summarily locate the city of New York for a prospective traveller located on another continent, the city is more specifically located with respect to the Hudson River. This change in point of view implies a smaller mental distance between the speaker and the target. At this distance, however, a river is not limited enough as a landmark to define the search domain. At the end of this chapter I will return to a discussion of nested locations and their use in the description of the preposition *à*.

In sum, the landmark of the preposition *à* must be significantly larger than the target, while remaining small enough to direct the prospective traveller. This takes into account the distance between the landmark and the speaker's location at the time of the utterance, or the point of view from which the landmark is conceptualized.

11.2.1.2 Relative movement of target and landmark

Although this cannot be an absolute condition, the target of most spatial relations is generally mobile with respect to the landmark, and the inverse occurs only under unusual circumstances. The preposition *à* reinforces this asymmetry in mobility between target and landmark. All the uses of this preposition with a mobile landmark seem as unacceptable as Ruwet's example (1969).

> (15) **Jean est couché à son tigre apprivoisé*
> Jean is sleeping at his pet tiger

The mobility of the target seems to improve the acceptability of *à*, even when used with atypical landmarks. I prefer examples (16) and (17), in which the target is mobile, over example (18).

> (16) *?le chien est à l'arbre*
> the dog is at the tree

> (17) *?la voiture est à l'arbre*
> the car is at the tree

> (18) *??le banc est à l'arbre*
> the bench is at the tree

These acceptability judgments do not refer to the possible attachment of the target to the landmark: example (16) would be acceptable if the dog's leash were tied to the tree, and (18) would be better if the bench were chained to the tree (to dissuade vandals, for instance).

11.2.1.3 The specific location of the landmark

The essential function of a localizing preposition is to situate a target whose position is unknown or uncertain by reference to a known landmark. The precision of the location of the landmark, that is, how precisely it is localized in the shared knowledge of the speakers, plays a role in the distribution of the preposition *à*. In this section, I will look at proper nouns, definite landmarks, and indefinite landmarks and their influence on the grammaticality judgments of utterances using *à*. A distinction will be drawn between landmarks introduced by a referential definite article and those introduced by a generic definite article. This contrast will be specifically addressed in section 11.3.

Beforehand, however, let me make a few remarks on the acceptability judgments proposed in this chapter. Since indefiniteness is generally characterized by the indefinite articles *un(e)* 'one' or *des* 'some', it will be introduced in the corpus by the use of these articles. Nevertheless, examples that are presented as unacceptable may in fact be acceptable in the rare cases where *un(e)* or *des* introduce definite locations. For example, the sentences below increase in acceptability from (19) to (21).

(19) ??*l'empereur est à une maison*
the emperor is at a house

(20) ?*l'empereur est à une maison infâme*
the emperor is at an infamous house

(21) *l'empereur est à une maison que tout le monde connaît*
the emperor is at a house everyone knows

In fact, the epithet in (20) specifies the nature of the house, whereas the subordinate clause in (21) informs us that the house is known to the discourse participants. Thus, the preposition *à* and the indefinite article are not incompatible; the problem lies in the use of *à* with an unspecified landmark—which is generally introduced by the indefinite article. Rather than focusing on the co-occurrence of *à* and the indefinite article, this section looks at the impossibility of using *à* in contexts in which the landmark is *nonspecific*. In the same way, the referential definite article should be understood as indicating specificity. If for some reason it did not serve this purpose, acceptability judgments would be modified.

Having voiced these concerns, I will now demonstrate that the preposition *à* is almost always acceptable when its landmark is designated by a proper noun; it is acceptable when the definite article introduces a landmark that is specifically located; and it is unacceptable (with a few notable exceptions) when the landmark is introduced by the indefinite article. Considering the above remarks, this results in the generalization that *à* is acceptable in proportion to the specificity of the landmark's position.

The landmark is a proper noun. Examples (22) and (23) present representative uses of *à* with a proper noun.

(22) *l'empereur est à Liège*
the emperor is in Liège

(23) *l'empereur est au Luxembourg*
the emperor is in Luxembourg

The use of *à* in conjunction with a proper noun is determined by linguistic convention. In fact, it is impossible to use this preposition in examples (24) and (26) to describe a situation analogous to that represented in (22) and (23).

(24) **l'empereur est à une ville appelée Liège*
the emperor is at a town called Liège

(25) *l'empereur est dans une ville appelée Liège*
the emperor is in a town called Liège

(26) **l'empereur est à un pays appelé Luxembourg*
the emperor is at a country called Luxembourg

(27) *l'empereur est dans un pays appelé Luxembourg*
the emperor is in a country called Luxembourg

Similarly, morphological or phonological criteria determine the choice of the preposition *en* for feminine place-names, or names of countries beginning in a vowel; other proper names for countries take the preposition *à*.[5]

(28) *l'impératrice est en Belgique*
the empress is in Belgium

(29) *l'empereur est en Urundi*
the emperor is in Urundi

(30) *le prince est au Katanga*
the prince is in Katanga

Rather than considering these to be arbitrary motivations, however, we can think of them as instances of conflicting motivations. While the preposition *en*, like *dans*, emphasizes the container/contained relation between target and landmark in examples (28) and (29), the preposition *à* highlights Katanga's function of localizing the prince in (30). Linguistic convention, which may only be explained diachronically by the phonological evolution of the language, is the criterion determining the choice between the two motivations.

Although the landmarks of examples (31) and (32) are indeed proper nouns, they are inadequate to localize an object.

(31) **l'empereur est à la Meuse*
the emperor is at the Meuse River

(32) **l'empereur est à Elisabeth*
the emperor is at Elizabeth (also: the emperor belongs to Elizabeth)

This has been explained in independent terms in sections 11.2.1.1 and 11.2.1.2. Taking into account the speaker's viewpoint, a river is too extensive a landmark to situate a target adequately. On the other hand, Elizabeth violates the condition that landmarks must be immobile. However, example (31) will be acceptable if the emperor has fallen into the Meuse, and (32) can metaphorically imply that he (in matters of sentiment) belongs to Elizabeth.

The following examples demonstrate the role of proper nouns in determining the acceptability of *à*.[6]

(33) **l'empereur est au rocher*
the emperor is at the boulder

(34) *l'empereur est au rocher de la Vierge Folle*
the emperor is at the boulder of the Vierge Folle

(35) **l'impératrice est au poteau téléphonique*
the empress is at the telephone pole

(36) *l'impératrice est au poteau téléphonique no. 3*
the empress is at telephone pole number 3

The only possible interpretations of examples (33) and (35) would have the target tied or chained up, going beyond simply situating the target by means of the landmark. In contrast, the proper nouns in (34) and (36) give the landmark the ability to localize the target. Only a location whose position is specified and well known by the entire community normally carries a proper name.

Landmarks introduced by the definite article. Not all landmarks introduced by the definite article permit the use of the preposition *à*, as the following examples illustrate.

(37a) *?? l'empereur est à l'arbre*
the emperor is at the tree

(b) *? l'empereur est à l'arbre que tu sais*
the emperor is at the tree that you know

(c) *l'empereur est devant l'arbre*
the emperor is in front of the tree

(38a) *?? l'impératrice est à la hutte*
the empress is at the shack

(b) *? l'impératrice est à la hutte que tu sais*
the empress is at the shack that you know

(c) *l'impératrice est dans la hutte*
the empress is in the shack

In fact, the definite article in examples (37a) and (38a) is not enough to give the tree or the shack the specific character that a localizing element demands. The two landmarks do have the requisite size and stability, however. As the (c) examples show, these landmarks are acceptable with other spatial prepositions, such as *devant* and *dans*.

If trees and shacks do not successfully situate a target, what can we make of the window and the beach in the acceptable utterances (39) and (40)?

    (39) *l'empereur est à la fenêtre*
        the emperor is at the window

    (40) *l'impératrice est à la plage*
        the empress is at the beach

Section 11.3 will focus on this type of example. For now let me point out that, in contrast to a target near a tree or a shack, a target near a window or on a beach will call to mind a social ritual in which the target participates. The preposition *à* is used in these examples to signal that the emperor and the empress participate in these routines.

We conclude from this section that the definite article (excepting its generic uses) is acceptable after *à* only when it introduces a landmark whose position is specific enough to localize the target.

Landmarks introduced by the indefinite article. As Lamiroy (1983) and Ruwet (1969) have pointed out for the preposition *à*, and as Hottenroth (1981) has shown for the Italian homologue of this preposition, indefinite landmarks are generally unacceptable following these prepositions.

    (41a) **l'empereur est à un arbre*
         the emperor is at a tree

     (b) *l'empereur est près d'un arbre*
         the emperor is near a tree

    (42a) **l'impératrice est à une tente*
         the empress is at a tent

     (b) *l'impératrice est dans une tente*
         the empress is in a tent

    (43a) **l'empereur est à une fenêtre*
         the emperor is at a window

     (b) *l'empereur est devant une fenêtre*
         the emperor is in front of a window

    (44a) **l'impératrice est à une plage*
         the empress is at a beach

     (b) *l'impératrice est sur une plage*
         the empress is on a beach

Other spatial relations, such as *près de, dans, devant,* and *sur* ([b] examples) accurately describe situations corresponding to the (a) examples.

However, there are circumstances in which the indefinite article is acceptable. In examples (45) and (46), several identical landmarks are brought together in a single location, and the target of the relation is localized with respect to one of these landmarks.

> (45) *l'empereur est à une table dans un café*
> the emperor is at a table in a café

> (46) *l'impératrice est à un guichet à la poste*
> the empress is at a window in the post office

Note that in these examples the landmark of *à* introduces nested locations: the primary, more general one (the café or the post office) and the secondary, more specific one (the table, the window).

Utterances (47) and (48) are also possible.

> (47) *l'impératrice est à un carrefour*
> the empress is at an intersection

> (48) *l'empereur est à un feu rouge*
> the emperor is at a stoplight

How can we account for the acceptability of the indefinite article in these utterances? I have demonstrated (Vandeloise 1987) that the preposition *à* after the verb *arriver* 'to arrive' is notable in that it is compatible with nonspecific and even indefinite landmarks. I accounted for this particularity by the way the verb describes a physical displacement. The use of the verb *arriver*, in fact, generally implies the presence of the speaker in the proximity of the target, or demands a complete knowledge of the landmark's position at the moment of utterance. This has the effect of specifying locations that otherwise would be too imprecise to serve as the landmark of the preposition *à*. Because of this character of the verb *arriver*, I will attempt to account for the acceptability of the indefinite article in examples (47) and (48). Although these sentences are constructed with the auxiliary verb *être* 'to be', because of their landmarks (*le carrefour* and *le feu rouge*) they in fact connote the idea of a target moving along a path. Here the auxiliary *être* is practically synonymous with the verb *arriver*. When *être* is used, the target appears to be immobile, because this auxiliary brings only a very brief period of movement to the conceptualization of the scene. Although movement is played down by the use of the auxiliary, it is emphasized by the landmarks in these utterances, landmarks that invariably imply movement along a path. The unusual acceptability of the indefinite article in these examples is attributed to the presence of these particular landmarks.

I wish to point out another set of examples in which the indefinite article is acceptable.

(49) *l'impératrice est à un bal*
the empress is at a ball

(50) *le roi est à une réunion*
the king is at a meeting

(51) *l'empereur est à un safari*
the emperor is on a safari

In these examples, however, the landmark does not designate the location itself, but the activity that takes place at that location. Note the contrast between examples (49) and (52) in this regard.

(52) **la reine est à une salle de bal*
the queen is at a ballroom

In this last example, the landmark designates the room in which the ball takes place, and the utterance is unacceptable.

We have now surveyed the different constraints on the target and the landmark of the localizing preposition *à*. These usages conform to the following usage rule:

A_1: *x est à y* if *y* localizes *x*.

For a landmark to localize a target ideally, both landmark and target must be ideal examples of their type. The qualities of the ideal landmark and target were surveyed in detail in the preceding sections. As Ruwet has pointed out, "the NP following *à* must itself have an intrinsic localizing value in some sense; this is not necessarily the case when we consider complements of the form *dans NP, sur NP,* etc." (1969, 320). This section has attempted to lay out in detail the elements that allow this nominal construction to situate an object.

11.2.2 Distance between speaker and landmark and its bearing on the use of *à* to localize a target

When omitted from an utterance, the landmark of a spatial relation often refers to the position of the speaker. Unless other contextual factors intervene, this is the interpretation of examples (53) and (54).

(53) *l'empereur est près*
the emperor is near

(54) *l'impératrice est à gauche*
the empress is to the left

When the preposition *à* is used, the landmark may not be omitted; in this way *à* resembles *dans* and *sur*. In contrast to *dans* and *sur*, however, the speaker may not serve as the landmark for *à*.

(55) *mon chapeau est sur moi*
my hat is on me

(56) *mon chapeau est à moi*
my hat is mine

While (56) is acceptable to indicate possession, it cannot be interpreted in a spatial sense. As for example (57), it is only acceptable if the speaker is *not* located in his own place.

(57) *le roi est à ma place*
the king is in my place

The landmark of the preposition *à* may refer to the speaker's position only in utterances in the first person singular.

Otherwise, the landmark of *à* must be distinct from the position of the speaker; furthermore, the use of this preposition improves when the landmark is distant from the place of utterance. In this way, examples (58) and (60) may be used only if the speaker is far from the football stadium or the arena.

(58) *le footballeur est au terrain de football*
the football player is at the playing field

(59) *le footballeur est sur le terrain de football*
the football player is on the playing field

(60) *le toréador est à l'arène*
the toreador is at the arena

(61) *le toréador est dans l'arène*
the toreador is in the arena

For a spectator in the stadium or in the arena, only examples (59) and (61) are acceptable. These facts, first noted by Herskovits, can be interpreted in several ways, though these interpretations are not necessarily mutually exclusive.

1. When the target and the landmark are both present in the field of vision, *dans* and *sur* are preferred; these prepositions describe the spatial configuration of their terms but are not restricted to locating the target with respect to the landmark (see chapters 12 and 13).

2. Distance tends to make the landmark unidimensional, facilitating a more precise definition of the search domain. This brings to mind the unidimensional character of *à* emphasized by H. H. Clark. However, rather than focusing on perceptual evidence, as Clark does, I believe that distant landmarks are preferred because they define the search domain more specifically. This hypothesis is justified if we imagine a speaker in the arena phoning to a friend.

> (62) *allo Majesté, je suis à l'arène*
> hello, your Majesty, I'm at the arena

Although the arena appears as a three-dimensional volume to the speaker, he will choose the preposition *à* because the landmark determines the path that will eventually lead the king towards him.

3. A greater distance between the landmark and the speaker increases the difficulty of localizing the target and thus emphasizes the importance of this notion. We will see that the preposition *à* stresses the importance of localization. A distant target can only facilitate the use of this preposition, since the construction emphasizes the search itself.

11.2.3 Situating the target with respect to a part of the object

I will conclude this section by sketching a systematic exception to the specificity of the landmark as discussed above. In fact, as the examples below illustrate, the preposition *à* is always appropriate to designate the parts of an object (see A. Borills 1988 for more details), even if the object is close to the speaker and does not otherwise allow the use of *à*.

> (63a) *le livre est au bord de la table*
> the book is at the edge of the table

> (b) *le livre est à l'extrémité de la table*
> the book is at the extreme edge of the table

> (c) *le livre est au coin de la table*
> the book is at the corner of the table

> (d) **le livre est à la table*
> the book is at the table

> (64a) *l'oiseau est au pied de l'arbre*
> the bird is at the foot of the tree

> (b) *l'oiseau est au centre de l'arbre*
> the bird is in the middle of the tree

> (c) *l'oiseau est au sommet de l'arbre*
> the bird is at the top of the tree

(d) **l'oiseau est à l'arbre*
the bird is at the tree

The (d) examples demonstrate that, as entire objects, the tree and the table are not acceptable landmarks. The use of *à* is also productive in the formation of prepositional expressions such as *à gauche, au-dessus de, auprès de*, etc.

(65a) *la reine est au-dessus de la table*
the queen is above the table

(b) *la reine est à gauche de la table*
the queen is at the left of the table

(c) *la reine est auprès de la table*
the queen is near the table

The contrast with entire landmarks is also evident when we note that either the first element of the landmark (the part) or the second (the entire object) may be introduced by the indefinite article.

(66) *le livre est à un bord de la table*
the book is at an edge of the table

(67) *le livre est au bord d'une table*
the book is at the edge of a table

Example (68) is questionable, however; here both the part and the entire object are indefinite.

(68) *??un livre est à un bord d'une table*
a book is at an edge of a table

Herskovits explains the use of the English preposition *at* in the English sentence corresponding to (63a), comparing this with the use of *on* in example (69).

(69) *the book is on the edge of the table*

According to Herskovits, in the first case the entire object is presented as a medium through which our imagination travels to choose a point; this is not the case if we substitute *on* for the preposition *at*. I will propose another interpretation to account for the acceptability of examples (63) and (64). This wider hypothesis does not exclude a priori the hypothesis proposed by Herskovits.

I return to the idea of nested locations, according to which a target may be localized more and more precisely by means of more and more restricted landmarks. Thus, example (70) contains several nested locations.

(70) *le prince est au Canada, à Montréal, à l'hôtel de la Couronne*
the prince is in Canada, in Montreal, at the Hotel de la
Couronne

The reader coming across this example passes through a series of
perspectives bringing him closer and closer to the prince. The entire
set of the target's possible positions on earth is first restricted to Canada, then to Montreal, and finally to the Hotel de la Couronne. These
landmarks, expressed by means of proper nouns, may be geographically located in more and more restricted domains. This is not the case
for the empress's hat rack, and example (71a) is unacceptable (if we
exclude the hypothesis of a hanging).

(71a) **l'empereur est au portemanteau de l'impératrice*
the emperor is at the empress's hat rack

(b) *l'empereur est au pied du portemanteau de l'impératrice*
the emperor is at the foot of the empress's hat rack

Why then is (71b) acceptable? Because the expression (*à* + name
of part + *de* + object) excludes any geographical interpretation of the
search for the target. By means of this construction, the object alone
(here the hat rack) represents the set of possible locations of the target. An example such as (72) will have the effects illustrated below.

(72) *l'empereur est au Canada, à Montréal, à l'hôtel de la Couronne, au pied du portemanteau de l'impératrice*
the emperor is in Canada, in Montreal, at the Hotel de
la Couronne, at the foot of the empress's hat rack

  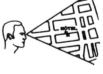

| 1) target geographically situated with respect to the planet Earth | 2) target geographically situated with respect to Canada | 3) target geographically situated with respect to Montreal | 4) target nongeographically situated with respect to the hat rack |

FIGURE 1

Note the discontinuity between the first three steps situating the target, which take into account the entire planet, and the last, which is made with respect to the hat rack, independent of its geographical position. The specification of the landmark at this point is no longer made with respect to the world, but by reference to the usual form of the object that the landmark calls to mind. As long as the speaker knows the usual form of a table or a chair, landmarks such as the foot of the table or the edge of the chair are perfectly specified, if the search domain of the target is known. These landmarks then allow the use of the preposition *à*.

Returning to examples (66) and (67), which introduced an indefinite element, we note that (66) resembles examples (45) and (46): it localizes the book with respect to some element in a set of identical elements (the edges of the table) situated at the same location (the table). As for example (67), depending on context, it may refer to some table within a specific set (for example, a table in a café), or it may refer to some table within the entire set of tables. In the latter case, only the more general image of a table will come to mind. How then do we interpret the hypothesis of the mental voyage through the object, which Herskovits has proposed? In particular, what is the starting point of this itinerary? Is it centripetal (from the edge—but which edge? —toward the center) or centrifugal (from the center toward the edge)? To evaluate Herskovits's proposal, all these implications must be considered.

Finally, the unacceptability of example (68) must not be attributed solely to the use of the preposition *à*, since (73) is strange as well.

> (73) *? un livre est sur un bord d'une table*
>   a book is on an edge of a table

11.3 *The preposition* à *and integrated landmarks*

In the preceding section, we saw that the preposition *à* in its spatial use is essentially localizing. To this end, it must be used with specified landmarks, often distinguished by a proper noun. The referential character of the definite article is not always sufficient to give *à* the needed ability to localize the target, however. This preposition is also permitted when the definite article is used in a generic fashion, as long as the landmark evokes the notion of a social ritual or routine in the mind of the discourse participants. The present section will be devoted to this type of usage, governed by rule A_2.

A_2: *x est à y* if the positions of *x* and *y* are associated in a routine evoked by *y*.

I will term this type of landmark an *integrated landmark* if it is capable of suggesting a routine within a sufficiently large linguistic community. The uses associated with these routines differ in three ways from strictly situating uses.

1. The routine evoked by *y* is more detailed in specifying the position of the different targets with respect to the landmark. In this way, the target is more precisely localized.

2. Since only targets capable of playing a role in the routine are permitted, this usage enforces additional constraints on the use of *à*.

3. Since the function of the landmark *y* is essentially to evoke a routine associated with the lexical category it represents, details that are specific to a particular element are superfluous and decrease the acceptability of the utterance.

I will now lay out in more detail the three characteristics of the use of *à* in conjunction with an integrated landmark.

11.3.1 The precision of the meaning of *à*

To show how the scenario evoked by an integrated landmark can specify the position of the target, I will describe the routine evoked by the window in example (39), repeated below as (74). The following examples bear on this analysis:

(74) *l'empereur est à la fenêtre*
the emperor is at the window

(75) *la plante est à la fenêtre*
the plant is at the window

(76) *les rideaux sont à la fenêtre*
the curtains are at the window

(77) *le radiateur est à la fenêtre*
the radiator is at the window

(78) *le drapeau est à la fenêtre*
the flag is at the window

In order to be appropriate, these utterances impose different conditions on the location of their target with respect to the landmark. While the emperor must be *near* the window, preferably looking out the window at the same time, the plant must be sitting *on* the window ledge or exposing most of its foliage to the sunlight coming through the window. The curtains must be hanging *above* the window, and the radiator must be standing *under* the window. The configurations brought to mind by the preposition *à* in these constructions correspond to the spatial relations *près de*, *sur*, *au-dessus*, and *en dessous*. As for the flag in example (78), it must be hanging *outside* the window; note that this contrasts with all the other targets (except perhaps the plant), which must be inside the house. If the targets are not found in the positions required by the social routine, the preposition *à* may not be employed. Imagine, for example, that the positions of the emperor and the plant are reversed. These situations will not be expressed by examples (74) and (75), but by (79) and (80).

> (79) *l'empereur est sur la fenêtre*
> the emperor is on the window

> (80) *la plante est (par terre) près de la fenêtre*
> the plant is (on the floor) near the window

If the curtains are placed in the usual position of a geranium, they too will be *sur la fenêtre.* As for the radiator, if it is in a position where (77) would be appropriate but has not yet been installed properly, I believe we would say it is *contre la fenêtre* 'against the window', rather than *à la fenêtre.* Finally, I cannot imagine what might be said if the emperor decided to position himself in the place of the flag at the window! It is impossible to understand the contrast between the various positions described by utterances (74)–(78) without understanding the role of windows in a linguistic community, a role that may change depending on whether the target is a human being, a plant, a curtain, a radiator, or a flag.

In section 11.1 we discussed the unacceptability of example (2b), repeated below.

> (81) **la cafetière est à la table*
> the coffeepot is at the table

We might consider this a counterexample to our analysis, since *à* should be acceptable before an integrated landmark. What more obviously evokes a social ritual than a table and a coffeepot? It is true that it is impossible to extract integrated landmarks in some automatic way from the total set of common nouns and then calculate their ability to localize each target. The hazards of linguistic convention will invariably influence this decision. Nonetheless, the preposition *à* cannot escape the force of ritual imposed upon the table by our civilization, as example (82) amply demonstrates.

> (82) *la cafetière est à table*
> the coffeepot is on the table

This example takes into account the factor of ritual, going so far as to eliminate the definite article before the landmark. The loss of the article renders the utterance more obviously conventionalized. A similar convention is evident in example (83).

> (83) *le roi est à terre*
> the king is on earth

As we have seen in examples involving the window, the routine of the table defines the position of the target more specifically than *à* otherwise would allow. The utterances in (84) bear witness to this.

> (84a) *le prince est à table*
> the prince is at the table
>
> (b) *le camembert est à table*
> the camembert is on the table

According to (84a), the prince is seated on a chair, facing the table, ready to eat, while (84b) represents the cheese placed on the surface of the table. If the positions of the two targets were reversed, the prince would be *sur la table,* while the camembert would be *sur la chaise.*

Other integrated landmarks that bring to mind an activity also locate the position of their target precisely. This is the case in examples (85)–(87).

> (85) *l'empereur est à son établi*
> the emperor is at his workbench
>
> (86) *le roi est au piano*
> the king is at the piano
>
> (87) *la princesse est à sa machine à écrire*
> the princess is at her typewriter

In these examples, the emperor, the king, and the princess must be positioned according to the proper use of the workbench, the piano, and the typewriter. It is the emperor's prerogative to use his workbench as a bed if he wishes, but in that case the preposition *sur* would be used to describe his position.

Examples (85)–(87) describe situations in which the target is precisely situated by the landmark. In examples (88a), (89a), and (90a), the target is associated with activities evoked by the landmark. Example (88a) might even refer to the king's studies, independent of the classroom building. This sentence is appropriate even if the king is not found at the university at the moment of utterance. This interpretation is impossible for example (88b), however.[7]

> (88a) *le roi est à l'Université*
> the king is at the university

(b) *le roi est dans l'Université*
the king is in the university

(89a) *l'empereur est à l'hôpital*
the emperor is at the hospital

(b) *l'empereur est dans l'hôpital*
the emperor is in the hospital

(90a) *le prince est au tribunal*
the prince is at court

(b) *le prince est dans le tribunal*
the prince is in court

The list of integrated landmarks recognized by a community is certainly long, but not infinite; the description of the characteristics of culturally ratified routines belongs to the field of anthropology rather than linguistics. A routine of this sort does not arise instantaneously, abruptly, but rather develops progressively over time. The ability to create an appropriate scenario also varies with the creativity of the speaker; thus example (37a), repeated in (91), was accepted by an informant who imagined the emperor pruning the tree.

(91) *l'empereur est à l'arbre*
the emperor is at the tree

This informant had succeeded in imagining a routine that would render the utterance interpretable. The influence of habit or custom on the use of *à* is also demonstrated in the comparison of (92a) and (92b).

(92a) **la reine est à l'armoire*
the queen is at the cupboard

(b) *?la reine est encore à l'armoire*
the queen is at the cupboard again

It seems to me that example (92b) is preferred over (92a), which is unacceptable under normal circumstances. In fact, the adverb *encore* informs the reader that, for the speaker, the cupboard is part of a routine, even though this routine may be unfamiliar to the reader.

I conclude this section with an example emphasizing the role of convention in the choice of an integrated landmark. Although there are certain structured rituals between humans and their motor vehicles, examples (93)–(95) are unacceptable.

(93) **la princesse est à l'auto*
the princess is at the car

(94) *l'impératrice est à l'avion
the empress is at the airplane

(95) *la reine est au bateau
the queen is at the boat

In contrast, examples (96)–(98) clearly distinguish the driver from the passengers, and the preposition à obviously is used in terms of an integrated landmark evoking a social routine.

(96) le prince est au volant
the prince is at the wheel

(97) l'empereur est aux commandes
the emperor is at the control panel

(98) le roi est au gouvernail
the king is at the helm

Perhaps these utterances are preferred over the earlier ones because they emphasize the active role of the pilot. As for the passengers, whether they are in a plane or on a boat, their position is described by (99).

(99) les passagers sont à bord
the passengers are on board

11.3.2 Constraints of an integrated landmark on the target of the preposition à

The routine associated with an integrated landmark has certain predictable but important consequences in the use of à. In particular, it introduces certain constraints on the choice of the appropriate target. While the (a) examples below seem questionable and the (b) examples are preferred, this is because neither the table nor the shirt customarily play a role in the routines evoked by the window and the table.

(100a) ?la table est à la fenêtre
the table is at the window

(b) la table est près de la fenêtre
the table is near the window

(101a) ?la chemise est à (la) table
the shirt is at the table

(b) la chemise est sur la table
the shirt is on the table

I have avoided mentioning selection restrictions in this section because they imply the possibility of absolute rules determining the possible lexical co-occurrences in a sentence. I do not believe that such decisions can be made mechanically by looking at the words of a sentence. Compare (100a) with the examples below.

> (102) *la chaise est à la fenêtre*
> the chair is at the window

> (103) *le coffre est à la fenêtre*
> the trunk is at the window

At first blush, example (103) is at least as questionable as (100a). How can we interpret (102)? Imagine a chair stationed by the window, from which one may look out at the street during the long winter months. Without a chair in the proper position, one could just as well sit on a trunk, or even a table—what then can we say about examples (100a) and (103)? These contextual clues allow us to sidestep certain conditions on the target, but do not weaken the importance of ritual. This flexibility demonstrates that the role of ritual is not solely lexical; that is, it is not associated with the specific lexical item evoking the ritual, independent of the context of utterance. The target is constrained by its capacity to participate in the ritual evoked by the landmark and is not restricted to a certain set of lexical items. If the target cannot easily participate in the relevant contexts, the utterance is considered unacceptable. Particular circumstances may integrate a target in a routine in which it normally does not participate, however. The exceptional co-occurrence of the target and the landmark is authorized by the routine in this instance.

In examples (88)–(90), the preposition *associates* the target with the activities practiced in the location of the landmarks and at the same time attributes additional qualities to the target. In fact, the (b) examples are exclusively spatial and thus neutral as to the activities of the target. In the (a) examples, the king, the emperor, and the prince must participate in the institutions designated by the landmark; in contrast, the (b) examples might refer to a plumber, or an occasional visitor. Here again, a target that cannot participate in the activities of the institution is unacceptable. Compare the (a) and (b) examples below.

> (104a) *?le chien est à l'école*
> the dog is at school

> (b) *le chien est dans l'école*
> the dog is in school

(105a) *??l'arbre est à l'école*
the tree is at school

(b) *l'arbre est dans l'école*
the tree is in the school

Since public education is not mandatory either for dogs or for trees, the (a) examples are questionable, while the (b) examples are perfectly natural. This conforms with what we saw in section 11.2; here too the mobile target in (104) is preferred over the stationary target (the tree). Furthermore, example (104a) is more natural when uttered by a speaker at a distance from the school (see section 11.2.2).

11.3.3 Generic character of integrated landmarks

The routine needed to interpret *à* is related to the lexical category of the landmark and not to a particular member of the category. It follows that the definite article is usually generic for this type of usage. As a result, the landmark does not allow any additional qualification that is specific to a particular member of the category. Qualifications specifying the spatial character of the landmark are of course acceptable, but here we leave the domain of integrated uses (rule A_2) and return to the function of localization (rule A_1). This transition is illustrated by the examples below.

(106) *le roi est à la caserne*
the king is at the barracks

(107) **le roi est à la caserne dont les barbelés brillent sous la pluie*
the king is at the barracks whose barbed wire glitters in the rain

(108) *le roi est dans la caserne dont les barbelés brillent sous la pluie*
the king is in the barracks whose barbed wire glitters in the rain

(109) *le roi est à la caserne Roi Albert*
the king is at the King Albert barracks

Except under particular circumstances, the landmark of (106) is generic. This is certainly the case if the utterance is appropriate when the king is not in the barracks at the moment of utterance (that is, when the utterance describes the king's activities rather than his location). In (109), in contrast, the proper noun specifies the landmark, and the landmark localizes the target. As for (107), it is unacceptable because the landmark has lost its generic character without becoming more specific. It appears that the preposition *à* in this example is hesitating between two rules: while the landmark is not specific enough for rule A_1, it is too specific to satisfy the conditions of A_2. Example (108) demonstrates that anecdotal information about the king's position is in fact possible with the preposition *dans*.

In his article on the French prepositions of location, Ruwet (1969) gives the landmark of *à* the function of localization but points out counterexamples such as *Pierre est à l'armée* 'Pierre is in the army', *Pierre est au soleil* 'Pierre is in the sun', etc. Here he implicitly recognizes the difference between specified landmarks and integrated landmarks. (Note that the example *Pierre est à l'armée* is distinct from example [106], and takes only Pierre's activities into account, as in [49] and [51]. In contrast, [106] may designate both the location and the activities of the king.) Ruwet also points out that the (b) examples below do not correspond to the (a) examples.

(110a) *ce film passe au cinéma de mon quartier*
      this film is playing at my neighborhood theater

  (b) **ce film passe aux cinémas de mon quarteir*
      this film is playing at my neighborhood theaters

(111a) *Pierre est à la maison/au lit*
      Pierre is at home/in bed

  (b) *?Pierre est à sa maison*
      Pierre is at his home

  (c) *??Pierre est à son lit*
      Pierre is at his bed

In my opinion, example (110b) seems possible in that *de mon quartier* situates the landmark spatially, although it removes its generic quality. The landmark is more specifically located in (112c).

(112) *ce film passe au deux cinémas de mon quarteier*
      this film is playing at the two theaters in my neighborhood

I concur with Ruwet that it is generally difficult to pluralize generic landmarks with the preposition *à*, as in the example below.

(113) **ce film passe aux cinémas*
      this film is playing at the theaters

In this case, the landmark is no longer generic but is not well enough specified to localize the target. The use of the possessive in (111b) and

(111c) also removes the generic character of (111a). The landmark of (111b) (his house) and (111c) (his bed) apparently influence the grammaticality judgments of these examples: since the first can be geographically specified more easily than the second, it may localize the target more readily (rule A_1).

This study of generic landmarks concludes with a comparison of examples (114)–(118).

(114) *le roi est à la maison*
the king is at home

(115) *?le roi est à la villa*
the king is at the villa

(116) *?le roi est au bungalow*
the king is at the bungalow

(117) *?le roi est au building*
the king is at the high rise

(118) *?le roi est à la tente*
the king is at the tent

In these examples, all the landmarks are dwellings of some sort. It appears, however, that the social routine of the home is attached to the lexical item *maison*, probably because this term is more general and more frequently employed. The contrast between examples (119) and (120) demonstrates this difference.

(119) *où peut-on être mieux qu'à la maison*
what better than to be at home

(120) **où peut-on être mieux qu'à la villa*
what better than to be at the villa

The use of the pronoun *on* 'one' and the sententious character of the utterance favor a generic interpretation, and the first utterance is preferred over the second. If examples (115)–(118) are acceptable, this is not due to a routine related to the villa, the high rise, or the tent. These landmarks are not integrated and will be acceptable only if they are topographically specified in the shared knowledge of the discourse participants. In that case these landmarks designate *the villa that you know, the bungalow you are familiar with*, etc.

This concludes our review of the principle characteristics of the second type of usage of *à*. We have seen that an interpretation of this use demands the shared knowledge of social routines. The preposition *à* depends on the immediate context of the utterance and on a more general social context. In fact, this is undoubtedly true for all entries in the lexicon; the extralinguistic context intervenes at various moments in the interpretation of each word. The uses of the preposition *à* are extreme examples in that they are unacceptable if the routine evoked by their landmark is not sufficiently conventionalized, or if their target cannot play a role in this routine. The part of linguistic convention in the selection of these routines should be not underestimated. The use of *à* with different parts of the house will prove my point.

In contrast to examples (121)–(123), example (124) is unacceptable.

> (121) *la reine est au salon*
>   the queen is in the living room

> (122) *la princesse est à la salle à manger*
>   the princess is in the dining room

> (123) *le roi est à la cuisine*
>   the king is in the kitchen

> (124) **l'empereur est à la chambre à coucher*
>   the emperor is at the bedroom

Do we conclude here that the habits and routines of the bedroom are less ritualized than the habits of the living room, the dining room, etc.? I doubt this, especially given the evidence in example (125), which is acceptable.

> (125) *le prince est au dortoir*
>   the prince is at the dormitory

It seems, rather, as if a convention related to the word *chambre* prohibits its use with *à* in (124). Herskovits has noted a similar restriction with the use of *room* after *at* in English. She claims that this preposition may not be used in conjunction with identical elements of a single larger set. In examples (126)–(129), the rooms/the neighborhoods/the provinces are individual elements making up the house/the city/the country; they are all equally unable to localize a target.

> (126) **le roi est à la chambre*
>   the king is at the bedroom

> (127) **la reine est à la salle*
>   the queen is at the room

(128) *la princesse est au quartier
the princess is at the neighborhood

(129) *l'empereur est à la province
the emperor is at the province

Since no routine is associated with any of these landmarks, only the localizing sense of *à* is possible in interpreting these sentences; this motivates the unacceptability of *à* in these cases. In fact, by their very precision, these utterances suggest that the target will be found in a domain limited to the house/the city/the country. From this perspective, however, the utterances cannot situate the target since they do not specify in which room/neighborhood/country it will be found. This argument does not hold for example (124), which clearly specifies where the emperor will be found. The ungrammaticality of (124) can be explained only from within the linguistic system: a number of separate cases motivate the unacceptability of the co-occurrence of *chambre* and *à;* an utterance with these lexical items remains unacceptable in (124), even though the specific motivation has disappeared. This convention does not extend to the word *salle,* as the acceptability of (122) illustrates. Furthermore, if a proper noun is employed, the use of *chambre* after *à* is permitted. Example (130) is appropriate in a hotel, and (131) is delightfully informative in certain establishments.

(130) *la reine est à la chambre 8*
the queen is in room 8

(131) *la princesse est à la chambre Rose*
the princess is in the Pink Room

11.4 Conclusions

The static uses of the preposition *à* have been described by two usage rules. Rule A_1 is based on the concept of localization; this notion maximizes the contrast between the target (the object sought after) and the landmark that is the point of reference. Rule A_2 associates the target of *à* with the routine called to mind by the landmark.

Despite the generality of its spatial uses, the preposition *à* is quite selective in its choice of landmarks. In particular, landmarks introduced by the indefinite article are rarely acceptable after this preposition. Place-names, on the other hand, are almost always acceptable. Landmarks introduced by the definite article constitute an intermediate case. It is an impossible task to describe the co-occurrences of *à* and the definite and indefinite articles distributionally; extralinguistic notions of localization and routine, on the other hand, give us a detailed explanation of the phenomena. Proper nouns easily localize the target since they function as ideal reference points.

This explains the frequent acceptability of proper nouns following the preposition *à*. The article *un*, however, introduces landmarks that do not localize the target adequately and that are inappropriate, in consequence. However, certain circumstances may render indefinite landmarks acceptable. Notably, I have demonstrated (Vandeloise 1987) that the perspective imposed by the verb *arriver* allows the article *un(e)* with landmarks of the preposition *à* after this verb. Finally, definite landmarks may be made acceptable by rule A_1 (referential definite article) or rule A_2 (generic definite article). In the first case, the landmark's position must be known by the discourse participants for it to enable them to locate the target. This is possible in the case of a house (*le roi est à la maison* 'the king is at home') but more questionable for a tree (? *le prince est à l'arbre* 'the prince is at the tree'). In the second case, the landmark introduced by the definite article must be integrated; that is, it must call to mind a routine established by the linguistic community. This is so in the case of a window (*la reine est à la fenêtre* 'the queen is at the window') or a beach (*la princesse est à la plage* 'the princess is at the beach'). Since the routine is not specific to a particular window or beach, the definite article has a generic sense, and the utterance is less acceptable if the characteristics of a particular window or beach are attributed to the landmark. This type of utterance is appropriate only if the target may, in some fashion, participate in the routine called to mind by the landmark.

The acceptability of indefinite articles and referential and generic definite articles is determined by two extralinguistic notions: the landmark's ability either to localize the target or to bring to mind a social ritual. This is not to say that linguistic convention does not play a role in the distribution of the preposition *à*. In particular, remember the example **l'empereur est à la chambre à coucher,* which can be explained only by analogy with the unacceptability of **l'empereur est à la chambre.* This grammaticality judgment is motivated by the indefiniteness of the landmark in a house containing several rooms; it remains attached to the word *chambre* by convention, even when this lexical item is further specified by the phrase *à coucher*. Both extralinguistic motivation (localization and ritual) and the conventions belonging to the system of the language account for the diverse uses of the preposition *à*.

12

The prepositions sur/sous *and the bearer/ burden relation*

Il est mort sur le coup de midi.[1]

A client in the Café du Bon Coin

At the beginning of this chapter I will present several characteristics of the prepositions *sur/sous;* each one has an exception. Taken together, these characteristics would provide a complete description of the prepositions under study, but the description would be redundant and overly general. For many uses of *sur/sous,* all the characteristics coincide; these are the characteristics of the bearer/burden relation. I will argue that this relation motivates the distribution of *sur/sous* in logical diachrony.

The characteristics of the preposition *sur* differ in many respects from those of the preposition *sous.* At first glance, it would seem that these prepositions are converse. So if the target of *sur* is held up by the landmark, the opposite should be true for *sous.* These prepositions are converse when their targets and landmarks are of approximately the same size. They are not converse, however, when the dimensions of subject and object are different. An examination of the preposition *sous* will also distinguish several ways an object may be inaccessible to perception.

Contact is often considered one important factor in the description of the preposition *sur;* this criterion is also found in the use of the prepositions *à* and *contre.* A comparison of these prepositions will illustrate how the bearer/burden relation allows us to predict the type of contact described by the preposition *sur.*

The distributions of the prepositions *sous* and *derrière* are also distinct. Both prepositions are used when the target is inaccessible to perception, but the choice of *sous* is explained by one specific trait of the bearer/burden relation.

12.1 *Characteristics of the prepositions* sur/sous

The *characteristics* of a word, we recall, apply at the level of observation, a stage that is, as much as possible, pretheoretical. Five character-

This chapter is a revised version of an article published in *Leuvense bijdragen* 2 (1985).

istics of the prepositions *sur/sous* will be discussed in this chapter. We will discover that the uses of these two prepositions are not absolutely parallel.

Order on the vertical axis. The scene below and the utterances describing it demonstrate that the target of *sur/sous* is generally higher/lower than its landmark.

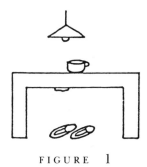

FIGURE 1

(1) *la tasse est sur la table*
the cup is on the table

(2) *le chewing-gum est sous la table*
the chewing gum is under the table

(3) *les pantoufles sont sous la table*
the slippers are under the table

Order along the vertical axis is not a sufficient condition for the use of *sur*, however, since example (4) is unacceptable.

(4) **la lampe est sur la table*
the lamp is on the table

Furthermore, the usual order implied by this relation may be reversed, as example (5) illustrates.

(5) *la mouche est sur le plafond*
the fly is on the ceiling

The order of target and landmark along the vertical axis is not automatically reversible, however, as example (6) demonstrates.

FIGURE 2

(6) *la lampe est sur le plafond*
    the lamp is on the ceiling

From the above examples, the following characteristic is deduced:

Characteristic A: If *a est sur/sous b*, the target is generally higher/lower than the landmark.

Contact. As example (1) has already demonstrated, the preposition *sur* generally implies contact between its terms. The lack of contact between the lamp and the table may explain why example (4) is unacceptable. The example of the table and the slippers in sentence (3) shows that contact is not a condition for the use of the preposition *sous*.

Different types of contact must be distinguished in an investigation of the preposition *sur;* contact may be vertical or horizontal, direct or indirect. Contact between two more or less horizontal surfaces will be termed *horizontal contact*. In contrast, *vertical contact* implies two nearly vertical surfaces.

(1) *la tasse est sur la table*
    the cup is on the table

(7) *le cadre est sur le mur*
    the frame is on the wall

The preposition *sur* may allow *indirect contact* between its terms. Figure 3 and example (8) are adapted from Herskovits (1982); figure 4 and example (9) are taken from Miller and Johnson-Laird (1976).

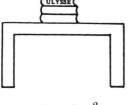

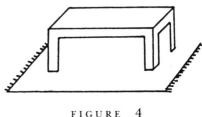

FIGURE 3   FIGURE 4

(8) Ulysse *est sur la table*
    Ulysses is on the table

(9) *la table est sur le sol*
    the table is on the ground

Although there is no direct contact between target and landmark in examples (8) and (9), *sur* is necessary in both cases. Not all instances of indirect contact allow *sur*, however, as example (10) illustrates.

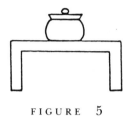

FIGURE 5

(10) **le couvercle est sur la table*
the lid is on the table

Similarly, figure 6 may be described by example (11), but not by (12).

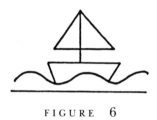

FIGURE 6

(11) *le bateau est sur l'eau*
the boat is on the water

(12) **le bateau est sur le sable*
the boat is on the sand

We will return to the contrast between examples (8), (9), and (11) on the one hand, and (10) and (12) on the other. Example (13) can be explained only by the notion of contact: this is a determining characteristic for the preposition *sur*.

(13) *le point est sur la ligne*
the point is on the line

Examples (14) and (15) present two different idealizations of the road.

(14) *il y a un obstacle sur la route*
there is an obstacle on the road

(15) *il y a beaucoup de maisons sur la route*
there are a lot of houses on the road

The first sentence refers to the road itself, while the second refers to the sides of the road.

Just as the preposition *à* may designate a place or a path leading to a place, there are dialectical uses of *sur* that emphasize the movement leading up to contact.

(16) *le curé va sur ses quatre-vingts ans*
      the priest is going on eighty years

(17) *le sacristain monte sur Rome*
      the sacristan is going up to Rome

Example (18) may be connected with this type of reference.

(18) *les cheveux de l'artiste tombent sur son col*
      the artist's hair falls over his collar

From the above examples, we can deduce a second characteristic applying to the preposition *sur* but not to the preposition *sous*, as figure 1 and example (3) demonstrate.

Characteristic B: If *a est sur b*, there is generally (indirect) contact between the target and the landmark.

Access to perception. The third characteristic I will discuss is a determining characteristic for the preposition *sous*. In the example below, neither order along the vertical axis nor contact between trajector and landmark can explain the use of the different prepositions.

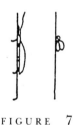

FIGURE 7

(19) *la mouche est sur le plâtras*
      the fly is on the plasterboard

(20) *le cafard est sous le plâtras*
      the cockroach is under the plasterboard

In fact, the two insects are located at the same height on the vertical axis, and both are in contact with the landmark. Here the characteristic motivating the choice of *sous* in (20) is access to perception: the fly, but not the roach, is visible to the speaker.

The cats in figure 8 are described by sentences (21)–(23).

FIGURE 8

(21a) *le chat est sous la table*
    the cat is under the table

  (b) *le chat est en dessous de la table*
    the cat is below the table

(22a) *? le chat est sous la lampe*
    the cat is under the lamp

  (b) *le chat est en dessous de la lampe*
    the cat is below the lamp

(23a) **le chat est sous le fil*
    the cat is under the clothesline

  (b) *le chat est en dessous du fil*
    the cat is below the clothesline

In these examples, it seems that the acceptability of *sous* decreases with the ability of the landmark to cover the target.[2] Neither of the first two characteristics, vertical order or contact, is able to express this contrast. As the (b) examples illustrate, the preposition *en dessous* is not sensitive to this criterion.

Note that, although the cat in the box is invisible, only the preposition *dans,* and not *sous,* is acceptable in this instance.

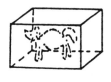

FIGURE 9

(24) *le chat est dans la boîte*
    the cat is in the box

(25) **le chat est sous la boîte*
    the cat is under the box

The contrast between the prepositions *dans* and *sur/sous* will be investigated in greater detail in chapter 13.

One final example will demonstrate the importance of access to perception in the use of *sous*. Judging from their order on the vertical axis, a stain on the underside of a table and a stain on the ceiling occupy the same space, but the preposition *sur* will be used for the visible stain on the ceiling, and *sous* will be used for the invisible stain.

(26) *il y a une tache sur le plafond*
there is a stain on the ceiling

(27) *il y a une tache sous la table*
there is a stain on the table

Access to perception therefore is a determining characteristic only for the preposition *sous* and may be expressed as follows:

Characteristic C: If *a est sous b,* the target is generally made imperceptible by the landmark.

The preposition *derrière* also expresses a certain kind of inaccessibility to perception. The two prepositional relations will be compared in section 12.6.

The target is smaller than the landmark. This characteristic is shared by most spatial relations (chapter 2). I bring it up again at this point because it will play an essential role in our discussion of the preposition *sous* (section 12.3).

The examples below illustrate this characteristic of *sur/sous.*

(28a) *la clé est sous la neige*
the key is under the snow

(b) *la neige est sur la clé*
the snow is on the key

(29a) *la poutre est sous le plâtras*
the beam is under the plaster

(b) *le plâtras est sur la poutre*
the plaster is on the beam

In fact, the most common readings of (a) and (b) are not synonymous. The (a) examples force a reading in which the target is entirely covered by the landmark, while for the (b) examples we imagine a few flakes of snow on the key, or a few crumbs of plaster on the beam. These interpretations respect the usual proportions of target and landmark: the latter commonly is larger than the former. This characteristic of *sur/sous* is formulated below.

> Characteristic D: In the relation *a est sur/sous b*, the target is generally smaller than the landmark.

Opposition to gravity. None of the characteristics discussed above explain figure 10, described by example (30).

> (30) *il y a des boutures sur la plante-ruban*
> there are a few buds on the spider plant

Here the target violates characteristic A, order along the vertical axis, and characteristic B, contact between target and landmark.

If we had to explain the use of *sur* in example (30), we would note that the plant *holds up* its buds. Pragmatically, this type of relation between a burden and its bearer generally implies characteristics A, B, C, and D, but this is not the case here. Nevertheless, the spider plant does share one general property with other supporting objects: it opposes the force of gravity pulling down on its sprouts. As we all know, this action takes place along the vertical axis. The opposition to gravity also plays a role in explaining example (7). Example (31) represents this characteristic as well.

> (31) *les feuilles sont sur l'arbre*
> the leaves are on the tree

The characteristic shared by all these examples is specific to the preposition *sur* and may be formulated as follows:

> Characteristic E': If *a est sur b*, the landmark acts on the target
> to oppose the weight of gravity.

This final characteristic concludes our discussion of the set of characteristics of *sur/sous*. Characteristic E' will be modified in section 12.4.

12.2 The bearer/burden relation and the impetus of the prepositions sur/sous

The distribution of the prepositions *sur/sous* has been discussed in terms of their various characteristics. We should expect a variety of responses if we were to ask French speakers what these prepositions mean. The characteristics of a preposition do not represent necessary and sufficient conditions for its use, in contrast to what we would hope for from a usage rule. Order on the vertical axis, as one example, is neither sufficient (see example [4]) nor necessary (example [5]). Selection restrictions that would render these characteristics sufficient do not have a reasonable, intuitive character (see chapter 4). Furthermore, the most characteristic uses of *sur/sous* are simultaneously motivated by many of these characteristics.

Synchronically, this complex network of characteristics does not necessarily pose a problem for the speaker: the memorization of linguistic conventions may allow the speaker to master the use of a preposition when it is not clearly predicted by the characteristics. I have proposed (chapter 4) that the existing symbolic relationship between the signifier and the signified of a spatial preposition must originally have been transparent. The actual distribution of these words derives from this simple original meaning, which I have called the impetus. For the prepositions *sur/sous*, I will demonstrate that this impetus is formulated on the basis of the bearer/burden relation, a family resemblance concept whose traits have been characterized above. This relation explains the complexity of the distribution of *sur/sous* and accounts for the numerous selection restrictions these prepositions demand.

The role of the bearer in the use of *sur* in sentences (30) and (31) has already been discussed. Given the nature of the world we live in, the characteristics of the prepositions *sur/sous* generally hold between a supporting object and its burden. In fact, it is true that

> the bearer is generally lower than the burden (characteristic A),
>
> the burden is generally in contact with the bearer (characteristic B),
>
> a part of the bearer is generally hidden by the burden (characteristic C),
>
> the bearer is generally larger than the burden (characteristic D),
>
> the force of the bearer works against the force of gravity on the burden (characteristic E), etc.

In the case of a cup held by the table, all these properties are present. For a fly walking on the ceiling, the first property is violated. The table in figure 4 and the ground bearing it up violate the second property but respect the others. As for the bud held up by the spider plant, it violates the first four properties but respects the fifth.

From these remarks, we conclude that the bearer/burden relation behaves like a family resemblance concept, a concept introduced by Wittgenstein (1953) and represented by different combinations of a set of characteristics or similarities. Although the entire set is present in the case of the cup on the table, only one characteristic of the bearer /burden relation explains the sprout held up by the plant. None of the traits of a family resemblance concept is necessary or sufficient. Note that the bearer/burden relation differs from the category *game* used by Wittgenstein since certain characteristic examples of the bearer/burden relation reunite all the properties of the family.

Among the traits of this family resemblance concept, we find the five characteristics of *sur/sous:* order on the vertical axis, contact, inaccessibility to perception, the dimensions of target and landmark, and opposition to the force of gravity. A direct relation between the bearer /burden relation and the use of the prepositions *sur/sous* may now be presented.

> S: *a est sur/sous b* if its target is the second/first element of the bearer/burden relation and its landmark the first/second element of this relation.

Rule S accounts for the later developments of the distribution of these prepositions, essentially depending on the bearer/burden relation, which includes among its traits the characteristics of *sur/sous.* Here we find one of the essential qualities required for the impetus of *sur/sous.* The match would be particularly close if we could find a direct symbolic connection between the bearer/burden relation and the signifiers *sur/sous.* This would presuppose that the bearer/burden relation is first understood by the child in its totality. This relation would then be a primitive of the description, although this does not mean that it could not be described by simpler elements (such as the individual characteristics of the prepositions *sur/sous*). Since the bearer/burden relation resembles a family resemblance concept, we cannot recover any logical relationship such as conjunction, disjunction, etc., between this concept and its traits.

Instead of proposing rule S, I could have explained the impetus of the prepositions *sur/sous* by rule S′, which is intuitively simpler.

> S′: *a est sur/sous b* if the target is borne by/bears the landmark.

I prefer the first formulation, however, because it emphasizes the role of the bearer/burden relation. Rule S explains sentence (32) better than rule S'.

(32) *le taureau est sur la vache*
      the bull is on the cow

If rule S' were taken literally, it would translate example (32) with the awkward paraphrase (32').

(32') *? le taureau est porté par la vache*
       the bull is carried by the cow

The first formulation does not allow for such confusion, because it does not directly associate the use of *sur/sous* with the use of the verb *porter* 'carry', but relates it to *some combination* of the traits of the bearer /burden relation. In example (32), only characteristics (A) and (B) play an essential role.

The idea of a family resemblance concept is fuzzy as we have defined it thus far. So we should not be surprised if it describes all of the circumstances where the prepositions *sur/sous* are used. How can we define situations where these prepositions are *not* used? I will respond to this question in sections 12.4–12.6. We will see that the impetus of the prepositions *sur/sous* explains the present distribution of these prepositions, and also explains the numerous selection restrictions bearing on these prepositions. First, however, we will attend to the preposition *sous*. While the distribution of *sur* and its impetus are directly related, this is less obvious for the preposition *sous* and its impetus. No bearer/burden relation, for example, connects the slippers and the chair in example (3), repeated below.

(3) *les pantoufles sont sous la table*
     the slippers are under the table

As for example (33), describing figure 11, this relation does exist but is reversed with respect to the impetus S.

FIGURE 11

(33) *la carte est sous la main*
      the card is under the hand

In fact, the object of the preposition here is the bearer and not the burden, although the impetus of *sous*[3] would predict the converse. The next section will discuss these differences.

12.3 The development of sous based on its impetus

Before continuing, it is important to note that there are advantages to choosing opposite impetuses for the prepositions *sur/sous*. In fact, contrary to what we would predict from their characteristics, the prepositions *sur/sous* are often considered to be converse. The impetuses of these prepositions justify this intuition, which obtains when target and landmark are in contact and their sizes are more or less equivalent. Examples (34) and (35) describe the same physical scene from different perspectives.

> (34) *le livre rouge est sur le livre bleu*
>   the red book is on the blue book

> (35) *le livre bleu est sous le livre rouge*
>   the blue book is under the red book

This is not the case when the target/bearer of *sous* is larger than its landmark/burden; this contradicts the general constraint on their respective dimensions, formulated in chapter 2. Because of the nature of the bearer/burden relationship, this constraint is more often violated than respected. This conflict draws our attention to an interesting implication bearing on the preposition *sous*. Here it is:

1. In order to respect both the impetus and the general constraint on the target and the landmark, the preposition *sous* must select for particular bearers that are, at least in one respect, smaller than their burden. One typical example is given by the terms in example (36).

> (36) *la table est sous la nappe*
>   the table is under the tablecloth

2. Since this type of bearer is smaller than its burden, it is necessarily hidden by the burden. A new characteristic of the preposition *sous*, the target's inaccessibility to perception, takes shape in the mind of the speaker.

3. Not just any burden can be the landmark of the preposition *sous*, as example (37) illustrates.

> (37) **la table est sous le porte-plume*
>   the table is under the penholder

In contrast, when the impetus of the preposition *sous* presents acceptable sentences, the burden always hides the bearer. The most regular characteristic takes precedence over the characteristic showing the greatest number of exceptions.

4. From this point in time, the impetus of the preposition *sous* may express inaccessibility to perception, even outside of the bearer/burden relationship, or when, exceptionally, a bearer hides its burden. This is the case of the hand holding the card in figure 11. This does not mean that the preposition *sous* has broken all ties with its impetus. At the end of this chapter, I will compare the prepositions *sous* and *derrière*. In fact, the latter also expresses inaccessibility to perception. I will show that the bearer/burden relation is needed to motivate the choice between these prepositions, a choice that otherwise appears entirely arbitrary.

Because inaccessibility to perception is central to the meaning of *sous*, this preposition may have a burden as its target and a bearer as its landmark, as long as the latter hides the former. The preposition *sous* at this point competes with the preposition *sur*. Their competition may be observed when we look at a piece of chewing gum stuck on the lower horizontal surface of a table. Although the chewing gum is the burden and the table the bearer, we would use the utterance (38) and not (39).

(38) *le chewing-gum est sous la table*
the chewing gum is under the table

(39) **le chewing-gum est sur la table*
the chewing gum is on the table

This illustrates the priority of inaccessibility to perception. Nonetheless, example (40) may describe the identical physical scene.

(40) *le chewing-gum est sur le dessous de la table*
the chewing gum is on the underside of the table.

Here the bearer/burden relationship prevails, in that the table—but not its underside—prevents us from perceiving the chewing gum. Finally, if the chewing gum were positioned slightly on the edge of the table, as in figure 12, this would be enough for both (38) and (39) to become possible utterances.

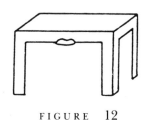

FIGURE 12

In tracing the development of *sous* from an impetus that is the inverse of the impetus of *sur*, I have demonstrated

1. why these two prepositions are considered the converse of each other, and

2. how the preposition *sous* takes on a new meaning, allowing it to express inaccessibility to perception in certain cases.

12.4 Comparison of the prepositions à and sur

Here the comparison of *à* and *sur* differs from that proposed in the French version of this book. At the time of that writing, I had not completed the analysis of *à* that is developed in chapter 11. When I was unaware of the role of ritual in the use of *à*, I believed that utterances such as (41)–(43) illustrate configurational uses of this preposition.

(41) *le tableau est au mur*
the painting is on the wall

(42) *le plafonnier est au plafond*
the ceiling light is on the ceiling

(43) *le chapeau est au portemanteau*
the hat is on the hat rack

I now believe that these uses do not demonstrate a spatial configuration; rather, according to rule A_2, they demonstrate the target's participation in the routine brought to mind by the wall, the ceiling, and the hat rack. These are routines in which suspension is indirectly implied. This conclusion follows also from the examples below.

(44a) **le tableau est à la paroi*
the painting is at the partition wall

(b) **le tableau est à la cloison*
the painting is at the dividing wall

(45a) **le plafonnier est à la voûte*
the ceiling light is at the archway

(b) **le plafonnier est à la tôle ondulée*
the ceiling light is at the corrugated-iron roof

(46a) **le chapeau est au clou*
the hat is at the nail

(b) **le chapeau est à la branche*
the hat is at the branch

Since examples (44)–(46) describe configurations identical to those in (41)–(43) (respectively: the contact of the target with a vertical surface, the contact of the target with a horizontal surface where the target is below the landmark, and a type of suspension), the differences in acceptability can be explained only in terms of the routines associated with examples (41)–(43). Landmarks such as *la paroi, la cloison, la voûte,* etc., are not equivalent to *le mur, le plafond, le portemanteau;* only the latter are capable of introducing the notion of a social routine. The relationship of (41)–(43) with rule A_2 and the ritual it brings to mind is confirmed if we consider the anomalous character of examples (47)–(49). In these examples, the target does not participate in the routine called up by the landmark.

(47) *?? le pain est au mur*
the bread is at the wall

(48) *?? le livre est au plafond*
the book is at the ceiling

(49) *?? la banane est au portemanteau*
the banana is at the hat rack

Examples (41)–(43) are associated with ritual, independent of the configuration adopted by the targets and landmarks. The criteria determining the boundary between the distributions of *à* and *sur* must therefore be modified. In the French version of this book, the following paradigm led me to consider the role of the orientation of the plane (vertical or horizontal) in the description of *à* and its comparison with *sur.*

(50) *la tasse est sur le (*au) bureau*
the cup is on (at) the desk

(51) *le tableau est sur le (au) mur*
the painting is on (at) the wall

(52) *le plafonnier est au (*sur le) mur*
the ceiling light is at (on) the wall

(53) *le chapeau est au (*sur le) portemanteau*
the hat is at (on) the hat rack

Note that example (50), which exemplifies all the traits of the bearer/burden relation, demands the preposition *sur* and prohibits the use of *à*. On the other hand, examples (52) and (53) exhibit the opposite behavior. Example (51), in which the landmark is vertical, plays an intermediary role, allowing both *sur* and *à*. To explain this paradigm by means of configurational differences, I postulated the existence of *ca-*

nonical, intermediary, and *marginal* bearer/burden relations. These were defined as follows:

1. In a *canonical* bearer/burden relation (example [50]), characteristics A–D are respected; furthermore, the plane of the bearer is (approximately) horizontal.

2. For an *intermediary* bearer/burden relation (example [51]), the plane of the bearer is vertical. Characteristic A is not respected, since the target is located at the same height as the landmark. The force of gravity is opposed by means of an intermediary, such as a nail or a hook, so that the dynamic characteristic (E′), as it has been formulated above, is not totally satisfied. This characteristic is partially respected, however, because of the potential force of friction which causes the wall to hold up the painting, preventing it from falling.

3. For a *marginal* bearer/burden relation (example [52]), characteristics A and E′ are violated, since the supported object is lower than its bearer and only the intermediary strength of screws prevent it from falling. The force of the ceiling bearing the ceiling light is indirect, since it is limited to holding the screws.

Given these three types of bearer/burden relations, we can establish a hierarchical ordering between *sur* and *à:* this forces the choice of *sur* for canonical relations, it allows both prepositions for intermediate relations, and it prohibits *sur* in the case of marginal relations (here preferring *à*). The preposition *à* plays an entirely passive role in this paradigm, as it is used only to describe configurations where *sur* is disallowed. In examples such as (51)–(53) the meaning of *à* is essentially one of opposition or differentiation.

The interpretation of this paradigm is entirely changed by rule A_2 and the role of ritual in the use of *à*. Not only is *à* now positively defined; furthermore, when *sur* is replaced by *à* in example (51) we can account for the difference in meaning. If by accident the princess's portrait had been hung backwards, facing the wall, we would prefer *sur le mur* to *au mur.* This brings us back to the routine that the landmark imposes on the interpretation: the object must be hung on the wall in its usual manner. Here, the portrait is a decorative object, but this cannot be the case for a portrait hung backwards. Therefore the use of *à* is not entirely acceptable in this example. The preposition *sur,* on the other hand, describes only the bearer/burden relation between the wall and the portrait.

Must we now dismiss the roles of shape and orientation, if we also rule out intermediate and marginal bearer/burden relations when choosing the preposition *sur?* It appears so, as demonstrated in the figures below.

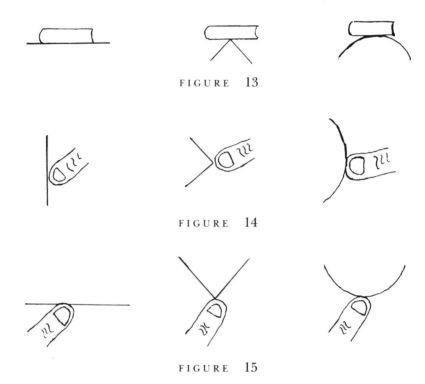

FIGURE 13

FIGURE 14

FIGURE 15

The landmark may be flat, angled, or round, but the preposition *sur* is used in each case to describe the position of the book in figure 13 and the finger in figures 14 and 15. Furthermore, the orientation of the landmark (horizontal or vertical) and the position of the landmark relative to the vertical axis (above, parallel to, or below the target) are unimportant. It remains the case that a vertical landmark such as the wall in example (51) allows both *sur* and *à*, while a horizontal landmark such as the desk in (50) allows only *sur*. This distinction is no longer explained by the bearer/burden relation, since it follows from the positive definition of *à* and the relation of this preposition with social routines.

Another property implied by the distinction among canonical, intermediate, and marginal bearer/burden relations remains useful in describing the preposition *sur*. This has to do with the *partial* opposition of the landmark against the weight of the target when an intervening object is present. This dynamic trait is manifested essentially by friction in the case of vertical surfaces. The effect of this complementary opposition seems evident in the following paradigm:

(54) *le papier peint est sur le (? au) mur*
    the wallpaper is on (at) the wall

(55) *le tableau est sur le (au) mur*
    the painting is on (at) the wall

(56) *le chauffe-eau est au (*sur le) mur*
    the water heater is at (on) the wall

Note that the targets in examples (54)–(56) are progressively heavier, so that the resistance a rough surface could provide against their fall becomes less and less significant when compared to the force of gravity. It is not mere chance that the preposition *sur* is less acceptable in (56), where the target is much heavier than in (54) and (55). To account for these nuances, I will reformulate characteristic E′ as follows:

Characteristic E: *a est sur b* if the action of the landmark opposes (significantly) the force of gravity on the target.

The potential force of the wall compared with the weight of the painting is enough to satisfy characteristic E as so reformulated. This force is negligible, however, for a heavier object, such as the water heater.

It is not always easy to determine when a target participates or does not participate in a social ritual. The contrasts between examples (57) and (58) point up this issue.

(57) *la mouche bleue est au plafond*
    the blue fly is on the ceiling

(58) **la mouche verte est au mur*
    the green fly is at the wall

Why should a fly be more easily associated with a ceiling, rather than a wall? We have discussed, above, two essential properties of the ritual imposed by these landmarks: the objects are attached and hanging, and play a decorative role. Neither normally applies in the case of the green fly. Note, however, that if a cruel child pins the fly to the wall, sentence (58) will be more appropriate. One aspect of the routine, namely attachment, would be fulfilled. Under normal circumstances, however, we do not think of the blue fly as attached to the ceiling. What then makes (57) appropriate? In the ritual related to the ceiling, objects hang suspended: in consequence, the supported object is lower than the bearing object. I believe that this aspect is essential in determining the rituals associated with ceilings. A fly suspended from the ceiling is a common everyday event, yet it never ceases to amaze young children. Perhaps this explains the contrast between examples (57) and (58). I am aware that this analysis comes perilously close to the borderline where fragile motivation becomes pure arbitrariness. However, I see a heuristic value in the type of research undertaken here, to push an explanation of the use of these words as far as possible. Example (57) is motivated by routines associating flies and ceilings, routines that do not hold for flies and walls, unless the fly is pinned to the wall.

12.5 Comparison of the prepositions contre and sur

I do not pretend to give a detailed analysis of the preposition *contre,* and here restrict my interest to its relation with the preposition *sur.* In summary, *contre* expresses contact between two forces, whether the elements be mobile, as in example (59), or immobile, as in (60).

> (59) *le curé se bat contre le ministre*
> the priest is fighting against the minister

> (60) *l'armoire est contre le mur*
> the cupboard is against the wall

I am particularly interested in situations where the contacting objects are immobile.

One contrast between *sur* and *contre* concerns the orientation of the elements in contact, which are vertical (or nearly vertical) for *sur,* and horizontal or oblique for *contre.* In examples (1) and (7), repeated below, the preposition *contre* is inappropriate.

> (1) *la tasse est sur (*contre) la table*
> the cup is on (against) the table

> (7) *la cadre est sur (*contre) le mur*
> the frame is on (against) the wall

In the first sentence, the weight of the cup and the reaction of the table are vertically aligned. In (7), the frame is supported by a nail, and the wall opposes gravity only by the pressure of the picture frame. This force, also, is vertical. In contrast, if the action and reaction of two bodies are aligned horizontally, the preposition *contre* will be preferred. This is illustrated by example (60), in which the cupboard leans against (*contre*) the wall. The preposition *contre* is also preferred if the interaction is oblique, as in the example of the broom in figure 16.

> (61) *le balai est contre (? sur) le mur*
> the broom is against (on) the wall

FIGURE 16

What scenes are called to mind by sentences (62) and (63)?

(62) *la carte bleue est sur la carte rouge*
the blue card is on the red card

(63) *la carte bleue est contre la carte rouge*
the blue card is against the red card

For the first utterance, I imagine two horizontal cards, one on top of the other. For the second, I see two horizontal cards juxtaposed or perhaps leaning against one another to form a child's house of cards. Once again, the preposition *sur* describes vertical force and leaves the care of horizontal and oblique forces to the preposition *contre*. If I place my leg against (*contre*) my leg, or my leg on (*sur*) my leg, two different movements are evoked: the inner part of my legs are in contact in the first case; in the second case, the upper side of one and the under side of the other are in contact. The use of *contre* then suggests horizontal interactions, that of *sur*, vertical interaction.

The preposition *sur*, however, may apply to a horizontal interaction if the landmark is vertical. Thus, watching the priest hang wallpaper on the walls of the sacristy, I might say,

(64) *le curé colle un tapis à fleurs sur (*contre) les fresques*
the priest is hanging flowered wallpaper on (against) the frescoes

Here the two prepositions are distinguished by a new trait: the interdependence of the positions of target and landmark. Indeed, the position of the target depends on the position of the landmark, but the inverse is not true. By the principle of transitivity, this remark holds true for an indirect bearer/burden relationship. The frame on the wall depends on the position of the nail from which it is hanging, but the nail depends on the position of the wall. In contrast, the preposition *contre*, which plays off two opposing forces, prefers the target and landmark to be independent. In the case of the broom leaning against the wall, they may be only partially independent. However, this is distinct from the example of the frame on the wall. In fact, the floor preventing the broom from falling does not depend on the position of the wall, in contrast to the nail. In a third example, two cards leaning against each other are not unequally interdependent in terms of the bearer/burden relation. Rather, the landmark and the target are mutually dependent. The use of *sur* is motivated in example (64) because the flowered wallpaper depends on the fresco it is glued to, and not the inverse, despite the horizontal alignment of contact.

Finally, the preposition *contre* may be used when the interaction of landmark and target is vertical, as long as the forces in play are stronger than the weight of the target. Thus example (65), but not (66), is impossible for a fly on the top surface of a table.

> (65) *la mouche est contre la table*
>   the fly is against the table

> (66) *la secretaire écrase la mouche contre (sur) la table*
>   the secretary swats the fly against (on) the table

In summary, if weight is the only factor, the criteria in the table are needed to decide between the prepositions *sur* and *contre* to express contact. If the force exerted by the burden is greater than its weight, the preposition *contre* becomes acceptable in both cases.

		sur	*contre*
a.	Vertical interaction between target and landmark.	yes	no
b.	The position of the target depends on the position of the landmark, but not the reverse.	yes	no

The conditions under which the preposition *sur* expresses contact are not arbitrary. Once again, they correspond to priorities of the bearer/burden relationship. More precisely, condition a is related to the fifth trait of this family resemblance: the bearer is in opposition to the force of gravity on the burden. Condition b is also a consequence of this trait, which may be reformulated in a more general fashion as follows:

> The bearer controls the position of the burden with respect to the force of gravity.

This formulation will demonstrate another advantage when we compare the prepositions *sur* and *dans* in chapter 13.

When the force exerted by the target is greater than that of gravity, it is evident that factors outside the bearer/burden relationship intervene between the bearer and its burden. These external factors allow, and may even prefer, the use of the preposition *contre*.

In conclusion, we have seen that a number of arbitrary restrictions must be included if we wish to define *sur* in terms of contact. However, the development of this preposition from the basis of the bearer/burden relationship explains why contact features among its characteristics, and also accounts for the specific types of contact *sur* is able to describe.

12.6 *The relation between the prepositions* derrière *and* sous

The preposition *sous* expresses inaccessibility to perception. In chapter 9 we saw that in certain contexts, the preposition *derrière* may play the same role. I will demonstrate in this section that the impetus of the preposition *sous,* tied to the bearer/burden relation, explains the distinction between these two prepositions. The preposition *derrière* expresses inaccessibility to perception in those contexts where *sous* is not required.

The preposition *sous* expresses inaccessibility to perception when this occurs perpendicular to the vertical axis. Thus example (3), repeated here, describes the slippers in figure 1, while example (67) is inappropriate.

(3) *les pantoufles sont sous la table*
    the slippers are under the table

(67) **les pantoufles sont derrière la table*
    the slippers are behind the table

This type of obstruction is a clear example of the bearer/burden relation. In fact, the burden generally hides the bearer perpendicular to the vertical axis. However, the preposition *derrière* is required if the ordinary order of target and landmark is violated, as in example (68). Here the target (the sun) is not below but above the clouds.

(68) *le soleil est derrière les nuages*
    the sun is behind the clouds

(69) **le soleil est sous les nuages*
    the sun is under the clouds

Furthermore, obstructions perpendicular to the horizontal direction generally require the preposition *derrière* also. Thus (71) cannot describe an upright tree.

(70) *l'arbre est derrière le mur*
the tree is behind the wall

(71) **l'arbre est sous le mur*
the tree is under the wall

The preposition *derrière* is always preferred when obstruction to perception occurs without contact. When the contact between target and landmark is perpendicular to the horizontal axis, the distributions of the prepositions *sous* and *derrière* interact in a very interesting way. Here, it might seem, begins the realm of the arbitrary.

I will demonstrate that, on the contrary, this division of labor is regulated by subtle details such as the thickness of the landmark and its extension with respect to the target. The preposition *sous* is preferred over *derrière* when the landmark is thin (example [72]), or when it covers a large surface area (example [74]). The preposition *derrière*, on the other hand, selects for a landmark that is thick (example [73]) or restricted in area (example [75]).

(72) *des fresques ont été trouvées sous (*derrière) une couche de peinture*
frescoes have been found under (behind) a layer of paint

(73) *il y a un trou dans le mur derrière (sous) le portrait*
there is a hole in the wall behind (under) the portrait

(74) *il y a un coffre sous (*derrière) le tapis*
there is a safe under (behind) the tapestry

(75) *il y a un coffre derrière (sous) la carte de Californie*
there is a safe behind (under) the map of California

In example (72), the preposition *sous* is preferred over *derrière* because the layer of paint is a thin landmark. The opposite choice is made for a thicker landmark, such as the portrait in (73). Because the tapestry covers the entire wall, the preposition *sous* is preferred over *derrière* in example (74). The latter preposition is chosen for the map of California, which only partially covers the wall. Since the landmark is thin, the preposition *sous* remains an option, however.

When contact is perpendicular to the horizontal axis, the criteria distinguishing between *sous* and *derrière* are so unexpected, they hardly restrict the arbitrary nature of these choices. Synchronically, we cannot consider them reasonable selection restrictions. They are based, however, in the development of the preposition *sous*. Recall that, according to the impetus of this preposition, the target is the bearer, and the landmark the burden. To satisfy the constraint on the dimensions of target and landmark, as discussed in chapter 2, the burden must be more extensive than the bearer. A table hidden by a tablecloth illustrates this type of relation well. Two pragmatic consequences follow from this observation:

1. the target/burden must be thin, to avoid crushing the landmark/bearer; and

2. the target entirely covers the bearer.

When the uses of *sous* and *derrière* coincide, these are the consequences motivating their distribution. The above examples provide spectacular illustrations of the power of the concept of an impetus. Language may present itself as a set of arbitrary rules, but this complex state has not arisen capriciously or casually. In certain cases, impetuses allow us to trace the development of language from the transparent and unambiguous relation between the signifier and the signified of each word, up to the most complex distributions. For spatial relations, research on this development is often possible even in the absence of historical evidence.

13

The prepositions dans/hors de and the container/contained relation

Mets quelque chose dans tes pieds![1]

Fabienne Guerens
Ode au clairon

Throughout this book I have attempted to show that the most comprehensive description of space is functional, rather than geometric or logical. The position of the target with respect to the landmark is not calculated in terms of absolute distance. Usage rules governing spatial prepositions include concepts of family resemblance, such as general and lateral orientation, or concepts that translate our ways of perceiving and making use of space, such as access to perception, potential contact, or the bearer/burden relationship. I will conclude this book by comparing a topological[2] definition of *dans/hors de* in terms of inclusion/exclusion, with a functional definition in terms of container /contained.

First I will present the topological solution, according to which *a est dans b* if the boundaries of the landmark *b* include the boundaries of its target *a*. This solution was presented in Vandeloise 1984. Such a definition is only valid if the two terms of the preposition are idealized appropriately. While a canonical rule demands the total inclusion of the target in the landmark, a derived rule allows the partial inclusion of the target. A certain number of selection restrictions bear on this latter rule.

This solution has one major defect: the idealizations of the two terms of the preposition, which are necessary for the correct application of the definition, cannot be defined without referring to the functional relation of container/contained. This relation, as we will see, is a family resemblance concept, and inclusion is only one of several of its traits. This introduces a new definition of the prepositions *dans/hors de* in terms of the container/contained relation. This relation minimizes the importance of the distinction between a canonical rule (where the landmark totally contains the target) and a derived rule

---

This chapter is a revised version of an article that appeared in *Leuvense bijdragen* 1 (1985).

(where the target is only partially contained). Another important trait of the container/contained relation is the force exerted by the container on the contained object. This trait introduces a development of the functional definition of *dans*, motivating the role played by the force of its landmark.

13.1 Topological relations between the objects of the prepositions dans/hors de

The examples and the scenes below illustrate the possible topological relations between the terms of the preposition *dans*.

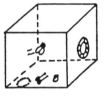      

FIGURE 1   FIGURE 2   FIGURE 3

(1) *la mouche est dans le coffre-fort*
     the fly is in the safe

(2) *les bijoux sont dans le coffre-fort*
     the jewels are in the safe

(3) *le chien est dans la niche*
     the dog is in the kennel

(4) *le vin est dans le verre*
     the wine is in the glass

(5) *la mouche est dans le verre*
     the fly is in the glass

If each object is represented by the set of its points, the five schemas in figure 4 illustrate their relative positions.
Note that these configurations exhaust the possibilities of inclusion/exclusion[3] in the two sets. The relation between the terms of the preposition *dans* varies from the total inclusion of the target within the landmark (schema I), through partial inclusion (schema III), to total exclusion (schema V). The boundaries of the target and the landmark may be in contact (schemas II and IV) or not (remaining schemas). The preposition *dans* is not influenced by contact.
The configurations permitted between the terms of the preposi-

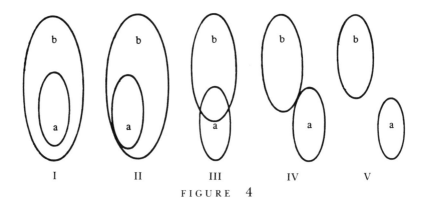

I   II   III   IV   V

FIGURE 4

tion *hors de* are more restricted. These are illustrated by the scenes and the utterances below.

FIGURE 5   FIGURE 6   FIGURE 7

(6) *le crayon est hors du sac*
    the pencil is out of the bag

(7) *le parapluie est hors du sac*
    the umbrella is out of the bag

(8) *l'oiseau est hors de la cage*
    the bird is out of the cage

(9) *le poisson est hors du bocal*
    the fish is out of the bowl

Only examples (8) and (9) are acceptable, so preposition *hors de* stipulates that its terms must be configured as in schemas IV and V; only there is the target external to the landmark.

When the terms of *dans* are represented by the set of their points, the uses of the preposition appear extremely complex. This line of topological reasoning demonstrates how far we are from the unified representation $a \subset b$ (illustrated by schemas I and II), which is generally attributed to this preposition.

The situation is simplified if, instead of considering the real forms of the prepositional objects, we replace them with appropriate idealizations. Each time the paradoxical representations IV and V arise, the landmark is an open container. One solution, proposed independently by Vandeloise (1979) and Herskovits (1982), is to close the glass with a dotted line (figure 8). If this contour is permitted, the pink fly and the blue fly in figure 8 no longer illustrate schemas IV and V, but II and I.

FIGURE 8

Another type of closure has been proposed by Langacker (1987a). Strictly speaking, the fish and the block of ice in figure 9 are arranged according to schema IV. In fact, the two prepositional terms share points only along their boundaries. Example (10) correctly describes this scene.

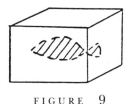

FIGURE 9

(10) *le poisson est dans la glace*
     the fish is in the ice

To avoid applying *dans* to schema IV, Langacker proposes that we close the block of ice as illustrated by the cross-hatching in figure 9. If we allow this idealization, the arrangement of the objects in figure 9 corresponds to schema II. A similar idealization is necessary to explain example (11), describing figure 10.

(11) *il y a un trou dans la route*
     there is a hole in the road

FIGURE   10

Appropriate idealizations allow us to reduce the configurations described by *dans* to schemas I–III. In section 13.4 I will discuss the problems posed by this type of idealization.

Schema III, illustrating the partial inclusion of the terms of *dans*, demands a more refined description in order to apply to the following utterances:

(12) *l'oeuf est dans le coquetier*
     the egg is in the eggcup

(13) *l'arbre est dans la terre*
     the tree is in the ground

(14) *la paille est dans le verre*
     the straw is in the glass

Schema III′ (figure 11), which takes into account the difference between convex and nonconvex shapes,[4] appropriately describes the topological relations of the elements of these sentences.

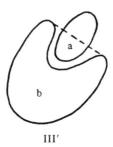

III′

FIGURE   11

Here we return to the partial inclusion described by schema III only by replacing the landmark *b* with its *convex closure b*. According to this new idealization, the terms of *dans* are topologically related in only two significant ways: total inclusion, expressed by configurations I and II; and partial inclusion, illustrated by configuration III′. These are respectively represented by the logical formulas $a \subset b$ and $a \cap b \neq 0$. The union of these relations conforms to the unified definition proposed by Miller and Johnson-Laird (1976) to describe the English preposition *in* (see section 1.2).

I have preferred (Vandeloise 1984) to describe the preposition *dans* by one canonical rule $a \subset b$ and one derived rule $a \cap b \neq 0$. The following section will lay out the reasons for this choice.

13.2 Total inclusion and partial inclusion

The preposition *dans* is best described by a canonical rule D_1, demanding the total inclusion of the target in the landmark, and a derived rule D_2, allowing its partial inclusion. These two rules are preferred over the single rule below.

D′: *a est dans b* if the boundaries of the landmark (partially) include the boundaries of the target.

My initial reason for adopting this description was intuitive. The uses of *dans* described by the first rule appear more representative than those described by the second rule. I have since learned that this intuition may be contradicted by evidence from first language acquisition (Herskovits, personal communication): children, it appears, use this preposition just as easily to express partial inclusion as to express total inclusion.

The second reason, based on selection restrictions, remains an important argument, however. Two selection restrictions apply to the derived usage rule but do not apply to the canonical rule. A complete description of the preposition *dans* must therefore treat these two rules separately.[5]

The first type of selection restriction is illustrated by examples (15)–(17).

(15) **la bouteille est dans le capuchon*
   the bottle is in the cap

(16) **le paquet est dans la ficelle*
   the package is in the string

(17) **le chat est dans le collier*
   the cat is in the collar

Although these uses of *dans* satisfy the derived usage rule, they are unacceptable. The condition $a < b$ prescribed by Cooper (1968) in his definition of the English preposition *in* is too extensive, however, and would eliminate the acceptable utterances below.

(18) *le fil est dans l'aiguille*
   the thread is in the needle

(19) *l'arbre est dans le pot*
    the tree is in the planter

In fact, these uses of *dans* are acceptable, although the target is larger than the landmark.

However, there are important differences between the inappropriate sentences (15)–(17) and the appropriate ones (18) and (19). For the first, the landmark is mobile with respect to the target: the cap is screwed onto the bottle and not the bottle into the cap; the collar is fastened around the cat's neck and not the other way around. In examples (18) and (19), in contrast, the target is mobile with respect to the landmark. The tailor threads the thread through the eye of the needle, and the tree grows out of the ground.

The importance of the movement of the target is illustrated again by the contrast between examples (20) and (21).

(20) **les fiches sont dans l'élastique*
    the index cards are in the rubber band

(21) *mets les fiches dans l'élastique*
    put the index cards in the rubber band

In fact, while example (20) suggests a movement of the rubber band towards the cards (figure 12), example (21) and figure 13, in which the rubber band is held steady by the speaker, suggest the reverse movement.

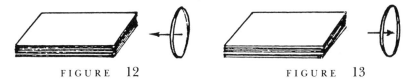

FIGURE 12   FIGURE 13

Similarly, another contrast can be imagined: it is awkward to say that *le doigt de l'évêque est dans l'anneau* 'the bishop's finger is in the ring'. However, if the bishop is administering the sacrament of marriage to a blushing and trembling bride, when she finally manages to slip the ring on her finger the groom might be relieved to think *le doigt est dans l'alliance* 'the finger is in the ring'.

Exceptions to the derived rule can be eliminated by condition C_1.

C_1: The landmark of the preposition *dans* may not be mobile with respect to its target.

Contrary to the condition $a < b$, condition C_1 does not eliminate examples (18) and (19). Note that condition C_1 bears on the derived rule (schema III), but not the canonical rule (schemas I and II). Although the net travels toward the butterfly, example (22) is, in fact, acceptable.

> (22) *le papillon est dans le filet*
> the butterfly is in the net

Here the net entirely contains the butterfly. Nevertheless, condition C_1 is too restrictive in that it would wrongly reject example (23), describing figure 14.

FIGURE 14

> (23) *le poisson est dans la main*
> the fish is in the hand

The landmark of this utterance is considered mobile with respect to the target. It is important to note, however, that the hand exercises a certain amount of force on the fish. The energy of the landmark, as we will see, has more general consequences on the distribution of the preposition *dans*. This influence is evident in the example below.

FIGURE 15

FIGURE 16

> (24) **le fil est dans la pince à linge*
> the clothes-line is in the clothespin

> (25) *le fil est dans la pince*
> the wire is in the pliers

Although the shapes of these objects are similar, the second example, but not the first, is acceptable. Only the energy of the landmarks distinguishes between them: the pliers, but not the clothespin, exercise a certain force on the target.

A different sort of example shows that the acceptability of the relation *a est dans b* depends on the energy of the landmark. As schema VI illustrates (figure 17), the preposition *dans* may express a reciprocal relation. Example (26) is acceptable, as well as (27), to express this relation.

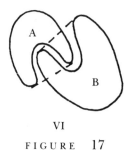

VI

FIGURE   17

(26) *A est dans B*
      A is in B

(27) *B est dans A*
      B is in A

This type of relation is also illustrated by example (28).

(28) *le curé et le ministre marchent la main dans la main*
      the priest and the minister walk hand in hand

Example (28) is acceptable only if the two hands exert comparable pressure. If the pressure is unequal, the stronger hand will be considered the landmark, as the contrast between examples (29) and (30) demonstrates. In a world where police and thieves are as they should be, the first sentence, but not the second, is acceptable.

(29) *la main du voleur est dans la main du gendarme*
      the thief's hand is in the policeman's hand

(30) **la main du gendarme est dans la main du voleur*
      the policeman's hand is in the thief's hand

From the examples above, we conclude that a restriction must be added to condition C_1 when the landmark exercises a force on the target. The restricted condition can be rewritten as follows:

C'_1: If the landmark does not exert force on the target, it may not be considered mobile with respect to the target.

The canonical usage rule and the derived usage rule, corrected by condition C'_1, correctly predict all the uses of *dans* that we have seen. However, a different type of use demands a supplementary condition bearing on the derived rule. This is shown by the examples below.

FIGURE 18   FIGURE 19   FIGURE 20   FIGURE 21

(31) *le nez est dans la tête*
      the nose is in the head

(32) *la flèche est dans la tête*
      the arrow is in the head

(33) *les roues sont dans la voiture*
      the wheels are in the car

(34) *les rochers sont dans la voiture*
      the boulders are in the car

When the target is a constituent of the landmark, as in examples (31) and (33), the utterance is unacceptable. Examples (32) and (34) are, in contrast, acceptable. The spatial configuration of the scene described by these examples is the same one described by (31) and (33). The contrast in these examples can be attributed only to whether or not the target is a constituent of the landmark. As Gilles Fauconnier pointed out to me, the acceptable utterance (35) contrasts with the unacceptable (31).

(35) *la reine a un joli nez dans un visage ovale*
      the queen has a lovely nose in an oval face

Here it is not the queen's face, but its oval form, that is the landmark of example (35). Because the lovely nose is not a constituent of this geometric form, this sentence is acceptable.[6]

As examples (36) and (37) illustrate, whether or not the subject is a constituent is important only for the derived rule and schema III'.

(36) *le cerveau est dans la tête*
      the brain is in the head

(37) *les sièges sont dans la voiture*
    the seats are in the car

Although brains and seats are indeed constituents of heads and cars, in both these examples the target is totally included in the landmark, and these sentences are acceptable. Condition C_2, bearing on the derived rule, is expressed as follows:

C_2: The target cannot be a constituent of the landmark.

To my knowledge, the preposition *dans* is now described by canonical rule D_1, paired with the derived rule D_2.

D_1: *a est dans b* if the boundaries of the landmark include the boundaries of the target.

D_2: *a est dans b* if the boundaries of the convex closure of the landmark partially include the boundaries of the target.

Conditions C'_1 and C_2 only bear on this second usage rule. Since they do not weaken the canonical rule, I considered this a good reason to describe *dans* by two rules rather than by one.

The schema below recapitulates the different types of use of *dans* presented here, and the rules governing them. Each type is illustrated by an example. The purpose of this schema is essentially mnemonic.

(a) *les bijoux sont dans le coffre-fort*
    the jewels are in the safe

(b) *le vin est dans le verre*
    the wine is in the glass

(c) **le nez est dans la tête*
    the nose is in the head

(d) *l'oeuf est dans le coquetier*
    the egg is in the eggcup

(e) *le poisson est dans la main*
    the fish is in the hand

(f) **la bouteille est dans le capuchon*
    the bottle is in the cap

13.3 The expression hors de *and movement*

The idealizations of the terms of *dans* are represented by schemas I–III' (figures 4 and 11). The terms of *hors de*, on the other hand, are described by schemas IV and V, so the two expressions are in comple-

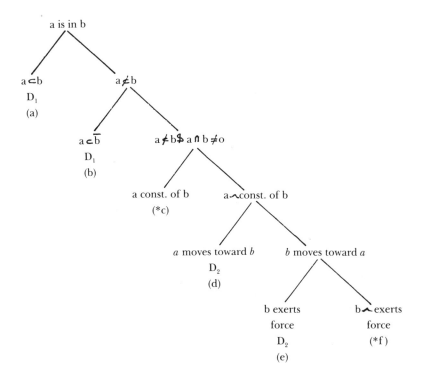

mentary distribution. Nevertheless, certain selection restrictions apply to the expression *hors de*. As examples (38) and (39) show, this expression is not always appropriate when the position of its terms is represented by schemas IV and V.

(38) **l'éléphant est hors de la boîte d'allumettes*
      the elephant is out of the matchbox

(39) **le ruisseau est hors de la maison*
      the brook is out of the house

Here again, the rule governing the use of *hors de* must be made more specific. The problem is intuitively evident: examples (38) and (39) are unacceptable because, obviously, the elephant/the brook never were in the matchbox/the house in the first place. In other words, it is not enough for target and landmark to satisfy schemas IV and V; the target must have previously been included in the landmark. This condition is graphically represented by schemas IV′ and V′.

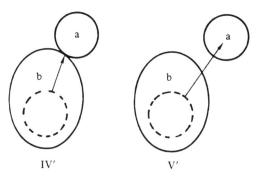

IV'   V'

FIGURE   22

The expression *hors de* implies a movement of the target initially located within the landmark, and rule H_1 must be

H_1: *a est hors de b* if the boundaries of the landmark *no longer* include the boundaries of the target.

Rule D_1/H_1 summarizes rules D_1 and H_1.

D_1/H_1: *a est dans/hors de b* if the boundaries of the landmark include/no longer include the boundaries of the target.

This explanation of the expressions *dans/hors de* in terms of inclusion/exclusion was proposed in Vandeloise 1984. Most descriptions of the English preposition *in* are similarly based on this topological relation. I will demonstrate now that these expressions cannot be completely described without recourse to the functional relation container /contained. Furthermore, this relation allows for a more satisfactory explanation of the preposition *dans*.

13.4 The container/contained relation

The idealization of open containers has played a major role in the description of *dans* in terms of inclusion/exclusion. Without this idealization, it would be impossible to demonstrate that *dans/hors de* are in complementary distribution. In this section I will argue that this idealization is impossible without referring to the container/contained relation. Definition D/H is formulated as a function of the container/ contained relation, and inclusion is one of its traits.

D/H: *a est dans/hors de b* if the landmark and the target are/are no longer the first and second elements in the container/contained relation.

This relation suggests a reformulation of selection restrictions C'_1 and C_2, such that the distinction between a canonical rule (total container) and a derived rule (partial container) loses its importance.

13.4.1 Need for the container/contained relation

If we limit the closure of the landmarks of *dans* to open containers, we are already letting the fox into the chicken coop. Elsewhere we have attempted to restrict objects idealized by rule D/H without appealing to the notion of a container. In fact, all open containers are sets of *nonconvex* points that may be bisected in more than two places by a straight line, and can be defined by this criterion. The problem is only provisionally resolved by this new definition, however. Herskovits (1982) has pointed out that the idealization of open containers does not correspond to their *convex closure,* the envelope closest to the container that cannot be bisected in more than two points by a straight line. Consider the examples below.

FIGURE 23   FIGURE 24

(40) *le vin est dans le verre*
      the wine is in the glass

(41) **la mouche est dans le verre*
      the fly is in the glass

(42) *l'oiseau est dans l'arbre*
      the bird is in the tree

(43) **la mouche est dans l'arbre*
      the fly is in the tree

The convex closure of the landmark is represented by the outside line. This erroneously predicts that the fly is in the glass/the tree. To allow examples (40) and (42) while excluding examples (41) and (43), Herskovits has proposed a geometric description of the tree and the glass in terms of their *outline,* the contour drawn with a dotted line. She is satisfied with a graphic representation of this notion. I have proposed (Vandeloise 1984) that the convex closure of the landmark be limited to its *containing* part, that is, the top of the glass in figure 23 and the leafy part of the tree in figure 24. This too admits that we need the notion of a container to describe the idealizations of the objects of *dans*. Since it is impossible to define this preposition in terms of inclusion/exclusion without idealizing the objects, we must be allowed to refer to the functional relation container/contained.[7]

This relation is more extensive than the inclusion/exclusion relation. It clearly demonstrates that the boundaries of a contained object are not always included in the physical boundaries of the container. The notion of inclusion/exclusion, in contrast, always implies the container/contained relation. Of course, water spilled into a cloth bag or a perforated box will not remain contained for very long; the bag and the box in these cases are poor containers, but containers nonetheless. In the same way, any object whose boundaries partially include the boundaries of another object partially contains that object. When an object is entirely included/excluded, the topological relation inclusion /exclusion then implies the functional container/contained relation; the reverse does not hold.

13.4.2 The advantages of the functional relation

It was demonstrated above that the container/contained relation is needed to describe the preposition *dans* completely. In this it figures among the primitive elements of the description of spatial prepositions, along with the bearer/burden relation. This is not to say that it cannot be analyzed into more simple elements, however. My analysis suggests that the container/contained relation could be globally perceived during the acquisition of language, well before the child begins to isolate its different aspects. Thus, although inclusion is a simple characteristic of a more complex relation, it may not be understood independently until a later time.

Definition D/H emphasizes the role of the container/contained relation in the distribution of these prepositions. I prefer this definition over the formulation in D'/H'; the latter may be more direct, but it allows for greater confusion.

D'/H ': *a est dans/hors de b* if the landmark (partially) contains / no longer contains the target.

It is not true, in fact, that *a est dans b* must always be synonymous, in colloquial French, with *b continent a*. To make definition D'/H' acceptable, a technical meaning related to the container/contained relation must be given to the verb *contenir* 'contain'. Definition D/H, as formulated, directly avoids any misunderstanding along these lines.

Rule D and the container/contained relation together motivate every detail of the distribution of the preposition *dans*. To illustrate this, I will employ the following traits of the container/contained relation:

1. The contained object moves toward the container and not the reverse.

2. The container controls the position of the contained object and not the reverse.

3. The contained object is included, at least partially, in the container or in the convex closure of its containing part.[8]

Since definition D associates the subject/object of the preposition *dans* with the contained/container, respectively, the terms of *dans* must also respect traits 1–3. These traits behave like the traits of a family resemblance concept. In particular, no single trait is necessary, and only total inclusion is sufficient.

No trait is necessary.

1. In example (22), the net (the object) moves toward the butterfly (the subject) and not the reverse, as trait 1 requires.

2. For *le doigt de la fiancée est dans l'alliance* 'the bride's finger is in the ring', the finger (the subject) determines the position of the ring (the object) and not the reverse, as trait 2 predicts.

3. Finally, even if there is no straight line intersecting both the pear and the bowl in figure 25, example (44) is still appropriate.

FIGURE   25

(44) *la poire est dans la coupe*[9]
      the pear is in the bowl

Only total inclusion is sufficient. Naturally, if a target heads towards a landmark, or if its position is controlled by the landmark, this is not enough for the target to be considered *dans* the landmark. The first two traits of the container/contained relation are therefore not sufficient.

As for the third trait, when we speak of the inclusion of the contained object in the containing part of the container, partial inclusion must be distinguished from total inclusion. The first is not sufficient, as figure 26 illustrates; here the cord described by example (45) is attached to the ceiling.

FIGURE   26

(45) *la corde est dans le verre*
        the cord is in the glass

On the other hand, although total inclusion is not a necessary condition, at least it implies the container/contained relation, as I have pointed out above. It is thus a sufficient condition for the use of the preposition *dans,* which explains its privileged status in the description of this preposition.

The properties of the container/contained relation suggest a reformulation of condition C'_1, which would apply to partial containers as well as to total containers. The principle argument in favor of using two rules to describe the preposition *dans* now loses its force. Remember that the evidence from language acquisition already poses a serious problem for this bipartite definition. It seems, in fact, that children use the preposition *dans* just as easily to express partial inclusion as to express total inclusion. The reasons for this similarity may be better understood in terms of the container/contained relation. An egg may be only partially contained in an eggcup, but it still satisfies the traits of the container/contained relation, just as well as the example of the jewels hidden in the safe.

In examples (15)–(17), the bottle, the package, and the cat are partially included in the bottle cap, the string, and the collar; these examples were eliminated by condition C_1, repeated here.

C_1: The landmark of the preposition *dans* may not be mobile with respect to its target.

In contrast, when the target is entirely included in the landmark, as in example (22), the utterance remains acceptable, even if it violates condition C_1.

(22) *le papillon est dans le filet*
    the butterfly is in the net

Returning to the characteristics of the container/contained relation, we note that condition C_1 prevents any violation of the first trait of this relation: the contained object must move to the container, and not the reverse. But examples (15)–(17) contradict the second characteristic of this relation: the container determines the position of the contained object, and not the reverse. In these examples, on the contrary, it is the contained object (the bottle, the package, or the cat) that determines the position of the container (the bottle cap, the string, or the collar). In contrast, example (22) respects this second characteristic. If condition C_1 is reformulated, it then applies equally to instances of total and partial inclusion.

C_1: The target cannot determine the position of the landmark.

This is not to minimize the importance of the first trait of the container/contained relation (stipulating that the contained object must move towards the container). Rather, this trait is needed to explain the contrast between examples (20) and (21), and the bride's finger in the ring.

A new trait of the container/contained relation, an object contains its interior but not its boundaries, allows a reformulation of condition C_2, which will apply to total inclusion, as well as to partial inclusion.

C_2: If the target is a constituent of the landmark, it may not share a boundary with the landmark.

Because the nose and the wheels are boundary constituents, in contrast to the brain and the seats, they cannot be said to be *dans* the head or *dans* the car.

Conditions C_1 and C_2, thus reformulated, apply equally to total or partial containers. They are not arbitrary in that both prevent target and landmark from violating the usual traits of the container/contained relation.

A restriction to condition C_1, related to the energy of the landmark, has been proposed in section 13.2. This concerns the acceptability of *le poisson dans la main* 'the fish in the hand' or *le fil dans la pince* 'the wire in the pliers'. Thus reformulated, condition C_1 no longer creates a problem by rejecting these examples. In fact the landmark (the hand/the pliers) determines the position of the target. Rather than saying that the hand (partially) *contains* the fish, we would prefer to say that it *holds* the fish. A derived rule, motivated by the second trait of the container/contained relation, can be written as follows:

D″: *a est dans b* if the landmark holds the target.

As formulated, rule D″ does not demand any additions. In fact, the force exerted by the container on the contained object is specifically part of the traits of the family resemblance of the container/contained relation. Note that French allows us to condense rules D′ and D″ in a single formula that perhaps reflects more than simple chance.[10]

a est dans/hors de b if the landmark (partially) contains or holds /no longer contains or holds the target.

The two examples below illustrate particularly well the advantages of the container/contained relation over inclusion/exclusion in defining the preposition *dans*.

(46) *l'aiguille est dans le champ de l'aimant*
the needle is in the field of the magnet

(47) **l'allumette est dans le champ de l'aimant*
the matchstick is in the field of the magnet

Although the two targets are included within the magnet's field, only the metal object, sensitive to the force of the landmark, may be contained within this field. The contrast between examples (46) and (47) can be explained only by the container/contained relation.

One final argument in favor of the description of *dans* by means of this functional relation will be proposed in the next section, which compares the prepositions *dans* and *sous*.

13.5 A comparison of the prepositions dans, sur, and sous

Remember that the impetus of the preposition *sur* is expressed in terms of the functional bearer/burden relation. One of the traits of this relation stipulates that the landmark must oppose the weight of the target. This trait was reformulated in chapter 12 as follows:

The bearer controls the position of the burden with respect to the force of gravity.

This reminds us of the second trait of the container/contained relation.

The container controls the position of the contained object and not the reverse.

As the contrast between these two traits points up, the difference between *dans* and *sur* can be expressed as follows: while the landmark of the preposition *sur* (the bearer) essentially controls the movements of its target (the burden) along a vertical direction, the landmark of *dans* (the container) controls the position of the target (the contained object) in every direction. The preposition *sur* will only be chosen when the landmark exclusively opposes the target's movement vertically. On the other hand, the preposition *dans* is used when force is exerted equally in every direction. This explains the choice of *sur* versus *dans* in sentences (48) and (49).

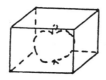

FIGURE   27

(48) *la pomme est dans la boîte*
       the apple is in the box

(49) **la pomme est sur la boîte*
       the apple is on the box

While closed containers exert total control over their contained objects, horizontal surfaces are able to exert only vertical control on the bodies they support. For these two types of objects either *dans* or *sur*, respectively, is most characteristic. For open containers, as their concavity decreases, the choice between *dans* and *sur* becomes less and less clear. As the examples below illustrate, this choice is often decided by convention.

Thus, we may use *dans* for an armchair but will prefer *sur* for a straight-backed chair.

(50) *l'huissier est assis sur (*dans) la chaise*
       the notary is sitting on (in) the chair

(51) *le chef comptable est assis dans (*sur) le fauteuil*
       the head accountant is seated in (on) the armchair

The deciding criterion for the preposition here is the *concavity* of the support, a common quality of containers. Note that, in examples (50) and (51), the use of *sur/dans* is largely conventional and may be related to the specific lexical item, rather than to the shape of the supporting object, as examples (52) and (53) illustrate.

(52) *l'huissier est assis sur (*dans) la chaise qui a la forme d'un fauteuil*
the notary is seated on (in) the chair shaped like an armchair

(53) *le chef comptable est assis dans (*sur) le fauteuil qui a la forme d'une chaise*
the head accountant is seated in (on) the armchair that is shaped like a straight-backed chair

In the examples below, once again the concavity of the supporting object determines the use of either *sur* or *dans*. For convex parts of the body, the bearer/burden relation and the preposition *sur* describe the scene (examples [54] and [56]); for the concave parts, the container/contained relation dominates, motivating the use of *dans* (examples [55] and [57]).

(54) *l'ambassadeur a des poils sur (*dans) la poitrine*
the ambassador has hair on (in) his chest

(55) *le ministre a des poils dans (*sur) l'oreille*
the minister has hair in (on) his ear

(56) *le chien a des poils sur (*dans) le dos*
the dog has hair on (in) its back

(57) *le trésorier a des boutons dans (*sur) le dos*
the treasurer has pimples in (on) his back

The use of the word *creux* 'hollow, sunken', implying concavity, is enough to motivate the use of the preposition *dans*.

(58) **l'archiduc embrasse l'archiduchesse dans le nez*
the archduke kisses the archduchess in her nose

(59) *l'archiduc embrasse l'archiduchesse dans le creux du nez*
the archduke kisses the archduchess in the curve of her nose

Depending on the circumstances, a bed may be considered flat or concave. If the minister is lying *sur son lit* 'on his bed', I imagine him awake and uncovered, thoughtfully considering affairs of state. If he is *dans son lit* 'in his bed', I imagine him under the covers, seeking a well-deserved rest. The following utterances illustrate an interesting contrast:

(60) *le ministre dort dans son lit*
the minister is sleeping in his bed

(61) *le ministre est sur son lit de mort*
the minister is on his deathbed

In both instances, the minister is covered up, but apparently the rigidity of death suggests a flat surface (preposition *sur*), while sleep suggests a more comfortable bed, shaping itself to the form of the sleeper.

A flat landmark does not authorize the use of the preposition *dans* unless the target penetrates the landmark.[11] This explains the contrast between examples (62) and (63).

(62) *l'arbre est dans (*sur) la terre*
the tree is in (on) the ground

(63) *l'antenne de télévision est sur (*dans) le toit*
the television antenna is on (in) the roof

If we compare the tree and the television antenna, however, we see that these targets occupy the same space with respect to their landmarks (the ground and the roof).

Finally, objects that have the same shape but different functions may motivate different prepositions. For example, a tray may be as deep as a shallow bowl. Nonetheless, even if they are similar in concavity, the preposition *sur* is used in the first case and the preposition *dans* in the second.

(64) *la pomme est sur (*dans) le plateau*
the apple is on (in) the tray

(65) *la pomme est dans (*sur) le plat*
the apple is in (on) the bowl

This is because the tray is used for serving, and the bowl is used for containing.

Let us examine here the division of labor between *dans* and *sous*. We saw in chapter 12 that the landmark of *sous* generally prevents the perception of its target when this is perpendicular to the vertical axis. Inasmuch as a container may also hide the contained object from perception, the two prepositions might overlap in these circumstances. Herskovits has remarked that the preposition *sous*, but not *dans*, is permissible in example (66).

(66) *le camembert est sous (*dans) la cloche à fromage*
the camembert is under (in) the cheese dish

Note that the cheese dish is nothing but an open container turned upside down; topologically, its convex closure does not differ from that of a bowl.

cloche à fromage   plat

FIGURE 28

If the preposition *dans* is defined in terms of inclusion/exclusion, we cannot explain why *dans* fails to apply to sentence (66) as well as to (67).

> (67) *le camembert est dans le plat*
> the camembert is in the bowl

If *dans* is defined as a function of the container/contained relation, on the other hand, this contrast is well motivated. It is an important trait of this relation that the position of the contained object depends on the container. This trait is violated in example (66) but not in (67): if we move the bowl, the position of the camembert changes, but the cheese does not move if we simply lift the cheese dish. The preposition *dans* may only be used in a situation that respects this one-way dependence.

We have seen that the cheese dish is an open container that is turned upside down: while containers generally open towards the top, this one opens towards the bottom. All solid objects exert a certain force towards the bottom because of the force of gravity. What happens when the target is not a solid but lighter than air? The force it exerts against a possible container is no longer directed downwards, but upwards. If the acceptability judgments of examples (66) and (67) have been motivated by the mutually dependent positions of the target and the landmark, we could expect a reversal in this novel example. This is indeed what we find in examples (68) and (69).

> (68) *le gaz précieux est dans la cloche à fromage*
> the rarefied gas is in the cheese dish

> (69) **le gaz précieux est dans le plat*
> the rarefied gas is in the bowl

These examples illustrate that the acceptability of *dans* is not motivated by the inclusion of the target within the closure of the landmark. On the contrary, it depends on the interaction of the two terms, influenced by the second trait of the container/contained relation. A glass is an acceptable container for bodies heavier than air, even if it does not totally include the boundaries of the targets. As for the cheese dish, it is an appropriate container only for bodies lighter than air.

These facts are summarized in the table below.

Containers opening upwards
  Targets heavier than air: *dans*
  Targets lighter than air: **dans*

Containers opening downwards
  Targets heavier than air: **dans*
  Targets lighter than air: *dans*

These contrasts, motivated by the second trait of the container/contained relation, would appear entirely arbitrary if the preposition *dans* were defined in terms of inclusion/exclusion.

13.6 *The expression* en dedans / en dehors

The prepositions *dans/hors de* always belong to the same grammatical category. Elsewhere, omitting certain frozen (example [70]) or archaic forms (example [71]), *dedans/dehors* are used in the adverbial expressions *en dedans/en dehors*.

(70) *sous des dehors souriants, le colonel est cruel*
  beneath a smiling exterior, the colonel is cruel

(71) *dedans mon coeur, la femme du juge est toujours la plus belle*
  deep within my heart, the judge's wife is still the most beautiful

These rare nominal and prepositional uses aside, the expressions *en dedans/en dehors* could be considered adverbs corresponding to the prepositions *dans/hors de*.

However, the examples below demonstrate that the distribution of *en dedans/en dehors* is more restricted than the distribution of *dans/hors de*.

(72a) *la caisse est en bois. L'orange est dans la caisse*
  the crate is made of wood. The orange is in the crate

(b) *la caisse est en bois. L'orange est dedans*
  the crate is made of wood. The orange is in it

(73a) *la prairie est verte. La vache est dans la prairie*
  the field is green. The cow is in the field

(b) *la prairie est verte. La vache est dedans*
the field is green. The cow is in it

(74a) *la plaine est verte. La vache est dans la plaine*
the plains are green. The cow is on the plains

(b) *? la plaine est verte. La vache est dedans*
the plains are green. The cow is in them

(75a) *la montagne est haute. Le juge est dans la montagne*
the mountains are high. The judge is in the mountains

(b) *? la montagne est haute. Le juge est dedans*
the mountains are high. The judge is in them

(76a) *l'angoisse paralyse un homme. Le général est dans l'angoisse*
fear can paralyze a man. The general is in fear

(b) **l'angoisse paralyse un homme. Le général est dedans*
fear can paralyze a man. The general is in it

While examples (72b) and (73b) are stylistically better than (72a) and (73a), examples (74b) and (75b) are questionable, and (76b) is frankly unacceptable.

Note here that *dedans* plays a pronominal role for the landmark of *dans* in the (b) examples. The acceptability of the (b) examples is related to the nature of the landmark: the utterance will be good if the landmark is a typical container, but bad otherwise. The use of *dedans* therefore is permitted for the crate and the field—these are clearly delimited, within a three-dimensional and a two-dimensional space, respectively. Its use becomes more questionable for the plains, whose limits are more vague, and the mountains, which do not (properly speaking) include the judge. Finally, a metaphorical container such as fear does not allow the use of *dedans* in (76b).

In sum, the adverbial expressions *en dehors/en dedans* demand a more canonical container as a landmark than the prepositions *dans/hors de*. The landmark for these expressions must be physical and clearly delimited.

CONCLUSIONS

This book presents a study of spatial prepositions in French. We have clearly seen that both geometry and logic are unable to describe the use of spatial terms adequately; I have appealed therefore to our knowledge of the world around us, and the ways in which we perceive and conceptualize our world, to present the most complete explanation of these words possible. Our intuitions are at least partially correct in associating our faculty of language with the entire set of our other cognitive faculties. Even if the existence of a specific linguistic intelligence is one day demonstrated, it is already certain that our general knowledge plays an important role in providing a detailed explanation of the mechanics of language. The parallel established here between the ways we perceive and conceptualize space, on the one hand, and the way we describe this space linguistically, on the other, provides supplementary evidence of this interrelationship, I trust.

Certain concepts used in this description, such as *access to perception, contact between two objects,* etc., are simple concepts. Others, such as *general orientation, the bearer/burden relation, the container/contained relation* (respectively describing the prepositions *devant/derrière, sur/sous, dans/hors de*), are complex concepts. None of the traits characterizing these complex concepts are either necessary or sufficient, and many different combinations of traits are capable of representing the global concept and motivating the spatial term with which the complex concept is associated. Such complex concepts behave like *family resemblance concepts.* However, for certain physical instances of general orientation or the bearer/burden relation, all the traits of the family resemblance are found together; this contrasts with the category *game,* first given by Wittgenstein as an example of a family resemblance concept.

The description of spatial terms is complex and demands numerous usage rules, often accompanied by selection restrictions whose arbitrary nature may surprise the reader. One example is the preposition *sous* which, in describing inaccessibility to perception, prefers a prepositional subject that is thin and extended with respect to its object. Synchronically, there is no reason to believe that the acquisition of such complex distributions poses an insurmountable problem for the speaker, or that a profound and abstract unit must be hidden behind these several rules. The speaker's knowledge of a word may, in fact, be explained by the recognition of different similarities among its uses and by the memorization of its most idiosyncratic uses. Diachronically, however, if we admit that language is symbolic in nature, a direct association between such complex signifiers and signifieds seems improbable to me, given the actual distribution of terms in our lexicon. For this reason, I have proposed the existence of an original simple signified for each word, which I term its impetus. The present distribution of the word is developed from this impetus. Although for many lexical items this evolution may be accidental and anecdotal, involving only etymology and diachronic change, this does not hold true for spatial terms. The development of spatial prepositions from their impetus to their actual distribution appears systematic, motivated by the nature of the world and the way we perceive and understand it. I have attempted to reconstruct this evolutionary path within a system of logical diachrony.

In the case of spatial terms, particularly those whose usage rules are formulated in terms of a complex concept such as the notion of general orientation, their evolution seems to develop along similar paths. The word described by such a usage rule, the preposition *devant* for example, applies first to the most characteristic forms of the family resemblance. These are instances where a maximum of traits of the family resemblance coincide. The family resemblance, at this stage, is understood globally. Eventually, different traits become detached from the whole and take on a relative independence, going so far as to motivate individually certain uses of the word describing the family resemblance concept. Thus, in an extreme case, the preposition *devant* applies to the dish of game located behind a deformed king, simply because the king's mouth (one trait characterizing the positive side of his general orientation) is located at the nape of his neck.

There are certain limits, however, on the autonomy of the traits of a family resemblance concept. For example, it has often been noted that the terms of the preposition *sur* contact each other. Nonetheless, this preposition describes only one type of specific contact, and numerous selection restrictions are needed to associate the use of this preposition with the type of contact it illustrates. It appears, in fact, that all instances of contact described by the preposition *sur* follow pragmatically from the usual configuration of a burden with respect to the object bearing it up: the two objects are vertically aligned, the support plays an active role, etc. Even when one trait of the family resemblance concept motivating a spatial term is autonomous in describing the distribution of a preposition, we see that this autonomy is restricted by the global concept (in this case the bearer/burden relation). The best evidence of the development of spatial terms from a single impetus to a more complex distribution is found in the motivation of selection restrictions bearing on the different usage rules of a word.

In this work, spatial terms have been described in relation to our knowledge of the world. We have here a kinetic and dynamic understanding, not simply a static knowledge. For reasons of descriptive ease, a static explanation of language is often given, just as it may be convenient for the film critic to stop the film for a moment to examine one image in greater detail. If he forgets to set it in motion again, however, he will lose an essential element of the cinema: the constant movement of images on the screen. I believe that the changes in situations motivating language have all too often been frozen for descriptive ease. This movement is nonetheless essential to the description of prepositions such as *avant*/*après*, when movement is related to real or potential encounter. Even in analyzing the dimensions of an object (Vandeloise 1988), characteristics that otherwise appear static, once again the factor of movement enabled me to present a unified description of the distribution of *la longueur* 'length'/*la largeur* 'width'.

NOTES

Chapter One

1. A more detailed analysis of adjectives of dimensions has been proposed in Bierwisch and Lang (1987).

2. The first feature classifies the dimensions according to their size; the second (± main) seems to imply that in every situation, thickness will be less salient than the other dimensions.

3. Although Bierwisch attempts to present a conceptual or referential interpretation of the semantic markers describing adjectives of dimension, he does not situate these concepts in the world around us; he locates them rather in "certain deep seated, innate properties of the human organism and its perceptual apparatus" (1967, 3). "Of course," he continues, "almost nothing is known at the moment about the structure of this apparatus of primitive conceptual elements and its relation to the real world" (4). I tend to share H. H. Clark's opinion that, while a certain a priori knowledge may play a part, the acquisition of spatial terms proceeds as a function of the faculties of memory, perceptual and motor ability, etc. "This *a priori* knowledge," Clark adds, "is separate from language itself and is not so mysterious" (1973, 28).

4. The expressions *au-dessus/en dessous* are perfectly converse expressions only in those situations where the prepositions *sur/sous* cannot be substituted.

5. The asterisk does not designate an impossible or agrammatical utterance; the use of these expressions in semantics, as Ducrot (1980) points out, is rarely justified, since "given a certain utterance, one can almost always imagine a situation in which it would be natural." Instead, the asterisk here indicates that example (15) is rendered unacceptable by the nature of the prepositional terms, where *derrière* otherwise would be acceptable.

6. I use *functional* in the sense of *utilitarian*. Geometrical and logical analyses describe spatial terms by means of formal concepts that are independent of context (distance, the number of the term's dimensions, etc.). In contrast, a functional description—I might even say a "utilitarian" description—depends also on nonspatial factors that are determined by the context and by the circumstances of the use of the prepositional terms.

7. At the time I was writing this book, I did not know "The Naive Physics Manifesto" (Hayes 1979). Like this author, I try to understand how our knowledge of the world is organized. In contrast to Hayes, however, I believe that formal characteristics of spatial terms are derived from their functional characteristics rather than the reverse. For example, I would not say that "the geometric *on* implies the support *on* because blocks are rigid and strong" (Hayes 1985, p. 14) but that the support *on* implies the geometric *on* because supports usually are two-dimensional planes.

8. As Benoît de Cornulier pointed out to me, *aller* can do without a spatial complement in the sentences *le curé va au pas* 'the priest is going at a walking

pace' or *le curé va droit devant lui* 'the priest is going straight ahead'. However, *va au pas* seems parallel to the verb *marcher* 'to walk', which does not describe movement so much as it describes the manner in which movement is accomplished. *Le curé va au pas* would then be acceptable in the same way *le curé marche* would be; I prefer the latter, in fact. Since these sentences describe the manner in which encounter takes place, they do not need to mention the second participant in the encounter. As for *le curé va droit devant lui*, although this sentence does not exactly specify the second term of the encounter, it does provide a certain amount of information about it. Once again this sentence is less acceptable than *le curé marche droit devant lui*.

Chapter Two

1. As note 5 in chapter 1 points out, it is not impossible to find certain contexts (for example, a detective novel or a treasure hunt) that would make sentence (2) acceptable. The question mark indicates that this sentence is unacceptable for most contexts that immediately come to mind. The example is slightly more acceptable here, however, than in those cases marked with an asterisk, although the distinction between the two marks is not precise.

2. *Trajector* and *landmark* are technical terms in cognitive grammar (Langacker 1987a). *Trajector* is used essentially for its suggestive value as an entity moving along a trajectory, and does not necessarily imply physical movement. *Figure* and *ground*, Talmy's terms, suggest an analogy with the terminology of perceptive psychology.

3. *La maison près du poteau* 'the house near the signpost' is acceptable as long as this noun phrase distinguishes between two or more houses. The localizing function of the verb *être* 'to be' is responsible for the ungrammatical reading of example (12) in most contexts.

4. The transfer principle is independently justified, providing for the fact that *every* omitted landmark acquires an egocentric interpretation. This principle is also needed to explain the choice between *l'arbre est à droite* 'the tree is on the right' and *l'arbre est à sa gauche* 'the tree is on his left', when used in identical circumstances. In the second utterance, the possessive adjective clearly shows that the speaker has moved to his addressee's position to describe the location of the tree.

5. This is probably what Larendeau and Pinard (1968) mean when they refer to *partial decentralization* in their discussion of the child learning to use *la gauche/la droite* with respect to a landmark other than himself.

6. Nicolas Ruwet has pointed out the syntactic differences between *de* and *par rapport à*. Inversion is possible in the case of the second, but not the first.

    (a) *par rapport à la chaise, je suis à gauche*
       with respect to the chair, I am on the left

    (b) **de la chaise, je suis à gauche*
       from the chair, I am on the left

Benoît de Cornulier also pointed out to me that the two expressions may co-occur.

> (c) *la table est à gauche de la chaise par rapport à la chaise*
>   the table is to the left of the chair from the perspective of the
>   chair

The noun phrase introduced by *par rapport à* adds to the objectivity and preciseness of the localization; it may be inserted optionally, at different places in the utterance, to modify the usual, more subjective description introduced by *de*.

7. Here I am ignoring the infinitive construction *bois un dernier verre avant de partir* 'have one last drink before leaving'.

Chapter Three

1. A convex shape has borders that cannot be intersected more than twice by a cross-section. The glass is not a convex form since a cross-section may intersect its perimeter at four points. The convex closure of the glass is the smallest convex shape encompassing the glass, and is represented by a dotted line in figure 2.

2. Herskovits calls these idealizations "geometric descriptions."

3. The relation connecting the church to its floor area may be a case of metonymy, rather than illustrating a projection. In fact, metonymy is a very general category of relations, many of which might be independently studied.

4. Lurcat (1976) offers another type of anthropomorphically oriented object, which she calls "readjusted objects." These include the cradle, the bed, the chair, etc. If children are asked to point out the head of the bed, they may indicate the uppermost part or that part where someone lying on the bed would place his head. This terminology, which Lurcat calls anthropomorphic, must be distinguished from the anthropomorphic cases discussed in this book. In the example of a cupboard, the speaker humanizes the object and calls the side resembling a human face the *front* of the cupboard. In the case of a readjusted object, however, when the child calls the *head of the bed* the part where he lays his own head, this does not mean that the child understands the bed to have human qualities.

5. In Thom's introduction to Lurcat's book (1976), the following terminology is proposed:

EGO	OBJECT	
left	left	
back × front	front × back	*reflection*
right	right	

	left	left	
	back × front	back × front	*translation*
	right	right	

	left	right	
	back × front	front × back	*rotation*
	right	left	

Translation here corresponds to what I term *tandem* orientation, and *reflection* corresponds to *mirror-image* orientation. An addressee facing me is oriented by *rotation*.

6. Tests conducted by Lurcat (1976) show that both tandem and mirror-image orientations are used by children up to age seven.

Chapter Four

1. For a semantic analysis of the distinction between active and passive voice, see Langacker 1982.

2. The study of spatial prepositions in other verbal environments promises to be extremely fruitful; the use of different verbs may modify the acceptability of sentences containing the same preposition. For example, if we take the case of a young tree planted in the ground, example (b) but not (a) is acceptable.

(a) *l'arbre est hors de terre*
the tree is out of the ground

(b) *l'arbre sort hors de terre*
the tree grows out of the ground

Note also the contrast between (a) and (b) below.

(a) *le curé est à un buisson*
the priest is at a bush

(b) *le curé arrive à un buisson*
the priest is coming to a bush

3. I borrow the opposition between *classical* and *natural categories* from the work of Rosch (1973) and Lakoff (1982, 1987) on prototypes in psychology and linguistics.

4. Certain members of the extralinguistic category designated by the signifier may be more or less representative of the category than others; the signifier itself is equally applicable to all the members of the category, however. In fact, as long as the speaker masters the conventions relating the members of a category to the signifier designating them, the choice of the signifier is equally direct for the prototypes of the category and for its more marginal elements.

5. This transparent association concerns only the origin of the acquisition of a spatial term. Obviously I do not mean to deny the role of arbitrariness and convention in language. I believe, however, that the linguistic description of space is less arbitrary than geometric or logical descriptive terms would suggest, if they are intended to be exhaustive.

6. It is worth noting that my description of *dans* and *sur* was elaborated with evidence from adult use only, that is, before I had any knowledge of relevant data on language acquisition.

7. The atomic feature of *contact* may be used to account for the fact that, when asked to place an object *x* relative to a reference object *y*, young children always try to put them into contact, whatever the spatial relation involved. At this early stage, then, contact *cannot* fulfill a discriminatory role for the choice of prepositions. This makes the explanatory value of contact in the definition of the preposition *on* very dubious. It also means that the absence of contact in a locative relation should be perceptually more salient for young children than contact itself. This fact might explain a curious finding of Bernstein (1984). Indeed, Bernstein discovered that, although young children learn *in* and *on* before *under*, there is a task in which they perform better with *under*. In Bernstein's experiment, children were presented with three configurations where neutral context-free objects illustrated the relationships *in, on,* and *under*. For each preposition, children had to point to the correct configuration. The reason children performed better with *under* might be that it was the only configuration where the objects were not in contact. Thus, even though in active tasks children cannot help putting the objects in contact with each other, in passive recognition they seem to pay more attention to the absence of contact. If Clark's "semantic feature hypothesis" were correct, it should treat *absence of contact* as a positive feature. Vandeloise 1986 and forthcoming propose another way of dealing with the incidence of contact in the distribution of *à sur,* and *contre.*

Chapter Five

1. "Always returning along the paths of time, we are neither ahead nor behind: late is early, near is far."

2. Increases in the price of a train ticket may also be a factor in varying the normal distance by which we measure *près de/loin de.* The influence of this factor is evident in the following examples:

    (a) *plus le train devient cher, plus Paris me semble loin*
        the more train fares go up, the further Paris seems to me

    (b) *plus le curé devient pauvre, plus Rome lui semble loin*
        the poorer the priest becomes, the further Rome seems to him

3. The notation A/B (X) C/D, where X indicates the context, reads A (X) C and B (X) D. The preceding phrase then reads, the target's access to the landmark *and* the landmark's access to the target.

4. If the expressions *près de*/*loin de* depended on distance alone, the unacceptability of the sentence *Paris est loin de 400 kilomètres* would be paradoxical.

5. Nicolas Ruwet pointed out to me that it is also possible to say *le curé se sent près de Platon* 'the priest feels close to Plato'. Furthermore, there are syntactic uses of *près de* that are impossible with *proche de*, such as *je suis près de partir* 'I am close to leaving' (compare **je suis proche de partir*). Nevertheless, examples (15)–(18) show that *proche de* is preferred outside of the spatial and temporal domains.

Chapter Six

1. "There are seven years in age between the first two and the third. I would have preferred to have him above the other two."

2. Not all the traits of a family resemblance concept have the same status. The direction of falling bodies naturally plays a more important role than the trajectory of a missile in shaping our knowledge of the vertical axis. I have introduced this minor, unexpected example to demonstrate how useless it would be to try to make an exhaustive list of all the traits of a family resemblance concept. I could just have easily included the traits of a German shepherd's ears, a kitten's tail, or the position of the chimney on a house. The principle traits of a family resemblance concept are enough to explain the majority of uses of the word that the concept describes.

3. This is observed, however, in some young children who associate the vertical direction with the line from their heads to their feet. When they lie down, *le haut* is above their heads, and *le bas* is at their feet. This trait then stands in opposition to all the other traits of the family resemblance characterizing the vertical axis. These uses of *haut* and *bas* are contrary to the conventions of language, and children later learn to recognize the absolute nature of the vertical axis and its independence from the position of the body.

4. In general, at least one of the traits of the family resemblance concept defining the vertical axis will indicate this direction. It is more difficult to determine the poles H and B when the speaker is faced with contradictory traits. As regards the vertical axis, however, this is so rare that the family resemblance concept is barely justifiable in a specific study. Nonetheless, I consider the family resemblance concept justified here since it provides a more global approach, and because family resemblance concepts will prove necessary for other prepositions treated in this study.

5. The use of *generally* will be avoided in the formulation of usage rules, although it will be permitted in the formulation of characteristics. When the usage rules are not necessary ones, a second usage rule must be added in order to define other uses of the word.

6. The complexity of lexical categories defined by spatial prepositions will be more readily apparent in the case of other prepositions.

Chapter Seven

1. "The feet in front of me, beneath me, behind me—these are my feet."

2. A study comparing the uses of *devant*/*derrière*, as developed in this chap-

ter, with the uses of these prepositions as laid out in chapter 9 has been published in *Le Français moderne*, no. 1/2 (1987).

3. It would of course be an exaggeration to say that a family resemblance concept might be represented by *any* combination of its traits, since it might in fact include traits that never coexist. The consequences of this qualification will be examined in detail in Vandeloise, "Family Resemblances."

4. The definitions of *devant/derrière* and *en face de/dans le dos de* differ in one single point: general orientation in the first definition is replaced by the frontal direction in the second. Although the positive side of general orientation covers one-half of the space around the speaker, the positive side of the frontal direction takes in only a narrow band about as wide as the speaker, located directly in front of the speaker.

Chapter Eight

1. More precisely, this refers to the vertical plane uniting the speaker's vertical position and line of sight.

2. It was Ron Langacker, gracefully turning himself upside down in an armchair, who suggested the possibility of this second type of transfer to me.

3. According to Lurcat (1976), the understanding of lateral asymmetry is acquired at the age of four or five, although left and right are not mastered until age six for one's own left and right, and around age eight for other objects.

4. These traits are not all equal in status, just as the traits of the family resemblance characterizing the vertical axis are not all equivalent. The position of the hand is of course more central than the position of the cerebral hemispheres—it is perhaps because *la main* 'the hand' is feminine in gender that *la gauche/la droite* are also feminine. This contrasts with other spatial nominalizations (*le devant, le dessus,* etc.), which in French are masculine.

5. In a case of total transfer, the speaker takes on the general and lateral orientation of the landmark; in a case of partial transfer, however, the speaker attributes his own lateral orientation to the landmark. The speaker may assimilate to the landmark either by adopting the landmark's characteristics or by attributing his own characteristics to the landmark.

Chapter Nine

1. "When we love something that resembles us (from the front), we force ourselves (from behind) as much as we are able (from the front) to make it love us in return (from behind)."

2. I wish to thank Annette Herskovits, George Lakoff, and Christophe Schwarze, who spent long hours in conversation with me during my stay in Berkeley, as I formulated these two solutions.

3. In *Traité des sensations*, Condillac demonstrates that a statue, without the sense of touch or movement, would perceive the world as a planar surface, flattened against its retina. However, I. Roch and C. S. Harris, cited by Lurcat, believe that the sense of touch does not contribute to the sense of sight and is

not a source of information for visual perception. Instead, vision apparently dominates the sense of touch ("Vision and Touch Perception: Mechanisms and Models," in *Readings from Scientific American* [1967]).

4. It might seem questionable that the distinction between the two versions of *devant/derrière* hinges on *derrière,* which is the more marked preposition. "Positive" terms, such as *haut* and *avant,* are often acquired before their corresponding "negative" terms, *bas* and *après* (H. H. Clark 1973). However, we saw in section 4.3 that this is not the case with *derrière.* Lurcat (1976) also has demonstrated that when children are asked to put a car *devant/derrière* a truck, they show a slightly higher rate of success with the second preposition.

Figure 14 is reproduced by permission from "Complex Primitives in Language Acquisition," *Belgian Journal of Linguistics* 2 (1987).

Chapter Ten

1. "I move ahead backwards."

2. Not wishing to die either by the cross or by the crescent, I should specify that Rome and Mecca are intended here only in their geographical senses.

3. The transitive sense of *avancer* corresponds to example (20).

4. These translations are obviously only approximate. The comparative study of spatial prepositions is uncharted territory, and full of possibilities. The works of Zubin and Svorou are admirable examples of this type of study.

5. A complete study of spatial nominalizations is presented in Vandeloise 1985.

Chapter Eleven

1. I would like to add that in Herskovits's detailed analysis (which was influential for many of the analyses presented here) the central definitions are accompanied by "type usages," idiosyncratic usages of the preposition that cannot be predicted on the basis of the core meaning.

2. The partial inclusion of *a* in *b* implies the inclusion of a part of *a* (the emperor or the chair) within the convex closure of *b* (the workbench or the table). This closure is located within the set of tangents to the object.

3. The relative sizes of target and landmark are certainly not the only factor influencing the acceptability of examples (9) and (11). Example (9) situates the target only if the speaker is near enough to the place to know its location. As we will see in section 11.2.2, the preposition *à* is more appropriate when its landmark is distant from the speaker. This factor alone could explain the unacceptability of (9). It does not bear on the acceptability of (11), however, which could be uttered at some distance from Evanston.

4. The different configurations represented by examples (11) (contiguity) and (12) (inclusion) could also account for the contrasting acceptability judgments. However, as we saw in section 11.1, the preposition *à* is relatively insensitive to these differences in configuration.

5. In the fifteenth and sixteenth centuries, *à* and *en* were written, respectively, *au* (pronounced /o/) and *o* when followed by the definite article. As a result of the variation in these two sounds, the preposition *en* before masculine place-names has been confused with the preposition *à*.

6. Although Hottenroth gives the Italian preposition *a* the role of situating a target, her corpus does not include prepositional phrases with place-names, institutions, or public spaces. As she claims, "This use of *a* evidently is not covered by the same conditions or restrictions as the use of *a* in prepositional phrases with common nouns" (1981, 68). I do not know if this is a difference between the two languages or merely a difference in interpretation, but landmarks represented by proper nouns seem to play a privileged role in the use of the French *à*. Because of their role localizing a target, they avoid constraints that restrict other landmarks of the same preposition. Otherwise, Hottenroth's article confirms many of my own analyses presented in section 11.3.

7. While the landmark of example (88a) may refer either to a building or to an institution, an example such as *Pierre est à l'armée* 'Pierre is in the army' (cited in section 11.3.3) refers uniquely to Pierre's activities.

Chapter Twelve

1. "He died on the stroke of noon."

2. Several readers of the first version of this chapter have doubted this intuition. I trust that examples (19) and (20) will justify characteristic C to the satisfaction of these readers.

3. I still remember the card (I think it was pink) used by Yuki Kuroda when he first explained that the impetus of *sous* could not directly account for its distribution. Kuroda's raised hand is at the origin of the following discussion.

Chapter Thirteen

1. "Put something in your feet!"

2. Topology is the study of the relative positions of geometric forms without taking into account their shapes or sizes.

3. Set a is included in set b if all the points of a coincide with points in b.

4. A shape is convex if its outline cannot be intersected more than twice by a straight line. The convex closure of a nonconvex shape is the smallest convex shape that includes the nonconvex shape.

5. As we will see below, this argument depends on the way the selection restrictions are formulated.

6. It is possible, however, to use *dans* in the following utterance: *la reine a un nez charmant dans un visage horrible* 'the queen has a lovely nose in a hideous face'. Perhaps the adjectives *charmant* and *horrible* transfer the sentence from the spatial domain to an abstract, esthetic domain. In this case, the hideousness of the face might contain the loveliness of the nose.

7. I owe this analysis to Yuki Kuroda, who led me towards a new interpretation of *dans* by pushing me to be more specific in defining the idealization of open containers.

8. In this final trait the reader may recognize the relation of inclusion. Characteristics specifying the movement of the prepositional terms, and their relative forces, combine with this otherwise purely formal trait.

9. This example was inspired by Herskovits.

10. In French: "*a est dans/hors de b* si le site (con)tient (partiellement)/ne (con)tient plus la cible."—Trans.

11. Does lack of penetration explain the unacceptability of example (31), *le nez est dans la tête* 'the nose is in the head', without taking into account the question of constituency? Although it is true that the nose is not rooted in the face, the nose is still totally included, since it is part of the face. On the other hand, the wheels of the car (example [33]) do penetrate the car body, and the contrast with (34) can only be explained by the fact that the wheels are a constituent of the car, while the boulders are not.

REFERENCES

Abkarian, G. 1982. "Comprehension of Deictic Locatives: The Object behind It." *Journal of Psycholinguistics Research* 11:229–43.

Bates, L., and Learned, J. 1948. "The Development of Verbal Space in the Young Child." *Journal of Genetic Psychology* 72:63–84.

Bennett, D. G. 1968. *English Prepositions: A Stratificational Semantics.* London: Longman.

Bernstein, M. 1984. "Non-linguistic Responses to Verbal Instructions." *Journal of Child Language* 11:293–311.

Bierwisch, M. 1967. "Some Semantic Universals of German Adjectivals." *Foundation of Language* 3:1–36.

Bierwisch, M., and Lang, E., eds. 1987. *Grammatische und konzeptuelle Aspekte von Dimensionsadjektiven.* Berlin: Akademie Verlag.

Bowerman, M. 1978. "Systematizing Semantic Knowledge: Change over Time in the Child Organisation of Word Meaning." *Child Development* 49:977–87.

———. 1985. "Beyond Communicative Adequacy." In *Child Language,* ed. K. Nelson, vol. 5, London, N.J.: Lawrence Erlbaum Associates.

Casad, E. H. 1982. "Cora Locationals and Structure Imagery." Doctoral diss., University of California, San Diego.

Casad, E. H., and Langacker, R. W. 1982. " 'Inside' and 'Outside' in Cora Grammar." *IJAL* 51:247–281.

Cassirer, E. 1923. *La Philosophie des formes symboliques. 1. Le Langage.* Translated from German by Ole Hansen-Lair. Paris: Minuit.

Clark, E. 1971. "On the Acquisition of the Meaning of *before* and *after.*" *Journal of Verbal Learning and Verbal Behavior* 10:266–75.

———. 1972a. "On the Child's Acquisition of Antonyms in Two Semantic Fields." *Journal of Verbal Learning and Verbal Behavior* 11:750–58.

———. 1972b. "Some Perceptual Factors in the Acquisition of Locative Terms by Young Children." In *Papers from the Eighth Regional Meeting.* Chicago: Chicago Linguistic Society.

———. 1974. "Non-linguistic Strategies and the Acquisition of Word Meanings." *Cognition* 2:161–82.

———. 1978. "Strategies for Communicating." *Child Development* 49:953–59.

———. 1980. "Here's the Top: Non-linguistic Strategies in the Acquisition of Orientational Terms." *Child Development* 51:329–38.

Clark, H. H. 1973. "Space, Time, Semantics, and the Child." In *Cognitive Development and the Acquisition of Language,* ed. T. E. Moore. New York: Academic Press.

Condillac. 1984. *Traité des sensations.* Reprint. Paris: Fayard.

Cooper, G. S. 1968. *A Semantic Analysis of English Locative Prepositions.* Bolt, Beranek, and Newman, report 1587.

Cox, M. 1979. "Young Children's Understanding of *in front of* and *behind* in the Placement of Objects." *Journal of Child Language* 6:529–45.

Cox, M., and Richardson, J. 1985. "How Do Children Describe Spatial Relationships?" *Journal of Child Language* 12:611–20.

Dinsmore, G. S. 1979. "Pragmatics, Formal Theory, and the Analysis of Presupposition." Doctoral diss., University of California, San Diego.

Ducrot, O., et al. 1980. *Les Mots du discours.* Paris: Minuit.

Fauconnier, G. 1984. *Espaces mentaux.* Paris: Minuit.

Fillmore, C. J. 1971. *Santa Cruz Lectures on Deixis.* Presented at the University of California, Santa Cruz. Indiana University Linguistics Club, Bloomington. Mimeograph.

———. 1975. "An Alternative to Checklist Theories of Meaning." In *Proceedings of the First Annual Meeting of the Berkeley Linguistics Society.* Berkeley: University of California.

———. 1982. "Towards a Descriptive Framework for Spatial Deixis." In *Speech, Place, and Action,* ed. J. R. Jarvella and W. Klein. London: John Wiley.

Flavell, J.; Shipstead, S.; and Croft, K. 1978. "Young Children's Knowledge about Visual Perception: Hiding Objects from Others." *Child Development* 49:1208–11.

Freeman, N.; Lloyd, S.; and Sinha, C. 1980. "Infant Search Task Reveals Early Concepts of Containment and Canonical Usage of Objects." *Cognition* 8:243–62.

Friedman, W., and Seely, B. 1976. "The Child Acquisition of Spatial and Temporal Word Meaning." *Child Development* 47:1103–8.

Friedrich, P. 1969. *On the Meaning of the Tarascan Suffixes of Space.* IJAL memoir 23.

Geeraerts, D. 1983. "Prototype Theory and Diachronic Semantics: A Case Study." *Indogermanische Forschungen* 88:1–32.

Gillis, S. 1982. "De verwerving van een woordveld door 4;5 tot 6 jarigen: Een verkennend onderzoek." *Antwerp Papers in Linguistics* 28.

———. 1985. "Description of the Use of *In.*" Manuscript.

Gougenheim, G. 1949. "L'Espace à deux dimensions et l'espace à trois dimensions en français." *Journal de psychologie* 17:35–52.

———. 1959. "Y a-t-il des prépositions vides en français? " *Le Français moderne,* 1–25.

Grieve, R.; Hoogenraad, R.; and Murray, D. 1977. "On the Young Child's Use of Lexis and Syntax in Understanding Locative Instructions." *Cognition.* 5:235–50.

Grimm, H. 1975. "On the Child's Acquisition of Semantic Structure Underlying the Wordfield of Prepositions." *Language and Speech* 18:97–119.

Hallet, S. J. 1967. *Wittgenstein's Definition of Meaning as Use.* New York: University of Fordham Press.

Hawkins, B. 1983. *Semantics of English Spatial Prepositions.* Doctoral diss., University of California, San Diego.

Hayes, P. J. 1979. "The Naive Physics Manifesto." In *Expert Systems in the Micro-electronic Age,* ed. Donald Michie. Edinburg; Edinburg University Press. 242–270.

————. 1985. "The Second Naive Physics Manifesto." In *Formal Theories of the Commonsense World,* ed. Hobbs, J. and Moore, R. New Jersey: Ablex Publishing. 1–36.

Herskovits, A. 1982. "Space and the Prepositions in English: Regularities and Irregularities in a Complex Domain." Doctoral diss., Stanford University, Stanford, Calif.

————. 1986. *Language and Spatial Cognition: An Interdisciplinary Study of the Prepositions in English.* Cambridge: Cambridge University Press.

Hill, C. A. 1975. "Variation in the Use of Front and Back by Bilingual Speakers." In *Proceedings of the First Annual Meeting of the Berkeley Linguistics Society.* Berkeley: University of California.

————. 1977. "Linguistic Representation of Spatial and Temporal Orientation." In *Proceedings of the Fourth Annual Meeting of the Berkeley Linguistics Society.* Berkeley: University of California.

Holzman, M. 1981. "From Memories of Instances to Abstract Featural Concepts: Where Is *under?* " *Journal of Psycholinguistic Research* 10:421–39.

Hottenroth, P. 1981. "Italian *a.* Allemand *an.* Une analyse contrastive." In *Analyse des prépositions,* ed. C. Schwarze. Tübingen: M. Niemeyer.

Johnston, J. 1984. "Acquisition of Locative Meanings: *Behind* and *in front of.*" *Journal of Child Language* 11:407–22.

Johnston, J., and Slobin, D. 1978. "The Development of Locative Expressions in English, Italian, Serbo-Croatian, and Turkish." *Journal of Child Language* 6:529–45.

Klein, W. [1980] 1983. "Deixis and Spatial Orientation in Route Direction." In *Spatial Orientation,* ed. H. L. Pick and L. P. Acredolo. New York: Plenum Press.

Kuczaj, S., and Maratsos, M. 1975. "On the Acquisition of *front, back,* and *side.*" *Child Development* 46:202–10.

Lakoff, G. 1982. "Categories and Cognitive Models." In *Cognitive Science Program.* Berkeley: University of California.

————. 1987. *Women, Fire and Dangerous Things: What Categories Reveal about the Mind.* Chicago and London: Chicago University Press.

Lakoff, G., and Johnson, M. 1980. *Metaphors We Live By.* Chicago: University of Chicago Press.

Lamiroy, B. 1983. *Les Verbes de mouvement en français et en espagnol.* Amsterdam and Philadelphia: John Benjamins and University of Louvain Press.

Langacker, R. W. 1982. "Space Grammar, Analysability, and the English Passive." *Language* 58:22–80.

————. 1987a. *Foundations of Cognitive Grammar.* Vol. 1, *Theoretical Prerequisites.* Stanford, Calif.: Stanford University Press.

————. 1987b. "Mouvements abstraits." *Langue française* 76:59–76.

————. 1987c. "Nouns and Verbs." *Language* 53:53–99.

Larendeau, M., and Pinard, A. 1968. *Les Premières Notions spatiales de l'enfant.* Paris: Delachaux et Niestle.

Leech, G. N. 1969. *Towards a Semantic Description of English.* London: Longman.

Levine, S., and Carey, S. 1982. "Up Front: The Acquisition of a Concept and of a Word." *Journal of Child Language* 9:645–57.

Lindner, S. 1981. "A Lexico-Semantic Analysis of English Verb-Particle Constructions with *up* and *out.*" Doctoral diss., University of California, San Diego.

Lurcat, L. 1976. *L'Enfant et l'espace.* Paris: PUF.

Miller, G. A., and Johnson-Laird, P. N. 1976. *Language and Perception.* Cambridge: Harvard University Press.

Nelson, Ka. 1977. "The Conceptual Basis for Naming." In *Language Learning and Thought,* ed. J. Macnamara. New York: Academic Press.

Rosch, E. 1973. "On the Internal Structure of Perceptual and Semantic Categories." In *Cognitive Development and the Acquisition of Language,* ed. T. E. Moore. New York: Academic Press.

Rosch, E., and Mervis, C. B. 1975. "Family Resemblances: Studies in the Internal Structure of Categories." *Cognitive Psychology* 7:573–605.

Rosch, E.; Simpson, C.; and Miller, R. 1976. "Structural Basis of Typicality Effects." *Journal of Experimental Psychology: Human Perception and Performance* 2, no. 4:491–502.

Ruwet, N. [1969] 1982. "A propos des prépositions de lieu en français." In *Mélanges Fohalle.* Gembloux, Belgium: N. Duclot. Reprinted in *Grammaire des insultes et autres études.* Paris: Seuil.

Schlesinger, I. 1979. *The Acquisition of Words and Concepts.* Jerusalem: Hebrew University.

Sinha, C., and Carabine, B. 1981. "Interactions between Lexis and Discourse in Conversation and Comprehension Tasks." *Journal of Child Language* 8:109–29.

Slobin, D. 1977. "Language Change in Childhood and in History." In *Language Learning and Thought,* ed. J. Macnamara. New York: Academic Press.

Smith, L. 1979. "Perceptual Development and Category Generalization." *Child Development* 50:705–15.

Spang-Hansen, E. 1961. *Les Prépositions vides en français moderne.* Copenhagen: Academic Forlag.

Talmy, L. [1980] 1983. "How Language Structures Space." In *Spatial Orientation,* ed. H. L. Pick and L. P. Acredolo. New York: Plenum Press.

Tanz, C. 1980. *Studies in the Acquisition of Deictic Terms.* New York: Cambridge University Press.

Teller, P. 1969. "Some Discussion and Extension of M. Bierwisch's Work on German Adjectivals." *Foundation of Language* 5:185–217.

Togeby, K. 1986. *Grammaire française.* Vol. 4, *Les Mots Invariables.* Copenhagen: Academic Forlag.

Tomasello, M. 1987. "Learning to Use Prepositions: A Case Study." *Journal of Child Language* 14:79–98.

Vandeloise, C. 1979. "Les Termes de dimensions en français." Master's thesis, University of Vincennes.

————. 1984. *Description of Space in French.* Doctoral diss., University of California, San Diego.

————. 1985. "La Description linguistique de l'espace et du mouvement." Doctoral diss., L'École des Hautes Études en sciences sociales, Paris.

————. 1986. "Length, Width, and Potential Passing." In *Progress in Cognitive Grammar,* ed. B. Rudzka-Ostyn. Amsterdam and Philadelphia: John Benjamins.

————. 1987. "La préposition *à* et le principe d'anticipation." *Langue française* 76:77–111.

————. 1989. "L'Expression linguistique de la relation de suspension." *Cahiers de lexicologie* 55:101–133.

————. 1990. "Representation, Prototypes, and Centrality." In *Meanings and Prototypes: Studies on Linguistic Categorization,* ed. S. L. Tsohatzidis, London and New York: Routledge. 401–434.

————. (In Press). "Structure of Spatial lexical categories and family resemblance" *Semantique du temps, de L'espace et du mouvement dans le Langage naturel,* ed. M. Borillo, and C. Vet, Paris: Hermes.

Walkerdine, V., and Sinha, C. 1978. "The Internal Triangle: Language, Reasoning, and the Social Context." In *The Social Context of Language,* ed. Markova. London: Wiley.

Weissenborn, J. 1981. "L'Acquisition des prépositions spatiales: Problèmes cognitifs et linguistiques." In *Analyse des prépositions,* ed. C. Schwarze. Tübingen: Niemeyer.

Wilcox, S., and Palermo, D. 1974. "*In, on,* and *under* Revisited." *Cognition* 3:245–54.

Wittgenstein, L. 1953. *Philosophical Investigations.* New York: Macmillan.

Zubin, D. A., and Svorou, S. 1984. "Perceptual Schemata in the Spatial Lexicon: A Cross-linguistic Study." In *Papers from the Parasession on Lexical Semantics.* Chicago: Chicago Linguistic Society.

INDEX

à: with *arriver*, 167, 185; asymmetrical character of, 159; with definite article, 165–66, 180, 184, 185; and dimensionality, 5–6, 158; distance between speaker and landmark of, 168–70; formal properties of, 157–59; with indefinite article, 162–63, 166–68, 171, 173, 175–76, 184, 185; and integrated landmarks, 173–84; when landmark is proper noun, 163–65, 185; and localization, 13–14, 160–73; precision of meaning of, 174–78; relative movement of target and landmark of, 161–62; relative size of target and landmark of, 160–61; situating target of with respect to part of and object, 170–73; specific location of landmark of, 162–68; *sur* compared to, 199–204; target and landmark of, 160–68, 200, 202; unidimensional character of, 170; usage rule for, 168

abstract domains, 138, 141, 142, 153

accessibility: facility of, 70; and the norm, 68–70; and *près de / loin de*, 67–73; types of, 70

access to perception: and *devant* and *derrière*, 42, 125–31, 152–53, 155; in functional description of spatial prepositions, 13, 14–16; and physical access, 70; and *sous*, 190–92, 198, 207

addressee: and accessibility and the norm, 69–70

àdroite; asymmetry of spatial relations, 21; derived uses of, 49; and direction, 3; and directional and functional preposi-

tions, 29, 30; and general and lateral orientation, 19, 109–21; and position of speaker, 77; prepositional terms of, 118–21; and relation of landmark and speaker, 26; usage rules for, 53

à gauche: asymmetry of spatial relations, 21; derived uses of, 49; and direction, 3; and directional and functional prepositions, 29, 30; and general and lateral orientation, 19, 109–21; and position of speaker, 77; prepositional terms of, 118–21; and relation of landmark and speaker, 26; usage rules for, 52

Akbarian, G., 62

aller: and potential encounter, 16–17, 239n.8

anthropomorphic orientation, 36–37; and contextual orientation, 97; and frontal orientation, 41; of projectors, 39

après: arrière compared to, 150; asymmetry of spatial relations, 21; asymmetry of subject/object relation, 11; coincidence with *derrière*, 154–55; contrasts with *derrière*, 155–56; as converse relation to *avant*, 147; and directional and functional prepositions, 29–30; distribution of, 152–56; domains of, 135–36; and order along a scale, 135–38; and potential encounter, 17–18, 148–50, 237; and relative movement, 138–48; relative size of target and landmark of, 160; scales of comparison for, 136–37, 139–40; symmetry of target and

255